John Thomas Codman

Brook Farm

Historic and personal memoirs

John Thomas Codman

Brook Farm
Historic and personal memoirs

ISBN/EAN: 9783337141981

Printed in Europe, USA, Canada, Australia, Japan

Cover: Foto ©ninafisch / pixelio.de

More available books at **www.hansebooks.com**

BROOK FARM

HISTORIC AND PERSONAL MEMOIRS

Brook Farm, West Roxbury, in 1846.

— BY —

JOHN THOMAS CODMAN

BOSTON, MASS.
ARENA PUBLISHING COMPANY
COPLEY SQUARE
1894

CONTENTS

CHAPTER V.

CHAPTER VI.

CHAPTER VII.

CHAPTER VIII.

CHAPTER IX.

CHAPTER X.

PREFACE.

THERE were two distinct phases in the Associated life at Brook Farm. The first was inaugurated by the pioneers, who introduced a school, and combined it with farm and household labors. The second phase began with an attempt to introduce methods of social science and to add mechanical and other industries to those already commenced. These different phases have been called the Transcendental and the Industrial periods.

Each individual had his special experiences of the life. The writer chronicles it from his standpoint. None, perhaps, was more interested in it than he, young as he was, but many were more able to elaborate it and write it in details, and did he not feel that it was an important duty neglected by all, these memoirs would have remained unwritten.

The record books of the institution are missing, and are doubtless long ago destroyed. These chapters have been compiled and written from few memoranda, at various times, very often after the arduous duties of days of professional life, and with a desire only to present the subject truthfully, faithfully and simply ; and also, not wholly to gratify curiosity. or to record the doings of the noble men and women who were wise before their time, but to whisper courage to those who, like their predecessors, are seeking some solution of the social problems that involves neither the too sudden surrender of acquired rights, the reckless abandon of old ideas to untried and crude radicalism. or the more to-be-dreaded feuds between classes, that mean desperation on one side and war on the other ; but to aid, if possible, in inspiring a belief that a peaceful adjustment of our surroundings will, in time, bring order out of chaos and harmony out of discord.

The reader will have observed long before he lays down this book, that the Brook Farm life and ideals were purely coöperative and philosophical, that all the elements of true society were recognized, and that the attempt was for the better adjustment of them to the changing and changed relations of their fellow-men, brought about by the pervading moral, scientific and social growth of the past and present centuries.

The nation is older, richer and wiser, since the Brook Farm experiment began. It is more tolerant of one another's opinions, more enterprising, progressive and liberal, and surely a few weak trials made half a century ago, are not enough to solve the majestic problem of right living and how to shape the outward forms of society, so that within their environments all interests may be harmonized, and the golden rule begin to be, in a practical way, the measure of all human lives.

The author, in closing, will confide to his readers the wish of his heart, that this sketch of his early days may inspire some who can command influence and means with an interest to continue the experiments in social science, along lines laid out with more or less clearness by the Brook Farmers.

J. T. C.

CHAPTER I.

EARLY in the present century, New England was the centre of progressive religious thought, in America. A morbid theology had reigned supreme, but its forms were too cold, harsh and forbidding to attract or even retain the liberal-minded, educated and philosophic students of the rising generation, or hold in check the ardent humanitarian spirit, that embodied itself in ideals that were greater than the existing creeds.

Yet nowhere prevailed a more religious spirit. It showed itself in tender care of masses of the people, in public schools and seminaries, in lectures, sermons, libraries and in acts of general benevolence.

From these conditions developed the idea of greater freedom from social trammels; from African slavery, which had not then been abolished; from domestic slavery, which still exists; from the exploitations of trade and commerce; from the vicious round of unpaid labor, vice and brutality. Protestations were heard against all of these evils, not always coming from the poor and unlearned, but oftener from the educated and refined, who had pride that the republic should stand foremost among the nations for justice, culture and righteousness.

The old theology was crumbling. A new church was springing from its vitals based on freer thought, in

1

which the intellect and heart had more share in determining righteousness. The fatherhood of God and the brotherhood of man became the themes of discourse, oftener than those of the vengeance of an offended Deity; and pity and forgiveness, oftener than those on everlasting punishment.

In truth, the new departure which had begun, soon attracted to itself the most cultivated persons of the time, some of whom, Sept. 19, 1836, formed a club that met at one another's houses and discussed all the important social and religious topics of the day. They were mostly young people, college-bred, learned, artistic and thoughtful, and of high ideals in intellectual acquirement, religion and social life. They were all agreed that there were many evils to be eradicated from society; in what way — individualistic, governmental or socialistic, or by a combination of ways — few were agreed.

The problem was an open one. The theories proposed and the discussions were extremely interesting, but no record of them is at hand, except a few essays published in the *Dial*, a quarterly magazine which was edited by members of the organization, which finally took the name of "The Transcendental Club." One of the *Dial* editors, as well as one of the founders of the Club, and at whose house it had its first meeting, was Rev. George Ripley, a Unitarian minister who was born at Greenfield, Mass., in the beautiful valley of the Connecticut River. He was of good farmer stock and had a fine physical presence, though of medium stature. He was a lover of books, a graduate of Harvard college, and a well trained and religious scholar. He was then settled over a Unitarian church worshipping on Purchase Street, in Boston, and faithfully fulfilled his duties. Above all things his head and heart sought righteousness for all men. He believed in the justice of God and the divine nature of man, His best creation. He believed man to be involved in an intricate and un-Christian social labyrinth, and with deep earnestness of purpose and thorough convictions of his personal duty in the case, set himself at work to evolve a way to extricate at least some of humanity from their vicious surroundings; and finally proposed to the Club a plan which he urged with his customary vigor and eloquence.

This plan was, in short, to locate on a farm where agriculture and education should be made the foundation of a new system of social life. Labor should be honored. All would take part in it. There should be no religious creeds adopted. The old, feeble and sick were to be cared for, the strong and able bearing the greater burden of the labor. There would be no rank, to entitle the owner of it to superior considerations because of the rank; and truth, justice and order were to be the governing principles of the society.

The theologians and philosophers of Europe, with whose writings and logic Mr. Ripley was well acquainted, had impressed him with the truth of the divinity of man's nature, or had convinced him more thoroughly that his own ideas of it were right. He had wrestled with progressively conservative giants, professors of colleges — notably Andrews Norton — and had won well-earned laurels. Norton was professor of sacred literature at Harvard, one of his own professors, sixteen years his senior, and made a point that the miracles of

Christ and the writings of the gospel were the only sure proofs existing of spiritual truths.

The Transcendental philosophy to which Mr. Ripley had become a convert, claimed that there was in human nature an intuitive faculty which clearly discerned spiritual truths, which idea was in contradistinction to the beliefs of the day, which declared that spiritual knowledge came by special grace, and was proven by the divine miracles ; this latter belief being largely joined to the doctrine of the innate depravity of man. Mr. Ripley's own words to his church on Purchase Street, declared that

" There is a class of persons who desire a reform in the prevailing philosophy of the day. These are called Transcendentalists, because they believe in an order of truth that transcends the sphere of the external senses. Their leading idea is the supremacy of mind over matter. Hence they maintain that the truth of religion does not depend on tradition nor historical facts, but has an unswerving witness in the soul. There is a light, they believe, which enlighteneth every man who cometh into the world. There is a faculty in all — the most degraded, the most ignorant, the most obscure — to perceive spiritual truth when distinctly presented ; and the ultimate appeal on all moral questions is not to a jury of scholars, a hierarchy of divines or the prescriptions of a creed, but to the common sense of the human race.

" There is another class of persons who are devoted to the removal of the abuses that prevail in modern society. They witness the oppressions done under the sun and they cannot keep silence. They have faith that God governs man ; they believe in a better future than the past ; their daily prayer is for the coming of the kingdom of righteousness, truth and love ; they look forward to a more pure, more lovely, more divine state of society than was ever realized on earth. With these views I rejoice to say I strongly and entirely sympathize."

The prevailing tone of New England life was Calvinistic. Its doctrines may be said to have entered every household, penetrated every sanctuary and influenced all the leaders of society. The new departure was not a going away from religious thought, but it joined intellect and heart. It ignored unreasonable extravagances of statement wherever found. It ignored faith alone. It did not believe that faith stood above works. It pointed always towards action. It summed up the lesson and meaning of all good doctrines, that man should *lead a better life here*, where the duties to our fellows should not be passed by as now, but fulfilled. It was a newer way of thinking, to be logical with religion and put it to the test of every-day life. If the new departure meant anything then, if it means anything to-day, its object is to accomplish a better life here on this earth. In his soul, penetrated by divine aspirations, Mr. Ripley heard these words ringing out: " A truer life, a more honest life, a juster life — accomplish it!"

It was at the Club that he again urged the realization of his plan. There gathered together were the brightest intellects, the highest minded, the most sympathetic, thoughtful and talented young men that New England contained. Preaching was good, but more than preaching was wanted — the Christian life ; could it not be commenced? Could they not educate the young in practical duties as well as in books, and by their own good example so surround them that the interior life could be awakened — the soul's inward goodness and the power to discern the true destiny of man?

Encouraged by the sympathy of his wife, sister and a few earnest spirits, Mr. Ripley started on his project. He was in his fortieth year. He was neither too young nor too old. A few years of life he could possibly spare for the experiment. He would then be only in his prime. He had no children to embarrass his movements. He could give all his strength of body and mind to it. He loved the country life. It was to be the fulfilling of what he had preached so long and what is, alas, still preached to-day with not much attempt to realize it — the Christian life. People would laugh at him! I doubt if that gave him one disturbing thought. It *was right;* as it was right he would do it. But maybe in his secret heart he thought that more of those who seemed to have been awakened, as he had been, to the divine call, would follow and join with him than did; for, singularly enough, not one of the members of the Transcendental Club, who first met together, joined Mr. Ripley's movement. They were all radical to the prevailing theology, stiff, rigid as it was, and never, in America, was there a group assembled who aimed higher, or did more, first and last, to elevate humanity; for the Club contained a galaxy of talent.

Mr. Ripley led them all in practical endeavor to form the Christian commonwealth that many of them had preached.

William Ellery Channing, in whose veins ran the blood of one of the signers of the Declaration of American Independence, a beloved preacher, was there, full of earnestness, tenderness, faith and love. With vigor he

poured out his eloquence to awaken thoughts for an enlarged theology, and with a sympathizing heart criticised
chattel slavery, social slavery and domestic servitude,
and afterward became one of the acknowledged leaders
of liberal Christendom.

Young Ralph Waldo Emerson was there, late from
the ministry, known better as poet, philosopher and
essayist; and James Freeman Clarke, talented writer
and preacher; and faithful and independent Rev. Cyrus
A. Bartol. Rev. Theodore Parker, son of a Lexington
hero, doughty, bold and brave, on whose head fell the
anathemas of the orthodox and the curses of the slave-
holders at a later day, showed his ever calm, pleasant
and earnest face at the board.

Rev. F. H. Hedge, Convers Francis, Thomas H.
Stone, Samuel D. Robbins, Samuel J. May and another
Channing — William Henry — were there; Christopher P. Cranch, divinity graduate, but now well known
as painter, poet and story teller; and beloved John S.
Dwight, famed mostly as writer on music, and musical
critic; and Orestes A. Brownson, prominent essayist,
who was, by turns, a Radical, Unitarian, Universalist,
Presbyterian and Roman Catholic.

All these above named persons were attached to the
clergy. There were others who, like A. Bronson
Alcott, were teachers, and sometimes lecturers. There
was Henry D. Thoreau, a charming writer who spent
two years in a hut in Walden woods; and Nathaniel
Hawthorne, the writer of many familiar romances; also
George Bancroft, the historian, Dr. Charles T. Follen,
Samuel G. Ward, Caleb Stetson, William Russell, Jones
Very, Robert Bartlett and S. V. Clevenger, sculptor.

As an innovation in clubs there were lady members,
among whom were Elizabeth P. Peabody, and her sister
Sophia, who became the wife of Hawthorne; Miss S.
Margaret Fuller, remarkable for her intellectual ca-
pacity, and who became the wife of Count D'Ossoli, of
Italy; Miss Marianne Ripley, sister, and Mrs. Sophia
Ripley, wife, of Rev. George Ripley.

Or if these persons were not all members of the Club,
of which there seems to be no list extant, nearly every
one was, and they can all be classsd as belonging to the
coterie or Transcendental circle; all at times attended
the meetings, participated in the discussions, and wrote
articles for the *Dial* and for what in those days were
called the radical journals and magazines.

The winter of 1840 had been the time of talk.
Early in the spring of the year 1841 it was announced
that a location was chosen at Brook Farm, West Roxbury, nine miles from Boston, Mass. Mr. Ripley
selected it. He and his wife had boarded there the
former summer. It was retired and pretty. Mr. Ellis
owned it; Mr. Parker, Mr. Russell and Mr. Shaw lived
not far away, and a small amount of cash paid down
would secure the place for an immediate commencement of the effort.

The party who went earliest to settle at Brook Farm
consisted of Mr. George Ripley; Sophia Willard Ripley,
his wife; Miss Marianne Ripley, his elder sister; Mr.
George P. Bradford, Mr. Warren Burton, Mrs. Minot
Pratt with three children, Mr. Nathaniel Hawthorne
and several others. Mr. William Allen acted as head
farmer. There were in all about twenty persons.
Doubtless there were blisters on the palms and aching

bones, in the first raw days of labor, and the poetry of life was often lost in the fatigue of the body.

Of the men of the Transcendental Club only Hawthorne and Dwight joined what was called " Mr. Ripley's community "; and though Mr. Emerson talked favorably of it he finally declined to join when asked to do so by Mr. Ripley.

The farmhouse, the only dwelling there was on the place, must have resounded with remarkable echoes as the pioneers of the new social order alighted on its threshold. They were of cultivated families, and were nearly all from the city and neighborhood of Boston. Their hearts were open to the tender influence of buds and blossoms, the fresh springing grass and the bubbling brook. They watched the birds of various plumage; the oriole, who hung his basket nest from the pendant branches of the elm, the robin redbreast who built close in the thick branches of the firs, and the sparrow who was contented with a less prominent nest, as he picked up hairs from the stable or from underneath the windows.

They were fond of cows, pigs and poultry. There was a flower garden to work in. There was a plenty of wild flowers in the fields and in the woods near by. There was delightful solitude and delightful society, and there was a wonderful novelty in all. There were contrasts of character, deep, strong natures to reason with, cheerful hearts to talk with, and great hopes everywhere. What wonder that they laughed, frolicked and sang, and got up little parties and masquerades to entertain the wonderful, wonderstruck and remarkable visitors who came to see them?

The place was a "milk farm" when the "Transcendentalists," as they were often called, entered on it. The surroundings were picturesque. Some one of the party started at an early hour in the morning with the milk for Boston, nine miles away.

All was new and had to be done by many for the first time. There was much hard work for the women, as it was not a well-proportioned family; pupils and visitors added to the labor, but poetry and enthusiasm changed plain names into elegance, as Deborah into "Ora," and beautified the laundry and kitchen with hopes and glories.

Immediately the school was set in operation. There were some promising pupils. The young and talented Dwight, whose heart was too full to preach what he might better practise in this ideal society, soon left his pastorate in Northampton, Mass., and joined as instructor, and was shortly followed by the capable Dana, who gained power for himself as well as gave it to the Association.

The following persons were nominated for positions in the Brook Farm School, fall term, 1842: —

George Ripley, Instructor in Intellectual and Natural Philosophy and Mathematics.

George P. Bradford, Instructor in Belles Lettres.

John S. Dwight, Instructor in Latin and Music.

Charles A. Dana, Instructor in Greek and German.

John S. Brown, Instructor in Theosophical and Practical Agriculture.

Sophia W. Ripley, Instructor in History and Modern Languages.

Marianne Ripley, Teacher of Primary School.

Abigail Morton, Teacher of Infant School.

Georgiana Bruce, Teacher of Infant School.
Hannah B. Ripley, Instructor in Drawing.

The infant school was for children under six years of age; the primary school, for children under ten; the preparatory school for pupils over ten years of age, intending to pursue the higher branches of study in the institution.

A six years' course prepared a young man to enter college. A three years' course in theoretical and practical agriculture was also laid out. The studies were elective, and pupils could enter any department for which they were qualified.

There were various other details, the most striking of which was that every pupil was expected to spend from one to two hours daily in manual labor.

Before the Association started from Boston, a constitution was drawn up. The following is a copy of the original: —

Articles of Agreement and Association between the members of the Institute for Agriculture and Education.

In order more effectually to promote the great purposes of human culture ; to establish the external relations of life on a basis of wisdom and purity ; to apply the principles of justice and love to our social organization in accordance with the laws of Divine Providence ; to substitute a system of brotherly coöperation for one of selfish competition ; to secure to our children, and to those who may be entrusted to our care, the benefits of the highest physical, intellectual and moral education in the present state of human knowledge, the resources at our command will permit; to institute an attractive, efficient and productive system of industry; to prevent the exercise of worldly anxiety by the competent supply of our necessary wants; to diminish the desire of excessive accumulation by making the acquisition of individual property subservient to upright and disinterested uses ; to guarantee to each other the means of physical support and of spiritual progress, and thus to impart a greater freedom, simplicity, truthfulness, refinement and moral dignity to our mode of life,—

We, the undersigned, do unite in a Voluntary Association, to wit : —

ARTICLE 1. The name and style of the Association shall be " (The Brook Farm) Institute of Agriculture and Education." All persons who shall hold one or more shares in the stock of the Association, and shall sign the articles of agreement, or who shall hereafter be admitted by the pleasure of the Association, shall be members thereof.

ART. 2. No religious test shall ever be required of any member of the Association; no authority assumed over individual freedom of opinion by the Association, nor by any member over another ; nor shall anyone be held accountable to the Association except for such acts as violate rights of the members, and the essential principles on which the Association is founded ; and in such cases the relation of any member may be suspended, or discontinued, at the pleasure of the Association.

ART. 3. The members of this Association shall own and manage such real and personal estate, in joint stock proprietorship, as may, from time to time, be agreed on, and establish such branches of industry as may be deemed expedient and desirable.

ART. 4. The Association shall provide such employment for all of its members as shall be adapted to their capacities, habits and tastes, and each member shall select and perform such operation of labor, whether corporal or mental, as he shall deem best suited to his own endowments, and the benefit of the Association.

ART. 5. The members of this Association shall be paid for all labor performed under its direction and for its advantage, at a fixed and equal rate, both for men and women. This rate shall not exceed one dollar per day, nor shall more than ten hours in the day be paid for as a day's labor.

ART. 6. The Association shall furnish to all its members, their children and family dependents, house-rent, fuel, food and clothing, and all other comforts and advantages possible, at the actual cost, as nearly as the same can be ascertained; but no charge shall be made for education, medical or nursing attendance, or the use of the library, public rooms or baths to the members; nor shall any charge be paid for food, rent or fuel by those deprived of labor by sickness, nor for food of children under ten years of age, nor for anything on members over seventy years of age, unless at the special request of the individual by whom the charges are paid, or unless the credits in his favor exceed, or equal, the amount of such charges.

ART. 7. All labor performed for the Association shall be duly credited, and all articles furnished shall be charged, and a full settlement made with every member once every year.

ART. 8. Every child over ten years of age shall be charged for food, clothing, and articles furnished at cost, and shall be credited for his labor, not exceeding fifty cents per day, and on the completion of his education in the Association at the age of twenty, shall be entitled to a certificate of stock, to the amount of credits in his favor, and may be admitted a member of the Association.

ART. 9. Every share-holder in the joint-stock proprietorship of the Association, shall be paid on such stock, at the rate of five per cent, annually.

ART. 10. The net profits of the Association remaining in the treasury after the payments of all demands for interest on stock, labor performed, and necessary repairs, and improvements, shall be divided into a number of shares corresponding with the number of days' labor,

and every member shall be entitled to one share for
every day's labor performed by him.

ART. 11. All payments may be made in certificates of
stock at the option of the Association; but in any case
of need, to be decided by himself, every member may
be permitted to draw on the funds of the treasury to
an amount not exceeding the credits in his favor.

ART. 12. The Association shall hold an annual meeting for the choice of officers, and such other necessary
business as shall come before them.

ART. 13. The officers of the Association shall be
twelve directors, divided into four departments, as follows: first, General Direction; second, Direction of
Agriculture; third, Direction of Education; fourth,
Direction of Finance; consisting of three persons each,
provided that the same persons may be a member of
each Direction at the pleasure of the Association.

ART. 14. The Chairman of the General Direction
shall be presiding officer in the Association, and together with the Direction of Finance, shall constitute a
Board of Trustees, by whom the property of the Association shall be managed.

ART. 15. The General Direction shall oversee and
manage the affairs of the Association so that every department shall be carried on in an orderly and efficient
manner. Each department shall be under the general
supervision of its own Direction, which shall select,
and, in accordance with the General Direction, shall
appoint, all such overseers, directors and agents, as
shall be necessary to the complete and systematic organization of the department, and shall have full authority to appoint such persons to these stations as they
shall judge best qualified for the same.

ART. 16. No Directors shall be deemed to possess
any rank superior to the other members of the Association, nor shall be chosen in reference to any other
consideration than their capacity to serve the Association; nor shall they be paid for their official service

except at the rate of one dollar for ten hours in a day, actually employed in official duties.

ART. 17. The Association may, from time to time. adopt such rules and regulations, not inconsistent with the spirit and purpose of the Articles of Agreement, as shall be found expedient and necessary.

[*This was signed by*]

GEO. RIPLEY,	WARREN BURTON,	SOPHIA W. RIPLEY,
MINOT PRATT,	SAM♦ D. ROBBINS,	MARIA J. PRATT,
D. MACK,	GEO. C. LEACH,	NATH. HAWTHORNE,
MARIANNE RIPLEY,	LEML. CAPEN,	MARY ROBBINS.

Not all who signed this document entered on the work. Mr. David Mack, whose name is attached, for some reason did not, neither did Mr. and Mrs. Samuel D. Robbins. Mr. Mack afterward founded the Northampton Association at Northampton, Mass.

It would be interesting to give a history of and describe all the persons who signed this original document, but room will not permit it. Mr. Ripley's biography is published; I refer the reader to that book for particulars of his life, but cannot refrain from selecting one pen-picture of him by the author, Rev. O. B. Frothingham, who writes : —

" He was no unbeliever, no sceptic, no innovator in matters of opinion or observance, but a quiet student. a scholar, a man of books, a calm, bright-minded, wholesouled thinker, believing, hopeful, social, sunny, but absorbed in philosophical pursuits. Well does the writer of these lines recall the vision of a slender figure wearing in summer the flowing silk robe, in winter the long, dark blue cloak of the profession, walking with measured step from his residence in Rowe Street towards the meeting house in Purchase Street. The face was shaven clean, the brown hair curled in close, crisp ringlets ; the face was pale as if in thought ; the gold-rimmed spectacles not

cles concealed black eyes; the head was alternately be
and raised. No one could have guessed that the m
had in him the fund of humor in which his friends
lighted, or the heroism in social reform which a fe
years later amazed the community. He seemed a sob
devoted minister of the gospel, formal, punctilio
ascetic, a trifle forbidding to the stranger. But ev
then the new thoughts of the age were at work with
him."

Minot Pratt was at one time foreman printer at t
office of the *Christian Register* — a finely formed, larg
graceful-featured, modest man. His voice was low, so
and calm. His presence inspired confidence and respe
Whatever he touched was well done. He was faithf
and dignified, and the serenity of his nature welled
in genial smiles. In farm work he was Mr. Riple
right hand. He was not far from him in age. Th
agreed in practical matters; indeed, Mr. Ripley deferr
to him. His wife was an earnest, strong, faithf
worker. They entered into the scheme with fervor, ar
it was often said of him that he was first to give M
Ripley the hand of fellowship in the practical work
organizing the society.

John Sullivan Dwight was born in Boston, and wa
keenly sensitive to harmony of all kinds; amiabl
thoughtful, kind. Touched with the divine desire t
do good to all, he entered into the work with his whol
earnest soul. Modest to a fault, but singularly pe
sistent in what he felt to be his duty, he never flinche
or failed to act when occasion required it. His taste
anywere of the most refined order. He shrank from coars
ciation act with an unusual degree of sensitiveness, bu
conside reat heart embraced all mankind in brotherhood.
tion; n

He graduated at Harvard College, and rumor says that he had more than ordinarily the goodwill of his classmates. He studied and made some fine translations from French and German authors, and was ordained to the ministry. He soon left the pulpit, feeling that it was better to try to actualize a Christian life, preaching it by deeds himself, than to preach it by words to others. He was supremely musical, though his musical feeling sometimes showed itself in verse, and he stamped Brook Farm with his musical influence. Short in stature, delicate in physical organization, the school claimed the major part of his services.

Mrs. Ripley was born under favorable stars and had superior mental talent and training, with hosts of friends and relatives. Her devotion to the "Community" caused a great flutter in her social circle. Her relatives were noted for their position, their personal dignity, and generally for a haughtiness of manner unknown in these days. In person she was tall, slender and graceful, with rather light, smooth hair, worn in the plain style of the day. Being near-sighted she was obliged to use a glass when looking at a distant person or thing. Her manner was vivacious and she was a good conversationalist. Mr. Ripley had changed since the description given of his appearance in earlier days, and had grown stouter; had lost his pallor and gained a good, healthy color. He had allowed a vigorous beard to grow, and shaved only his upper lip.

A young man of education, culture and marked ability was Charles Anderson Dana when from Harvard College he presented himself at the farm. He was strong of purpose and lithe of frame, and it was not

long before Mr. Ripley found it out and gave him a
place at the front. He was about four and twenty
years of age, and he took to books, language and literature. Social, good-natured and animated, he readily
pleased all with whom he came in contact. He was
above medium height; his complexion was light, and
his beard, which he wore full but well trimmed, was
vigorous and of auburn hue, and his thick head of hair
was well cut to moderate shortness. His features were
quite regular; his forehead high and full, and his head
large. His face was pleasant and animated, and he
had a genial smile and greeting for all. His voice was
musical and clear, and his language remarkably correct.
He loved to spend a portion of his time in work on the
farm and in the tree nursery, and you might be sure of
finding him there when not otherwise occupied. Enjoying fun and social life, there was always a dignity remaining which gave him influence and commanded respect.
If you looked into his room you saw pleasant volumes
in various languages peeping at you from the table,
chair, bookcase, and even from the floor, and they gave
one the impression that for so young a person he was
remarkably studious and well informed.

George P. Bradford had the department of Belle
Lettres. Of him, after his decease, his former friend
and pupil, George William Curtis, wrote as follows in
Harper's Monthly for May, 1890 : —

"The recollection of George Bradford is that of a
long life as serene and happy as it was blameless and
delightful to others. It was a life of affection and
many interests and friendly devotion; but it was not
that of a recluse scholar like Edward Fitzgerald, with

the pensive consciousness of something desired but undone. George Bradford was in full sympathy with the best spirit of his time. He had all the distinctive American interest in public affairs. His conscience was as sensitive to public wrongs and perilous tendencies as to private and personal conduct. He voted with strong convictions, and wondered sometimes that the course so plain to him was not equally plain to others.

" It was a life with nothing of what we call achievement, and yet a life beneficent to every other life that it touched, like a summer wind laden with a thousand invisible seeds that, dropping everywhere, spring up into flowers and fruit. It is a name which to most readers of these words is wholly unknown, and which will not be written, like that of so many of the friends of him who bore it, in our literature and upon the memory of his countrymen. But to those who knew him well, and who therefore loved him, it recalls the most essential human worth and purest charm of character, the truest manhood, the most affectionate fidelity. To those who hear of him now, and perhaps never again, these words may suggest that the personal influences which most envelop and sweeten life may escape fame, but live immortal in the best part of other lives."

Among the signers was also Nathaniel Hawthorne, the writer, and it may not be out of place to make here a few comments on his relation to the Brook Farm life, so often alluded to by writers.

Hawthorne was an idealist in its broad sense. The idea of a juster and more rational social state pleased him. He felt himself honored, and was very grateful for the appreciation of the men and women by whom he was surrounded in the literary circle of the Transcendental Club, but he never surrendered the well-matured plan of his youth, to be a writer of stories.

When he went to Brook Farm he thought that his
manual labors might in a small way do a trifle towards
aiding the formation of the ideal state, and evidently
felt that in his leisure hours he could compose, write
for magazines, and the like; but the hard, unwonted
though self-imposed labor, the peculiar surroundings,
the buzz and hum of the large family in which he could
not fail to take an interest, distracted him from his
purpose.   James T. Fields, the publisher, said of him,
" He was a man who had, so to speak, a physical affinity
with solitude."   He could not put his mind to his special
work.   The seclusion in which he had worked before,
he could not find, and though "no one intruded on
him," as he says, yet he was not in his best element.

Had he stayed longer, this newness of situation
would doubtless have worn off, and he would have
found a seclusion little dreamed of at first acquaintance
with the life.   He was in haste to be at his writing;
so after a few months of manual labor, bidding adieu to
the farm, he found himself back in Boston.   There were
other interests that carried him there, for we find that in
the next year he married Sophia Peabody of Salem,
Mass.   Critics have said that the Brook Farm life was
hurtful to his genius.   He never once intimated it, but
said afterwards to Emerson that he was "almost sorry
he did not stay with the Brook Farmers and see it out
to the finish."

The most ingenuous, the most simple-minded of all
men in matters of ordinary business, in relative values
and exchanges, and unwilling to act as teacher, he could
only be counted as an ordinary day-laborer, except
where he could use the twin gifts of intellect and imag-

ination with which he was so highly endowed. His allusion to his "having had the good fortune, for a time, to be personally connected with it," and "his old and affectionately remembered home at Brook Farm" speak volumes, as does also this little passage from "Blithedale Romance":—

"Often in these years that are darkening around me, I remember our beautiful scheme of a noble and unselfish life, and how fair in that first summer appeared the prospect that it might endure for generations, and be perfected, as the ages rolled by, into the system of a people and a world. Were my former associates now there — were there only three or four of those true-hearted men still laboring in the sun — I sometimes fancy that I should direct my world-weary footsteps thitherward, and entreat them to receive me for old friendship's sake. More and more I feel we struck upon what ought to be a truth. Posterity may dig it up and profit by it."

In "Years of Experience" the writer, Georgiana (Bruce) Kirby, one of the early associates, says:—

"Hawthorne, after spending a year at the Community, had now left. No one could have been more out of place than he in a mixed company, no matter how cultivated, worthy and individualized each member of it might be. He was morbidly shy and reserved, needing to be shielded from his fellows, and obtaining the fruits of observation at second-hand. He was therefore not amenable to the democratic influences at the Community which enriched the others, and made them declare, in after years, that the years or months spent there had been the most valuable ones in their lives."

Messrs. W. B. Allen, Minot Pratt, Warren Burton, Charles Hosmer, Isaac Hecker and George C. Leach, with Mr. Hawthorne, devoted most of their time to out-door farm work.

Many of the pupils became interested in the new life with which they came in contact. It influenced them for good, and in after years they were full of gratitude and praise for the help and moral tone it imparted to them. An extract from a letter from Mr. Richard F. Fuller, the father of Margaret Fuller, to Mr. Ripley at this time reads as follows : —

"A lady asked me not long since where she should send her daughter to school. I said at once, to the *Community*, for there she would learn for the first time, perhaps, that all these matters of creed and morals are not quite so well settled as to make thinking nowadays a piece of supererogation, and would learn to distinguish between truth and the ' sense sublime,' and the dead dogmas of the past. This is the great benefit I believe you confer upon the young."

The pupil who became the most prominent was George William Curtis, who always acknowledged the beneficial effect it had upon all his future career.

New England and New York sent in their share of pupils until the accommodations were crowded. The school flourished. It was not large, but select. It was necessary to have more room, and a neighbor's cottage was hired. Enthusiasts wished to build on the place. Plans of procedure for the Association were indefinite. The central idea of justice to all men and women was ever uppermost. Mrs. Olvord, a lady of means, built a small gabled cottage of wood, which, owing to ill health, she was able to occupy but a short time. At the highest point of the domain, on a ledge of " pudding-stone," the Association erected a small, square, wooden building which was named " the Eyrie," and at another period a large double or twin house was built to be conjointly occupied by two brothers from Plymouth, Mass., of the name of Morton; it was called " the Pilgrim House." The original farmhouse was christened " the Hive." The cultivation of the farm proceeded, and some ornamentation in the shape of flower-beds was done around the houses. It was soon found that much milk was needed at home, and the sale of it was discontinued.

A few individuals making a common family on a farm near a city, would seem to be too unimportant a matter to excite much comment now, even though the people who did it were superior in attainments, of high purpose, and above criticism in their moral and social standing; but at this date of our country's history, all thoughtful people in New England seemed to be gaping at them with curiosity and wonder, and comments were unlimited. As they were neither dogmatists, nor active fanatics who brandished anathemas of terror and destruction at those who followed not in their ways, but simply and unostentatiously attended to their own business, and seemed to care very little for what any one said derogatory to their proceedings, the conditions appeared so unique, that interest in their doings increased day by day.

Mr. Ripley wrote of it a few months after its commencement: " We are now in full operation as a family of workers, teachers and students. We feel the deepest convictions that, for us, our mode of life is the true one, and no attraction would tempt any one of us to exchange it for that we have quitted lately." And it would be an impertinence now to penetrate into its private circles and bring its members and doings to the gaze of an investigating and curious public, were it not that its doings and its members have become, from their relation to social science, a part of public history.

The pressure of life was off at Brook Farm, for the nonce. What anyone did that was out of the common, might cause smiles and laughter but no frowns or scoldings. Each felt and believed in the demonstration of his or her own individuality, and, as a first consequence, there was something that was often mistaken, by strangers, for rudeness and want of order. Some forgot that it was especially work they came for, and were anxious to have their theories discussed. Independence in dress was universal. The Mrs. Grundys were all away, and if the young ladies thought it was prettier to exhibit the grace of flowing tresses than to bind them up in "pugs" behind their heads, who should, who could, object?

Prim Margaret Fuller, who was a visitor — and never a member of the community as has often been stated — professed herself disturbed, at first, by the easy and perhaps indifferent manner in which they listened to her long conversations, as they sat on the floor or on crickets; but on a later visit, she expressed herself as better pleased. Doubtless some of the individual angularities had been rubbed off, by this time, by the pleasant but close contact of the Community life — and some of hers as well.

CHAPTER II.

Two years of the experimental and "idyllic" life ran rapidly away, and the Community had gained something of position and name in the outward world. Personal contact had modified the extreme views of many of the founders. Changes had taken place in the individuals composing it; some had departed. Six of the original stockholders remained. The number had increased to about seventy, including some thirty who were pupils. The financial success had not been all that was desired. Everything else was getting more settled. The social life was charming. Improvements in material matters, in comforts, in discipline and in grace of manners were visible. But what was to be developed next among all the things desirable? Was it to push the school still further in progress, to attach mechanical industries to the organization, to work up the farm life into more prominence, or what?

It could not be expected that this large number of persons, whose early surroundings and ideas had been so varied, could at once agree as to what next steps were necessary to take, or to what definite end the Community should be shaped. There was need, certainly, of some central purpose strong enough for all to unite upon to inspire permanence.

Neither Mr. Ripley nor any of his co-workers had heard of Charles Fourier — the French exponent of industrial association — or his doctrines, unless in a most casual way, and certainly they had not studied them when they started the Community. They were independent workers in a field of social science; but when they became acquainted with his ideas, especially his ideas of industry made attractive by organized labor, and its relation to the higher standard of work and liberal belief they had adopted and maintained thus far, their enthusiasm was awakened for them and they resolved to graft some of his formulas on their institution. The little Community, with its bright, cheerful school and its happy members, was not paying its way. There were philosophers enough in it. There were plenty of sweet, charming characters and amateur workmen in it, but the hard-fisted toilers and the brave financiers were absent.

Still, it was not entirely absence of financial success that led the responsible men of the Community to make the change in the organization that they did, but truly because the grand and reasonable ideas of the distinguished Frenchman bore such internal evidences of harmony with human nature and with God's providence and laws that they carried conviction to the great and sympathetic minds of Brook Farm. Fourier argued that there was a sublime destiny for mankind on this earth, that the Creator was infinitely good, that all the instincts of our nature, when not subverted by bad conditions, pointed towards that destiny, and that humanity was on its way upward — that the past progress argued what the future might be.

I give as illustrations, a few extracts from "The Social Destiny of Man," by Albert Brisbane, page 269:—

"Four societies have existed on the earth — the savage, patriarchal, barbarian and civilized. Under these general heads may be classed the various social forms through which man has progressed up to the present day. *If four have existed may not a fifth, or even a sixth, be discovered and organized?* Common sense would dictate that there could, although the world has entertained a different opinion."

Page 293: "If the barbarian asserts that the lash is the only means of forcing the slave to labor, the civilized is not far behind him in his reasoning, for he will assert with equal confidence that necessity and want are necessary stimulants to industry. The barbarian is as ignorant of the levers which civilization puts in play as is the civilized of the powerful incentives to action which the groups and series will call forth."

Page 464: "If He [God] has not known how or has not wished to give us a social code productive of justice, industrial attraction and passional harmony: — *if he has not known how*, how could he have supposed our weak reason would succeed in a task in which he himself doubted of success? *If he has not wished*, how can our legislators hope to organize a society which would lead to the results above mentioned, and of which he wished to deprive us. . . . What motive could he have had to refuse us such a code? Six views may be taken on the subject of this omission.

"*First — either he has not known how* to give us a social code guaranteeing truth, justice and industrial attraction; in this case why create in us the want of it, without having the means of satisfying that want which he satisfies in creatures inferior to us, to which he assigns a mode of existence adapted to their attractions and instincts:

"Second — *or he has not wished* to give us this code; which thus supposes the Creator to be the persecutor of mankind, creating in us wants which it is impossible to

satisfy, inasmuch as none of our codes can extirpate our
permanent scourges:

"Third — *or he has known how and has not wished;*
in which case the Creator becomes a malignant being,
knowing how to do good, but preferring the reign of
evil:

"Fourth — *or he has wished and has not known how;*
in this case he is incapable of governing us, knowing
and wishing the good which he cannot realize, and which
we still less can attain:

"Fifth — *or he has neither wished nor known how;*
and we must attribute to him both want of genius and
evil intention:

"Sixth — *or he has known how and has wished;* in
this case the code exists, and he must have provided a
mode for its revelation — for of what use would it be
if it were to remain hidden from men for whom it is
destined ? "

Page 468 : "If the human race were at the commencement of their social career — in the first ages of civilization — they would perhaps be excusable for founding
some hope of social good upon human science, upon
the legislation of man; but long experience has proved
the impotency of human legislation, and shown clearly
that the world has nothing to hope from human laws
and civilized constitutions."

Page 260 : " Either the passions *are bad* or the social
mechanism *is false*, for evil prevails, and to a melancholy
extent. If the former be true, then there is no hope of
a better state of things, for every means of repression
and constraint that human ingenuity could invent has
been applied to regulate their action; but all in vain —
they have remained unchanged, and in the eyes of the
moralist as perverse as ever. If, however, the latter be
true — that is, if the social mechanism be false — then
there is a chance for a better future ; for our incoherent
and absurd societies are changing more or less with

very century. They are at the mercy or whim of a tyrant, or of a revolution of the mass; they may therefore be reformed or done away with entirely."

These grand words and this powerful logic, if even too strong for some of the readers of this book, were not so for the brave hearts of the leaders of Brook Farm, and for Mr. Ripley in particular. The tentative feeling, the search for science to back up the social impulses, seemed at last to have found something solid in a society conceived by the Creator; the man created by him, fitted to it by him; the society fitted to the man; the one the counterpart of the other. Albert Brisbane, Parke Godwin and Horace Greeley, with the *Tribune*, were arousing the thinkers in New York; Gerritt Smith was agitating the land question and giving away to actual settlers vast tracts of land owned by him. The works of the communist Owen and others were read. Antislavery, anti-war and non-resistance societies were vigorously prosecuting their claims. It was an era of great social activity. Thousands were aroused. "Communities," "Associations" and "Phalanxes" were springing up in various quarters. It seemed that the tide of change from social chaos to order was fast rising. A great wave of reform was sweeping over the land. Should the Community moor itself where it was, or be borne on with the flood?

This was the question of moment; and while the young danced or played, acted in charade or masquerade, and the youths wove garlands of green around their straw hats, and amused themselves by wearing long tresses and tunics, the sedater heads were solving this important question. And they must decide it, but first

of all Mr. Ripley's wishes must be consulted : the key
to the situation was in his hands.   What would he do?
Would he, and should they, take among them men and
women endowed only with practical, everyday talents,
able to be honest and make shoes and sew garments ; to
strike with a sledge and a blacksmith's arm; to be adepts,
maybe, in all the cares for the outward wants of the
body, but who had never read Goethe or Schiller, and,
possibly, neither Shakespeare, Scott nor Robert Burns;
and might not care to read or study Latin, French, German or philosophy !   It was for Mr. Ripley to decide.

Did he then think of the little church in Purchase
Street, and of what he had solemnly said to the listening congregation ?   Had he not told them that in every
soul was a divine fire that aspired to the right no matter
how deeply it had been covered from sight or buried by
the troubling cares and surroundings that environed it :
that there was a divine equality of spirit at the base of
all human lives ?

Did he not hear reverberating in his soul the sublime
passage, " If I be lifted up, I will lift all others up to
me " ?   Had he not been lifted up ?   Had he not been
supremely blest with health, strength, education, talent,
friends, companionship with the great and his cup filled
full of the sweet and sublime accords of the Christian
faith ?   Had he not been lifted up, not in crucifixion,
but by myriads of silent blessings, and was it not Christlike to aid in lifting all others up also?

Alas for those who speak of Mr. Ripley's action at
this time as " Ripley's fall " !   These were the moments
when he achieved his glory, when the greatness of his
character arose, almost without exception, above all

ers of the Transcendental School, who hovered
und, and wished to claim him as a bright example of
man separated from the common herd of humanity, as
eader of a select group of men and women, cultivated
ellectually and socially. Then, as before, when he
w what he deemed right, or, rather, when the in-
itions of his soul told him his duty, he did not hesi-
te.

Soon he was practically deserted by Emerson and his
oterie, by some of the associates and pupils of the
School, and boarders, who were scared out of their propriety by the fear of losing social caste, and they
howed their disfavor by leaving him alone; but, in-
trenched as he was, and surrounded by a multitude of
friends, new and old, and many secretly admiring his
intrepid spirit, they could only vent their disfavor in
by sneers and hints that Mr. Ripley, and, of course, his
followers with him, had fallen from their high estate.
Yes, they who sat near by on the fences and crowed reform the loudest — they who had never soiled their ink-
stained fingers with the grass-green sod of old Brook
Farm in practical example of work — found most fault
with him, because he chose to remain and risk his social
standing still more than he had already done, in his
magnificent work and experiment.

In order to show more clearly some of the philosophy
under which the leaders of Brook Farm based the
changes in their theories and organization, let us pause
a few moments to give a slight sketch of the growth of
human society from its primitive formation to the
present time, trusting that the time spent on it may not
be unworthily used, and the patience of those to whom

these ideas are old is asked for the benefit of others
whom they are new.

It is evident that, at some time, there was a beginning of social life. To those who have full faith in the
Mosaic record it was in the Garden of Eden; but that
may be considered as before society, as such, was fairly
begun. It was the very dawn of the childhood of our
race. To those who recognize the fact that the primitive man was a weak, unskilled, uncultivated savage,
the conclusion must come that the first social life of the
race was very crude; that men lived in trees or in caves
and rude huts, and that they formed societies or hordes
for protection from the huge and formidable wild animals that roamed the uncultivated earth.

Upon the slain beasts, wild fruits and grains they
existed. They hunted and fished, and although the
passions of friendship, love and ambition implanted in
their souls by their Creator shone out at times, at other
times they quarrelled like the brutes they slaughtered.
This state of crude society is named *savagism*.

But as the beasts became less formidable foes, and
were much diminished in numbers by being slain and
possibly from other causes, it is probable that at times
the race suffered hunger, and finding that the ground
readily produced from seed, the primitive race or races
began to plant, and finding also that they had slain so
many of the wild animals that they could keep herds of
cattle without great danger of their destruction by them,
the life of the herdsman began. But as the herds began to be numerous, it was found necessary to travel
with them in order to give them new pasturage, and
then the nomadic or wandering life was fully installed.

With their cattle and their wives, and their limited
owledge of cultivation, the patriarchal tribe moved
ʼom place to place; sometimes to find water, some-
ᵗnes to find pasture for their horses and cattle, and at
ʰarvest time they returned to their fields to harvest the
ʰain which had been planted for all. This, as you see,
ᵗscribes crudely the second state of society, which is
ʰe "*patriarchal*" state.

As population increased, the difficulty of constantly
ʰanging the place of residence was more and more ap-
ᵖarent; and as some arts had sprung up, such as the
ʰanufacture of pottery, farming implements and de-
ʰensive weapons, which could not be equally well car-
ᵗied on in all places, towns, and afterwards cities, sprang
ᵗᵤp, where the artisans resided; and being often liable
ᵗⁿo marauders, especially when the outside population or
ᵗribes were wandering away from them, they enclosed
ᵗhem with walls. By industry some wealth was ac-
ʲquired; some luxury and comparative splendor were
introduced. Prominent and naturally ambitious indi-
ᶠviduals and families raised themselves into power, and,
placing themselves at the head of armies, with the new-
est weapons of war, made by their own hands, went
forth to conquer. Thus the third, or what is called the
"*barbaric*," state was established.

Still moving on in the same direction, a great variety
of class distinction was made. Woman arose steadily
from a condition of almost hopeless slavery to be the
one companion of man, and direct slavery of man to
man was abolished. Invention was stimulated, and
means of dissemination of knowledge, such as the printing press and the university, came to light. Kings

and princes reign by law, which is fully established, an
commerce and trade flourish. These things inaugurat
the advent of civilization ; but perhaps the most marke
types of civilization are the *independence of the indi-*
vidual, monogamic marriage and *free competition.* Thu
was established the fourth societary condition.

Society having progressed so far, and gone through
so many changes, is it reasonable that it must now stop
at what we call "*civilization*" as the *ultimatum* of its
progress? With a little thought it will be seen how
surely man has, through all these changes, emancipated
himself from physical surroundings until he stands
forth free and independent, but without, however, any
positive relation or duty binding him to maintain the
independence of all the human brotherhood. His independence is for himself alone, and in that relation he is
forced by *conditions of his surroundings* to neglect and
trespass on the rights of his fellow-man to keep his individual supremacy, and to develop various promptings
of his soul, which are ofttimes good, great and noble.

In the early days of civilization, free competition de-
velops the resources of man. The prospect of wealth,
and the power it brings with it, encourages trade to
seek the ends of the earth, and from its products vast
enterprises are built up. As every fruit has in it that
which causes its final dissolution, and within it also the
germs of a future and higher life, so civilized society
carries in it the germs of its decay and dissolution, society being a natural product, as fruit is, of God's providence. *Free competition* is the destructive agent, or
one of the most important agents in its dissolution.
Observe that the power which ripens a natural fruit

ses, in the end, its destruction.   Observe also that
competition, which in the early stages of civilization glorifies and typifies it, by continuing at its work
will finally destroy it.

There is another element which is called capital.   In
savage life there is hardly anything which can be called
capital.   The amount of capital depends on the wealth
of the community.   As society advances, wealth increases; from savagism to civilization, from early civilization to the present time.   This wealth, this capital,
comes from the reserved products of labor; "dried
labor," it has been called, for labor is its only source of
production.   This wealth belongs to the community
that has earned it, saved it and inherited it.   It is the
grand moving power of society as it now stands, and
without it we would return to the savage state.   Society
can never be too wealthy, any more than it can be too
powerful, and the one is the synonym, to a great ex-
ent, of the other.

But capital with interest, as the agent and assistant
of competition, is destructive.   Capital joined with
labor builds manufactories, railroads, towns, and is the
great moving power of civilization; but in the growth
of civilization vast amounts of it have accumulated, and
being unevenly distributed, there are those who are constantly seeking its use to help them to business and to
elevation, and have been ready to pay a royalty, which
we call interest, for the use of it.   This has made capital a commodity.

The progress of arts and inventions has been, in
modern days, in such increased ratio to the increase of
capital that it has created so great a demand that a

monopoly has been made of it; more is paid for the u
of it than its real worth, so that wealth, even in t'
democratic country, is piling up in colossal fortunes
being drawn from the great body of society. Con
quently, classes of people grow relatively poorer as fa
as other bodies of people or individuals grow riche
the extremes of riches and poverty constantly increasin

Every advance in the producing capacity of machin
ery gives organized capital a better hold on labor, be
cause capital owns the machinery, and, in homely
phrase, labor " is the under dog in the fight " all of the
time. It makes no practical difference to it whethe
the laborer becomes capitalist or no, for the moment h
becomes so he is engaged in the same crusade. He .
no better nor worse than the one whom we called cap
italist yesterday. It is the *unnatural position* or *rel*
tion of *capital and labor* that makes him what he is
To change this relation to a more just one was among
the grandest ideas of the Brook Farmers, and the only
way it could possibly be done, in their estimation, was
by reorganizing society on a new basis; by combinin ·
the capital of the workers and others interested an
using it so as finally to control machinery for the bene
fit of labor, and to reduce its hours of toil so that th
laborer could have time for self-improvement.

Having traced the progress of society from its earliest
forms to our present civilization, it can be easily
shown how the supreme or governing power is first in
the hands of the most powerful physically; then passes
to the one most able by prowess to sway a tribe or people; then passes into the hierarchy of the church, that
rules by swaying mental terrors; next into the hierarchy

he state, that rules by both mental and physical forces; and, in our present civilization, has passed or is passing rapidly into the hands of a moneyed class ruling with powers according to the amount of capital swayed; and it can be proved that these changes are but the natural result of forces that are as sure and constant as sunlight and electricity.

This present form of social power, it is argued, is transient, and like the others, will pass away and be replaced, and can only be replaced by a failure, or by a hierachy of organized talent arranged in serial order from the most talented down to the humblest laborer, and this is another of the grand ideas of the Brook Farmers. From the seeds of this civilization will spring — is springing — a higher order. It is an order that the teacher Fourier called "*guaranteeism.*" It is an order in which the *governing power* passes from the moneyed aristocracy into the hands of *organized bodies.* It is an order in which the spiritual and material truths are incorporated into organic societies and governments which guarantee to everyone support in sickness and protection from dangers of various sorts; an order which, in fact, abounds in mutual guarantees covering by degrees all the numerous necessities and wants of life — hence its name; and finally, in the process of time, placing all the material wants of the people under protective guarantees.

This fifth condition of society must pass into the sixth order, which is the *associative order*, or the coöperative phase of society in which it will be proven by practical works that, by adherence to principles and proper organizations, we may avoid a large share of the

miseries we have in the past so unsparingly l t t
charge of the Deity as discipline for us, but u are
the results of our own ignorance. The "nonic
order " is associated life of a high type, and ndes
association of families, economy of means, unif interests, labor made attractive, equitable distribu of
profits, integral justice, etc., in such a way as ting
about very great happiness among *all* people, tide-
serving its grand name. From the commencem of
the age of harmony, which is a higher octave of fe,
society begins a new era, the beauties and accoi ict
which no one can do more than speculate upon. opt

This sketch of the progress of the human rac rse
seem trite to many readers. It may have a f om-
sound, but it is necessary to our narrative. It wa ro-
mulgated many years before our modern writers me
into the field with their evolutionary theories, and is
at least a theoretic base for social scientists to bld
their hopes of present and future progress on. To ie
Brook Farm leaders it was new; it was sensible; t
was reasonable. Communism they did not favor, f
their motto was, " Community of property is the grav
of individual liberty." Instinctively they rebelled
against it.

The organized communities held everything in common — houses, lands, moneys and goods ; even prescrib-
ing what garments should be worn, and also electing a
religious creed for their members. It was not compatible with the greater ideas of freedom held at Brook
Farm. It was not a free life and it could not be a true
life, for they all believed in the motto, " The *truth* shall
make you *free*," and instead of freedom, the " Com-

munities " used mental constraint and tyranny to hold themselves together.

The Brook Farmers believed that the laborer owned value of his labor ; if it was used, it was credited to , and a part of the increased value of the domain belonged to him. It never belonged to the organization; that is, the value of it — but by mutual consent might retained, invested and added to the laborer's stock. Theoretically the result would show that the person who was the most capable, active and industrious would in time own the most accrued capital. This the Brook Farmers claimed was right and according to nature. and, combined with *yearly diminishing interest*, could not be structive, as capital is now.

They had fallen unwittingly, it may be said, on ideas that coincided with those of Charles Fourier. There was an agreement between them, unknown at the start. Their idea that certain mutual guarantees were to be in the constitution, such as immunity from labor in extreme age and youth, care in sickness — a certain " minimum " rights according to the prosperity or wealth of the institution — and that an "integral education" was a duty of the Association — an education not of the mind alone, but of the hands, heart and affections — coincided exactly with Fourier, and it was easy to adopt the motto of " *coöperative labor*," for they had already adopted the principle ; also " *association of families*," for that had been agreed on. It was easy to adopt the formula of " *honors according to usefulness* "; they believed in it.

Usefulness, not wealth, station or any artificial distinction, was to receive the highest rank and the greatest honors and favors from the body politic. It might be

an invention of the mind; it might be some Herculean
or disagreeable labor of the body, or it might be some
enthusiasm imparted from some brilliant soul, that would
win the honor; but it could be given to none except
those who had won it by superior usefulness, when
that usefulness came from doing the work in the "sacred legion " — who were a body of persons who
unattractive work from a sense of duty — or in any other
body or group.

It was easy to adopt " *attractive industry*," another of
Fourier's mottoes, for were they not trying mind
body to make it so? And finally, it was easy to add
the aphorism that the attractions of life in the univ...
are in proportion to the destinies they assist in accom-
plishing — " *attractions are proportionate to destinies*,"
as it is translated. Certainly it was simple and easy
grasp and believe, when explained so well as it had be
by Fourier, and by Brisbane and Godwin, his Americ
translators. And lastly, if all these things were tru
why not say so and adopt them? They were outsid
and free from modern society. They had one of thei
own. They were happy in it. They had adopted truth
as their guide — truth as they saw it, and whenever and
wherever they saw it.

Thus closed the first chapter in the history of this
little society. They had gathered together without any
idea of scientific organization, but from profound convictions of the present wrong relations of the human
brotherhood, from religious convictions of duty, and in
the belief that they would increase in love to one another, and draw to themselves by their example the good
and wise; believing also that if they planted the seeds

of truth and unity they would be watered with deeds of
faith, and by degrees overtop and destroy the evil under-
growth that abounded in the so-called civilization all
around them.

Now came to the leaders a new revelation! It was of
science applied to society. Mr. Ripley had great faith
scientific agriculture. Was there to be science applied to society? Was it true that the actual laws
applicable to social life had been discovered? Were
they immutable as the laws of earthly bodies — of
the sun, the stars and the universe? And did they
actually agree with the laws of music, color and mathematics? It seemed so. They could but try them. And
with a faith for which, during all these succeeding years,
they have been laughed at by cynical philosophers, they
went to work to apply them, as far as possible, to the
actual life they were then leading. All honor to
them!

When the resolution was finally taken to join with
the movements that seemed to be, as it were, a new impulse for humanity's sake — an outpouring of spirit
upon the children of men, instanced by the very great
and sudden interest taken by numerous bodies, societies
and individuals along the line of social reform — it was
not entirely palatable to all who had looked on the little Community as their pet property, their ideal home;
for the sainted individualists, for cultivated book-worms,
for theorists who could read Latin and Greek but
whose ideas of labor extended only to planting flowers
or washing with care a few muslins to adorn their
beautiful selves; and fearing a loss of selectness some
departed. The motive extended to the school, and,

although many of the former pupils left, their places were soon filled by others.

The responsible men looked at the matter from another standpoint. They felt that the labor on the farm had been the least success of anything, and that to organize and improve it was one thing important, if not *the* one thing needful. Many good men stood at the outer gates waiting for entrance. The members of the "Direction" were firm, and brave. They felt that the experience of the first two years was a permanent advantage to them, and they reorganized under the same name as before. With the new constitution was published a preliminary statement from which the following is extracted : —

"All persons who are not familiar with the purposes of Association, will understand from this document that we propose a radical and universal reform rather than to redress any particular wrong, or to remove the sufferings of any single class of human beings. We do this in the light of universal principles in which all differences, whether of religion, or politics, or philosophy, are reconciled, and the dearest and most private hope of every man has the promise of fulfilment. Herein, let it be understood, we would remove nothing that is truly beautiful or venerable ; we reverence the religious sentiment in all its forms, the family and whatever else has its foundation either in human nature or Divine Providence. The work we are engaged in is not destruction, but true conservation; it is not a mere resolution, but, as we are assured, a necessary step in the progress which no one can be blind enough to think has yet reached its limit.

"We believe that humanity, trained by these long centuries of suffering and struggle, led on by so many saints and heroes and sages, is at length prepared to enter into that universal order toward which it has perpetually moved. Thus we recognize the worth of the whole past, and of every doctrine and institution it has bequeathed us; thus also we perceive that the present has its own high mission, and we shall only say what is beginning to be seen by all sincere thinkers, when we declare that the imperative duty of this time and this country, nay, more, that its only salvation and the salvation of civilized countries, lies in the reorganization of society according to the unchanging laws of human nature, and of universal harmony.

" We look, then, to the generous and helpful of all classes for sympathy, for encouragement and for actual aid; not to ourselves only, but to all who are engaged in this great work. And whatever may be the result of any special efforts, we can never doubt that the object we have in view will be finally attained; that human life shall yet be developed, not in discord and misery, but in harmony and joy, and that the perfected earth shall at last bear on her bosom a race of men worthy of the name."

[*Signed by the Directors.*] GEORGE RIPLEY.
MINOT PRATT.
i CHARLES A. DANA.
Brook Farm, Mass., Jan. 18, 1844.

This constitution was largely like the first one, but varied from it in the following particulars: —

" The department of Industry shall be managed in groups and series as far as is practicable, and shall consist of three primary series, to wit : Agricultural, Mechanical and Domestic Industry. The chief of each group to be elected weekly, and the chief of each series once in two months by the members thereof, subject to the approval of the General Direction."

" Persons wishing to become members must first reside on the place as applicants for one month."

"Applicants who have passed acceptably through their term may become candidates, and remain in this new relation a month more, when they may be admitted as Associates."

"Personal property may be received as stock by the Direction of Finance when it shall be deemed advantageous to the Association."

"Persons shall, on becoming residents on the domain, deliver an exact inventory of all the furniture and implements which they may retain as private property, to be filed for reference in the office of the Direction."

"New groups and series may be formed from time to time for the prosecution of different and new branches of industry."

"Three hundred days shall be considered a year's labor. The hours of labor shall be from the first of October to the first of April at least eight hours daily, and from the first of April to the first of October at least ten hours daily, and no person shall be credited for labor beyond that time."

"No debt shall be contracted in behalf of the Association by any person whatever."

"Articles furnished to the Associates shall be charged at cost as nearly as the same can bo ascertained."

"The period of education shall extend from birth to the age of twenty years, and shall be divided into three stages: Infancy to six years, Pupilage from six to sixteen years, and Probation from sixteen to twenty. The education during probation shall be in the practical duties of Associates."

"No public meeting for business or amusement shall be protracted beyond the hour of ten P. M."

Many persons who have heard of the Community life at Brook Farm have idealized it into a little coterie of choice spirits who sat around the study lamp at early eve, after the light toil of the day had ceased, and discussed the intellectual problems of the German philosophers who had given much of the impulse to the Transcendental Club, and brought so many young men forward as leaders of thought : but this was only partially true.

Mr. Ripley at first endeavored to instruct the assembly and impart to them some of his own intellectual enthusiasm. Evening classes were formed ; readings took place from some of the prominent poets — Goethe, Schiller, Shakespeare ; from Carlyle and Cousin as well as Emanuel Kant ; but when the industrial period began he had more than his hands full, and he laid his books on the shelf. They were his tools — they were the ladders on which he had mounted to his high estate. Why should he worship them ? They had taught him, as had the Hebrew writers, faith in the Creator ; faith in His creation, man ; faith in reason, faith in right, faith in magnificent human destiny. Why should he spend his life in singing praises of them ? To work ! To begin to shape society to higher ends ! That was indeed the worthiest end in life, and his worthiest homage to the writers and their books.

CHAPTER III.

It was a pleasant afternoon in March, 1843, when I left Boston, in a small omnibus, that started from Brattle Street for West Roxbury Village and Brook Farm. My father's family of three had preceded me, he remaining behind to close his business; it was a question of but a few days when we should be all embarked in the new and untried life to which we were looking forward with pleasurable emotions.

The nine miles of interval was passed, riding through an undulating country, by pleasant farms surrou. bel with the stone walls so common in Massachusetts bol the eastern states, and by pretty white houses, witl green window blinds and little front flower gardens with fruit and shade trees standing sentinels on thei borders. Here and there a ledge of "pudding-stone' cropped out, and the scenery grew more primitive as we neared the vicinity of the farm. Slowly we rode, on, leaving passengers and parcels by the way until it showed signs of deepening twilight, when we reached by a slight acclivity the door of the farmhouse that was, at the entrance of the place, where I was soon joined by my relatives who took me in charge and made me presentable for supper; but I was too late to join with the family, and took my first meal with them the following day.

Looking out of the window the next morning, I found it overlooked the farmyard and the broad meadow that lay south of the house. What awakened me was the sound of a trumpet or horn, blown by some one for rising or breakfast. I dressed leisurely, as I found it was the first or "rising horn," and went out of the front door for a survey. Before me was the driveway. A wooden fence, and a row of mulberry and spruce trees stood guarding the two embankments that were terraced down to the brook and meadow. On the embankments were shrubs and flower beds. A couple of rods to the right stood a graceful elm, beside a gateway that opened on a pathway to the garden and fields.

Passing by the front of the house I found that two wings had been added to it in the rear, leaving shed and carriage room beneath. Directly in front of me, and facing due east, was a large barn raised upon stone posts, which was open on the south side to the large barnyard, and between the barn and house was a drive-way or road, leading over the premises.

In the kitchen, which was directly in the rear of the dining room, there was a clatter of dishes, and a few persons were going from place to place outside.

Some one was in the barn attending to the cattle. He had on a tarpaulin straw hat, and a farmer's frock of blue mixture that hung down below the tops of his cowhide boots. I looked sharply at the man, and found it was Mr. George Ripley. The "second horn" sounded; it aroused the dog, who howled pitifully or musically — in bad unison with it. Soon the persons from the other houses came to breakfast, strolling leisurely along.

I found that all the people, unless ill, took their meals at the farmhouse dining room. A little quaintness of dress, some picturesque costumes — such as the blue tunics with black belts of leather, that the men wore; the full beards, that were not common then as now; the broad hats and graceful, flowing hair of the young ladies; the varied style of garments of the students and the boarders — all interested me.

The long, low dining room had rows of tables, some six in number, seating on an average fourteen persons each. White painted benches supplied the place of chairs. The tables were neatly set in white ware; white mugs served for both cups and drinking glasses. There were white linen table cloths, and everything was scrupulously neat.

At the farther end of the room sat Mr. Ripley. The garments of the husbandman and farmer had all been laid aside, and, neatly dressed, he was smiling and laughing, his gleaming eyes seeming to reflect their brilliancy on the golden bows of his spectacles. At his right sat his wife, and near by his sister, who poured the morning libation of tea or coffee. Most of the pupils were at this table. Mrs. Ripley, tall, graceful and slim, was, like her husband, near-sighted, but only on occasions would she raise a gold-bowed eye-glass to look at some distant object or person. The fare at the table was plain; good bread. butter and milk from the farm were present. It is hardly necessary to say that I looked around with peculiar interest on those who were to be my new friends and companions. It was not a dismal or sober meal. There was a happy buzz that indicated to me a probability of great future happiness.

How well do I remember the old dining-room with its familiar forms and faces — too many to describe now! There were the young and pretty Misses Foord; the one a dimpled blonde, lovely, rosy-complexioned, with large, wonderful blue eyes; and her sister with her clear skin and dark hair and eyebrows, both wearing their contrasted and unbound tresses flowing over their graceful shoulders. And hark! 'tis Dolly, dear Dolly Hosmer, with her rollicking, noisy laugh. And pretty Mary Donnelly — oh, how pretty! with the dimples and the peach-bloom on her face, her white teeth and coal-black hair — ever pretty whether she was smiling at you or peeling potatoes. And Charles Newcomb, the mysterious and profound, with his long, dark, straight locks of hair, one of which was continually being brushed away from his forehead as it continually fell; with his gold-bowed eye-glass, his large nose and peculiar blue eyes, his spasmodic expressions of nervous horror, and his cachinnatious laugh. There were sturdy Teel, and heavy Eaton, and frisky Burnham, and bluff Rykman, with round-eyed Fanny Dwight and another graceful Fanny, and oh! so many more men and women, friends and workers striving for a sublime idea. I could describe very many of them and the minute details of all the houses and surroundings, but it would unwisely overcrowd these pages.

Mounting the central and highest portion of the farm I found it was beautifully situated in an amphitheatre

surrounded by hills on all sides, and formed a charming
picture. There was a young orchard of apple trees, and
here and there stood a few shade trees by the walls and
roadside. There were fields, or rather patches, where
corn and vegetables were grown for family use. Some
of them were exposed on the southern faces of the hills,
and some were in the hollows. In front was the broad,
meadow, like a pleasant sea of green, stretching far
away.

From the first house, the old farmhouse called now
" the Hive " — a pretty and well-chosen name — the
driveway led to the other houses. It descended nearly
to the level of the meadow, and did not rise again until
it neared the " Pilgrim House," the most distant one.
From that it turned on itself on the high ground toward
the " Cottage " and " Eyry," the remaining houses.

The " Pilgrim House," an oblong double house, oc-
cupying a commanding position, was plain and white,
without ornamentation, and squarely built like most of
the New England country houses of its date. There
were no trees around it, and it was the least attractiv
house on the place.

The " Cottage " had four gables, and was also plai
and unpretending; it had only some half-a-dozen room
and was painted a dark brown color. It was situate
on a little knoll, with flower beds in the rear, and greer
sward all around it.

Beyond and nearer to the " Hive," in the centre
the domain, was the " Eyry " (this is the way Mr. Rip
ley spelled it; some spelled it " Eyrie " and some
" Aerie "). It had for its base a ledge of Roxbury conglomerate called " pudding-stone," and it was banked

up with two greensward terraces. It had the highest
and finest location, with a background of oak and maple
woods, and looked out on the orchard, commanding a
fine view. It was a square, smooth, wooden structure,
painted a light gray, sandstone color. It was made of
smooth, matched boards, and had a large, flat cornice or
flange that surrounded it near the top, which saved it
from extreme plainness. Yet it was pleasing to the eye,
and it had low, French windows that open like doors out
on to the upper terrace.

As I looked in it for the first time I saw that a few
pictures adorned the walls : pressed fern leaves filled
the mantel vases, and the bright remnants of last
autumn's foliage were in some places fastened to the
walls. There was also a piano, over which hung an oil
painting, and in the opposite room was a large array of
Mr. Ripley's books. It was " the library," and many of
the works were in German. In particular, there was a
set of fourteen volumes, " Specimens of Foreign Literature," edited by Mr. Ripley, that attracted my
attention.

At the Cottage were the school-rooms principally for
the younger children ; and the Pilgrim House was used
mostly for family lodgings.

For a time my sleeping apartment was with others in
the upper room of the rear wing of the farmhouse, dignified by the name " Attica." My companions were all
single men ; good, reliable fellows who were working
for a principle and would ordinarily have declined such
a lodging-place, but under the circumstances were not
apt to grumble, but made the best of it. It was like
camping out, and all its mischances were turned into

fun. My roommates were called "the Admiral," "the Dutchman," "the General" and "the Parson," — nicknames given each one of them for some personal peculiarity.

There were advantages as well as disadvantages in living in "Attica." It was nearest the centre of the life and business of the place. In the winter mornings there was no long walk to meals, as those had who lived at the other houses. We were near the warm kitchen; and when the house was still and work suspended — all save the baking of bread, which often proceeded in the evening in the range ovens — a group would gather around the fire and talk and gossip — for we were not beyond the last; speculation, theory and argument went pleasantly on until bed-time.

No, Attica! I have not forgotten the days spent inside thy walls, thy strange inhabitants, or the mysteries that surrounded thee on my first entrance into thy domain! I have not forgotten the long, low roof and projecting beams, or the half dozen bedsteads that were standing around; the two large chimneys that arose in the centre and the number of stove-pipes that came from below and entered them; or the skylights that were thy only means of illumination save the window at "the Parson's" end, which looked out on the pleasant fields and the houses beyond; or the plain, uncarpeted floor, the washstands by the chimneys and the clothing hung up around.

Neither have I forgotten the nights when lying in bed I have heard the rain pouring and pattering above thee and me; or when I saw by the dim light of a single oil lamp, as I lifted myself on my elbow in bed, one of the occupants moving his cot bedstead from some gentle leak that was getting too familiar with his bedclothes; or when in the dreary winter the Storm King howled around and bore some fleecy flakes on his windy gusts through a stray hole in the roof, and morning showed us a miniature white mountain on the floor.

No, to this day a vision of the "Parson" (Capen) comes to me, reading by the light of an oil lamp placed on a shelf at the head of his bedstead, long after others were asleep; lying in bed at the furthermost portion of thy space; now chuckling to himself, then drowsily reading on and on, with his spectacles dropped down on to the point of his long nose — as the passage was either witty or dry; or visions of the early risers, waking betimes and disturbing the dreams of the later ones by the preparations of the toilet; or the sound of the morning horn as it rose from beneath us on the clear air!

I was seventeen years of age, and having passed the time when I could have been by right a pupil in the day school, was assigned to manual labor. You will see by the Constitution that I was a "Probationer." It was fortunate that I loved the grass and trees, and the routine of farm life. My youth excused and deprived me of the council meetings and the right to vote, so that many hours spent by some, though but a little older than myself, in meetings, were absolutely mine to rove in, or to use as I liked. Though born to city life and work I dearly loved the country and a farm, but did not know its duties, nor had I the strength for heavy labor, so I assisted in work in and about the houses in the early hours of the day, and in some of the lighter farming, as planting, hoeing, weeding and driving the oxen, horses and cows; in fact, taking a lad's place in the farm and house employments.

Owing to the amount of labor and the disproportion of female help, some of the young men under age oftentimes assisted after meals in wiping dishes and supplying hot and cold water. It was a matter of rivalry between parties to see which could beat in a match, the washer or wipers. Two lads of near my own age supplied dishes and hot water as fast as it was needed, and one young lady washed the plates, saucers, mugs and the like, the same young men doing the wiping.

There was plenty of plain crockery piled up and it was rushed into a capacious receptacle and washed with great dexterity. Then wipe, young men, wipe! Will you allow a young lady to wash faster than two can wipe? *Never, boys, never!* and with incredible speed the surface of the plates and dishes was changed into mirrors. There was one young lady who was hard to beat; often when the parties thought they had nearly succeeded she would cry out for "hot water"! and one would have to supply her with it, and by that time his partner would be overwhelmed with a stock of unwiped crockery. Need I say that at times I was one of those boys?

There were none of the modern conveniences for water, and the pump had to do its share of work. The rooms were supplied daily by a water carrier who went from house to house filling the pails and pitchers in the rooms and halls.

I was willing and tractable. The fresh air, the simple diet and the free life began at once to tone up my organization. I soon found that the Eyry steps and the Eyry embankments were where the air was freshest of an evening, and the tones of the piano presided over by the "poet's sister," Fanny Dwight, attracted me more and more. The pupils and those of their ages grouped naturally together. I did not care to go among the arguers and the disputants who talked anti-this and anti-that, the new sciences of medicine — the water cure and homœopathy; who disputed the doctrines of community of property, western lands, politics, approaching war with Mexico, etc., etc. Nor did I care to group with the few who played euchre and smoked "conchas," and the book of nature had very often more charms for me than any other.

Our family rooms were small, and as stated I was sandwiched in with others, in rather unpromising quarters. But I almost only slept there. My interested parents often spent the evenings as well as the days in domestic duties, so I was much alone. I cared not. I could thoughtfully contemplate the climbing constellations, and sometimes one of the many who grew friendly to me would point out the planets and name the stars for me, and I would watch the moon rise slowly above the horizon. The beautiful meadow was below me, and above and around the whole eastern hemisphere of sky. Or I would wander around the houses to see what was going on, meeting groups of promenaders by the way. At the cottage the piano would be playing, and likely as not Lucas and José or Willard and Charles were waltzing with Anna and Abbie or Katie and Agnes to Louisa's playing. Or it was singing school, and all joined it; or Mrs. Ripley was going to read "Margaret"; or the "Professor"

(Dana) wanted most in his German class; or it was full moon and we would walk a mile or two down the highway, or make a moonlight visit to the pines. Otherwise I was dreaming day-dreams to Fanny's piano playing.

Ah! do you think I was indolent? Not so! In my meditations I was working out social problems and solving theories of life and religion. I was nursing kindliness of heart, love to all men. I was awakening a crushed nature, and absorbing influences that made the mottoes of "Unity of man with man," "Unity of man with God," "Unity of man with the universe," seem like real, tangible things. But who can say how much was also due to the low, soothing harmonies that floated out of those graceful windows with parting sashes that opened like doors down to the windowsills?

In time I explored every cranny and hollow of ground. I wandered in the woods, found every wild flower, knew every tree; knew where the trailing evergreens grew; could go to the spot where I could find what I wanted for bouquets, and surprised the Community with their ample size and beauty. I came in with wreaths and garlands; gathered varieties of grasses untold; picked rhodoras in early spring, saracenas and orchids in summer, asters and gentians in the late fall, and innumerable flowers in various places of a neighborhood wonderfully rich in botanical specimens.

CHAPTER IV.

THE INDUSTRIAL PERIOD.

WHEN I arrived, Hawthorne, Bradford, Hosmer, Hecker, Burton, Leach and Allen had gone ; as had also the Curtis brothers, George and Burrill, the Bancroft boys, sons of the historian, and Barlow (since General Barlow) — all pupils; as well as some of the ladies — Miss Dora Gannett, niece of Rev. Ezra S. Gannett, Miss Georgianna Bruce, (afterwards Mrs. Kirby), Miss Allen, Miss Sarah Stearns; and the phase of the Brook Farm life jocosely or seriously alluded to by the after-comers as the "Transcendental Days" or "Community Times," gave place to the "Associative or Industrial Period."

In the place of the Transcendentalists came other men and women, new and untried, with not so much of Greek and Latin, not so much suavity of manners, not so much "cultivation," but warm of heart and brave of purpose. The magnificent idea was a revelation of truth to some but also a great temptation for many shivering poor and impatient outsiders. They could thrive on it. They felt it was their right, their destiny, having failed in the civilized fight for bread and butter and comfort, to have from some source food, shelter and protection; and it struck them that Brook Farm was just the place to go for it. So the Association was inundated with applications of all kinds by person and by letter.

It is my fortune to possess the originals of a number of these interesting letters, specimens of which may be found in the appendix. The replies by Mr. Ripley were drafts of the letters sent; they are all in his fine hand-writing and *bona fide* documents which the writer personally secured at Brook Farm many years ago, after the organization had broken up.

The Directors used discretionary power, and if there was any probability that the applicant would be useful, his case was presented for action at a general meeting of the Association.

I was not long on the farm before I became acquainted with many of the Associates besides those before mentioned — those who belonged entirely to the Associative period ; and among the unique figures there was no one that struck my young fancy more than that of Peter, or, in familiar talk, " the General."

Peter M. Baldwin was about his work when I was introduced to him, and as he put forth his hand I saw that his arms extended no little way through the sleeves of a common green baize jacket; and that his large feet, which were encased in an old pair of slippers, had descended some six inches below a pair of blue overalls before they touched the ground. If he had been inclined to corpulency, his frame was ample to build upon for a man of Websterian proportions, but he was not so inclined; on the contrary, he simulated other great men in his personality — Jackson, or our modern Abraham Lincoln. He was spare, bony, nervous. His heavy eyebrows, his dark hair well sprinkled with gray, which arose straight upward from his high, indented forehead, and his large, half-Roman nose, prominent cheek-bones and thin cheeks reminded one so forcibly of the pictures of General Jackson that he was by unanimous consent nicknamed " the General."

He shook me by the hand warmly and asked me a few questions, and it was not until after this first interview that I discovered he had an impediment in his speech. A rapid talker, he would rattle on in conversation and then stop as suddenly as though you had put your hand over his mouth. You would look up in astonishment, and then find by the contortions of his face that he was trying to speak some troublesome word but could not. The word once recovered, his speech flowed on as before and perhaps for a long while, until he stumbled upon another fence-like one ; when he would dismount, take down the bars, or jump it, and proceed as before.

This impediment, strange to say, never troubled the General when he had prepared a piece for recitation, for he would then speak with dignity and precision, and made the very beau ideal of " the lean and hungry Cassius."

He was a universal favorite, on account of the kindness and benevolence of his disposition. This generosity was superabundant, for if any of the younger portion of the family wished for the sweets of the storeroom, over which he presided, they had only " to coax the General " to succeed in obtaining their wishes.

" The General " was the baker and made the bread, cake and some of the pastry. He also assisted the " kitchen group " in domestic cookery. Beyond this he was particularly fond of three things — disputation, the newspapers and a cigar. He was thoroughly devoted to the doctrines of " united industry " and to Brook Farm He was among the first up in the morning and last at night, attending to his ovens and his bread.

Peter's room was at first in Attica with others, where I saw him often, and his favorite pastime was a game of euchre, which had not then worked itself into general favor. I did not care to play it then, or any cards; I was too much charmed with the life of the place, with the society of the young, with social games under the inspiration of the hostess, with love of dance and music and the ever-changing face of nature, to care for such dull solace as the pasteboard games.

But the General did; he conversed, he smoked, he read the newspapers, he argued, stuttered and talked the " water cure," and one day I was surprised on going into the room to find him fully embarked for the cure of a desperate headache. What had he done? Why, taken the wash-bowl and filled it with water, placed it on the floor, stretched himself out at full length on the floor also, and, with a pillow at his shoulders, laid the back of his head into the wash-bowl. But being of an active temperament he could not be quiet and idle long, so, calling for a newspaper and lighting a cigar, he gently puffed the weed and read the news, lying still in position while the " cure " was progressing. It was a funny sight !

My attention was soon drawn to a large, portly gentleman who carried his head erect and had an easy, familiar way about him ; for he was acting as host, being charged with the reception of guests and strangers who came to visit or to look about the place. He walked with the grandeur of a Falstaff and the dignity of a sachem. His capacious gray coat and broad-brimmed hat might suggest to a stranger that he had been at some time a member of a Shaker community, but his closely cut gray hair and his heavy, o'erhanging eyebrows and brave visage gave the lie to any such suggestion. Aye, aye, every hair that stood bristling up on that front of his seemed to stand in rebellion against such a charge, seemed saying, and growing more bristly every moment, "I, a Shaker? Not I!" A large mouth was an appropriate companion to a ponderous throat and chin, which were daily shaven with scrupulous adherence to the first principles of warm water, soap and a sharp razor, and a practice of thirty years gave a polish to his face unknown to those less adept in the art.

On one occasion, some of the members fled from the tyranny of the brutal blade and let their beards grow in uncut stubble, not, however, without criticism from our host, who said in answer to their argument that it was natural for the beard to grow, "Art is the perfection of nature! Look at this garden!" It was after dinner, and some were taking a few moments' rest in front of the Hive, lounging on the fence and looking down the terrace into what was called "her majesty's garden" and toward the bubbling brook. "What would it be without its walks, flower-beds and arrangement?" he continued. "And these fields — what would they be without the art of cultivation? You see it is art that perfects nature."

Then some wag suggested that he was trying to cultivate "the field of his face," but nothing could disturb the imperturbable gravity of his composition. Gravity, solid gravity, was one of the basic elements of his nature.

When, however, he lighted his enthusiastic lamp, and his warm heart gushed forth in song or story — I think I hear him singing now, " A man's a man for a' that!" — he carried his audience with him.

The " Omniarch," as Mr. Ryckman was called, was a man of family, his short, sprightly, nervous little wife acting as hostess and attending to the lady visitors.

Many visitors asked the question of him, " Mr. Ryckman, do the Brook Farmers hold all their property in common ? "

With a bland smile he would say to them : " Certainly not ; the idea of a Community, as it is generally understood, is a society that owns or holds all the property or capital of its members as its own, in its own corporate right — that no one can remove, but everyone can use portions of at will, or in turn. If the ideas of the first projectors were not all definite on this point, we now stand boldly as champions of individual property. It is one of our watchwords. For what is property ? It is but the extension of the individual ; wings to fly with ; hands to work with ; dried labor ; labor's product laid away for future use, to bless oneself with. It is the bottom and foundation of material society, for none exists without it, and the greater the amount, distributed fairly and justly, the greater the power and strength of the society that holds it. We take human nature as it is — as God made it. We do not propose to remake it; that is the folly of reformers and theorists, and more especially moralists in and out of the church. The desire, the personal desire, to acquire property is a fundamental trait of character more or less strong in every individual. If a society cannot be adjusted to that trait

it will fail.   We think one can be.   We think ours is
so, as fairly as the nature of our transitory conditions
will allow.   We want capital here.   That we can make
it here in time, there is no doubt, but we must labor
long to secure a plus of labor that we can dry and store
for future use.   Meanwhile we want to build a suitable
unitary building, which is almost an absolute necessity ;
farming implements and various appliances are wanted
to suit the new conditions under which we live, and
many things for comfort, too numerous to mention."

The host was not sparing of his words, especially when
stimulated by charming questioners, in ways like these:
" Tell me more, Mr. Ryckman."   "What are you living
here for?"   " Can you expect anything from this
life ? "

" Yes, madam, we expect a great deal.   The theory
of our life is that a great saving can be made over ordinary ways of living.   It now takes one hundred houses
for one hundred families, and one hundred housekeepers,
and probably, on the average, one hundred servants, one
hundred kitchens, one hundred fires, and as many cooking stoves or ranges, and everything in proportion.
Now by combining together the saving on the cost of all
these houses and cooks, kitchens, coal and wood, dispensing with all unnecessary servants and labor, a house
of magnificent proportions adapted to the wants of the
combined families could be built, with elegant parlors
for lectures, assemblies and music; dining-rooms,
kitchens and laundries which would not cost as much
as the separate households full of inconvenience and
discomfort.

" This economic side of our life is easily seen, but

there are many other sides or phases that are not as readily comprehended. We are here as a protest to the unnatural life of our crowded cities. We are here to build society anew on juster principles, believing that if we once get a fair foothold, the institution will be self-supporting, and so attractive that we shall have no need to seek for true, earnest workers; they will seek us, rather than we seek them, and we shall be able to choose of the best material for an eternal city where all will be rich in the fulness of the surrounding life, and the children will be educated from the start to industry, goodness and justice."

Among the pleasant pictures of memory is that of Thomas Blake as he appeared after he had changed his civilized clothes for a Brook Farm tunic of blue plaid, a " tarpaulin " straw hat and a neat broad rolling shirt collar of large dimensions that gracefully tended towards his square shoulders. I see again his dark, manly countenance lighted up by his keen brown eyes; his Roman features; his closely curling hair; his intellectual forehead and pleasant smile, and his very neat, " trig " appearance. The new life seemed to fill him full of pleasure, and he was always ready for his share of work, study or enjoyment. His short, nautical figure and his name, Blake, soon earned him the complimentary title, which with one accord we gave him, " the Admiral." A nearness of age brought us together, and a strong sympathy of tastes cemented our friendship. We worked, played, danced and sung together, and wandered up and down the paths and roads discussing social problems and all sorts of subjects, ever returning in our talks to our home life, its pleasures, aims and duties.

I thought that there was a little of the dapper look about John Glover Drew who arrived the same day with the Admiral, as I met him for the first time near the corner of the Hive. He seemed stiff and formal in dress and manner, and his face had in it the cool, matter-of-fact element which did not attract me; in fact he looked too "civilized." His clothes were of fine materials; dress coat, silk vest and dark pantaloons. His stylish and plump person filled them out thoroughly. A tall silk hat set a trifle back on his head exposed his large forehead; a fob and seal that hung below his vest, in contrast to the Brook Farm dress, made an added conspicuousness to his appearance. I can see him now, in my mind's eye, lift his watch out of its secret enclosure and examine it to secure promptness of his engagements.

His large head was covered with dark, slightly curling hair. His smooth face, toned by a delicate beard and fine arching eyebrows, reminded one of the portraits of Shakespeare. His nose was short and round and his nostrils dilated when in animated conversation. The muscles of his firm mouth were ever on the play and gave life to his countenance, which when in repose assumed a heavy and somewhat stern appearance. The union between his head and body was made, apparently, by a high, stiff, black neck-stock.

He was fully of medium height, and healthy, but if one in his presence tried the blowing of a flute or the tuning of a violin it would set him in agonies, and the end of his wrath was not forthcoming. He was wholly alive. There was not a point where you could touch him and not appreciate that the nerves of sensation vibrated and quivered. Droll and jocose in manner, he was constantly quoting from Shakespeare or the poets, of whom he had been a constant reader. He was witty, too, and did not disdain a pun, or repartee.

He had the elements of a good mercantile training, and was therefore just the man needed in the young Association, and soon arose from one position to another, winning the meaner laurels of "chief of group" and "head of series," and in time became the "commercial agent" and member of the "Industrial Council." Thenceforth and ever after, he was more bustling than before, both in and out of doors; hovering around the barn with its horses and wagons; ever tackling up teams and starting for the city; unpacking boxes, bales and barrels; ever in conference with the chiefs, inquiring what was needed — anyone could see that almost everything was needed — and showing by his exterior the busy brain that worked within. Mr. Drew was an especial admirer of some of Byron's poems, and it was rumored around that the corners of newspapers had occasionally been garnished with the fruits of his pen.

Here let me say that first impressions in this case gave no index to the manly, brave spirit that was in him, which, true as steel, bore to the end witness to his belief in the truth and the divinity of the associative and coöperative ideas.

There was in the farming group a healthy-looking young man, of ruddy countenance and fair skin, with brown hair and beard that grew luxuriantly, who soon made himself conspicuous by his individuality, his good nature and cheerfulness. There was a positive side to his character; he was in earnest, and he put himself by his earnestness into a positive way that to the superficial seemed to savor of the important, so that Irish John nicknamed him "John Almighty," and it stuck to him, as an old simile says, "like a burdock to a boy's trousers." His devotion was rewarded by chances to lecture. He became one of the faithful, and faithful he has always remained. Amid all the changes of life that have come to him since, and notwithstanding the many persons indoctrinated with Fourier's ideas, he has been for years almost the only man among them broadly advocating them and directly working for the laboring man by endeavoring to organize societies and industrial unions of various sorts for their benefit. I sincerely honor the devotion of John Orvis, continued through so many years of his life.

But what would be the use in sketching the characters that throng around me by the hundreds, who were associated with this new life? Good-natured, full-faced Frederick Cabot, of Boston, whose capacities were devoted to the bookkeeping department and who was clerk of the corporation, who was in the vigor of young manhood, unique of face and beard, with stout neck and low, rolling collar, when beards were absent and collars high; and plain, unpretending Buckley Hastings, who could work like a Trojan — were of them; and the corps of farmers and workers, male and female, who made the body politic, all were interesting, but they must be left out of this narrative, along with the great number of kind and sympathetic persons whose dear hearts encouraged, and whose dearer presence stimulated the Association in its labor.

But it will hardly do to leave out John Cheevers from the list of strange characters on the farm, because, though he did not belong there as member and was as a barnacle on the body politic, he was so quaint and queer. He was Irish and came to America as valet to Sir John Caldwell, who died very suddenly at the Tremont House in Boston. Pity, compassion or the like induced Mr. Ripley to befriend him, and being introduced to the life he became, as may be said, omnipresent. His education, his refined tastes, seemed to spring from a crude and vigorous soil. Travel and contact with high and low made his conversation interesting, and the mystery of a supposed relationship with Sir John added a romance to his life.

His affection for many of the residents was very great. He was introduced into associative life in " Transcendental days," and many a tale he told of the departed ones, often alluding to them as "extinct volcanoes of Transcendental nonsense and humbuggery."

Like many of his countrymen, he carried things to extremes. Extremes in language were the most common, for he had all the oiliness and glibness of an Emeraldic tongue, and in conversation, when a little excited, the words tumbled out with headlong velocity or flowed like molten brass into the mould of the founder, and, to carry the simile farther, some would sputter over. He had in his storehouse of language, many queer phrases and sayings that he brought out to embellish his conversation, some of which were only used as a *corps de reserve*, or brought into action when all others failed in argument.

He prophesied that all people, no matter how high they might carry their heads, would sooner or later "find their level." He believed in the practical. All "folly" and "nonsense" were eschewed by him, and yet no one was more fond of a joke than he, excepting when it was played on himself. John professed great love for the mother church if you attacked it; but if anyone spoke earnestly in its favor he was equally persuaded by him not to believe in such "Jesuitical nonsense and folly." His tunic dress, instead of being a blue one like what most of the men wore, was made of green plaid, but on Sundays, a dark blue "swallowtail" coat with brass buttons made its appearance, and with shoes newly polished he was ready for church.

Unlike the majority of the men, who wore the hair moderately long, his was cut short to his pate, not a straggling hair protruding itself beyond the others. In deference to the seventh day, he exchanged his shirt of blue cotton for a white, well-starched linen one, and donned a high black lasting neck-stock and dark vest, and shaved his face so clean that it reflected his own sunshine if not the solar ray. In person he was of medium height, with a head of thick, dark, almost black hair, slightly sprinkled with gray, and his small dark eyebrows were high above his full eyes which were set almost flush with his forehead. The muscles of his face were prominent, and deep lines were marked around his large mouth with its long under lip, which half the time was on a broad grin.

He walked with a headlong sort of gait, his body

slightly bent forward, deriving its motion from the lower portion of his frame, without that swaying of arms and chest so common, and which gives grace to motion. He was ever moving, bustling about; ever inquiring — now for this one, then for another; occasionally taking from his pocket a small paper parcel into which he thrust finger and thumb mysteriously and guardedly, and turning half away from you would make the cabalistic motions common to imbibers of "old Rappee"; and having satisfied the desire of that extraordinary pug nose of his, would be off in a twinkling to some distant part of the farm, where you may be sure that he was edifying his hearers with a specimen of good-nature, and the peculiar intonations of a mellow voice flavored with genuine brogue.

There are two friends of the movement who cannot be left out, who were often on the farm, whose characters were very unlike and almost at antipodes; yet both were impressed with the associative theories. One of them viewed them from a Christian and moral side, believing that Christianity favored them, that they were productive of the earthly end toward which the sublime doctrines of Christianity pointed; and the other believed that scientific social organization alone would act so powerfully as a stimulant and teacher to humanity, that mankind and human nature would gravitate to their own sublime places at once if an organization was presented suitable to their needs. They were Albert Brisbane and William Henry Channing.

Among the devoted friends there was no one for whom we had greater admiration and esteem than Rev. William Henry Channing. He was a Unitarian

minister and a nephew of the celebrated Rev. William
Ellery Channing. His figure was tall and stately,
though rather slender. He carried himself finely, and
walked with head erect. His features were sharp cut,
clean and regular. His hair was dark and curling,
and worn a trifle long for these days. His forehead
was high and slightly retreating. His eyes were sharp
and piercing, deeply set, with delicate dark eyebrows.
His complexion was warm and brilliant, his beard
closely shaven. He had a pleasant smile which, when
it deepened, showed a fine set of white teeth. All of
these physical signs were in his favor, but there was
about his face, so handsome at times, an earnestness
that seemed almost painful, when, devoted to the cause,
he spoke with the burning, eloquent words he so often
uttered.

In social life he was charming. His voice was soft and
melodious; his education and talents were of the finest
order. He was a firm believer in the mission of Jesus
Christ to bring peace, order and justice out of our
social chaos. He was an Associationist from the Christian side, if I may so speak. His belief in Christ was
so thorough that it made him think all things possible
that were Christlike, and he believed that associated
life contained more of the spirit of Christ in it than any
other form of society, ancient or modern.

He desired to join the organization with his wife and
young children, but Mrs. Channing did not, and we
were deprived of his union with us, as well as of the
company of a charming woman and her family. But
he was around us like a protecting spirit. He spoke
on social occasions to us. He was full of inspiration

and full of hope, though his education was not of a
practical sort after a worldly standard. He couldn't
calculate market values. Neither could he organize
a workshop or build a barn. His thoughts were for
greater things; for everything that elevated large numbers of people — education, morals, faith, peace, antislavery and the good government of his country.

One Sabbath afternoon we were invited to meet with
him in the nearby beautiful pine woods, for religious
services; and like the Pilgrims and reformers of old, we
there raised our voices in hymns of praise, and listened
to a sermon of hopefulness from his eloquent lips.
Would we had a picture of that marked company as
they were seated around on the pine leaves that covered the ground, following their " attractions " by joining in groups with those they most admired or most
sympathized with — young and fair, bright and cheerful,
as they mostly were, with the warm sunlight glinting
through the sighing pines; hearts and eyes illuminated
with great thoughts; hands and faces browned with
working for great, world-wide ideas. Memory is the
only photograph of it, and be assured the picture is a
beautiful one.

The church was Channing's first love, but he found
it bound with creeds, and not broad enough to cover
all humanity, as his great bounding heart did. After
music and an inspiring address under the trees, and the
arches of Nature's temple, looking heavenward, he said,
" Let us all join hands and make a circle, the symbol of
universal unity, and of the *at-one-ment* of all men and
women, and here form the Church of Humanity that

shall cover the men and women of every nation and every clime."

Who shall say that it was not so? — that then and there was not formed one of the impulses of life, one of the branches of the spiritual church that shall live forever! Their daily toil, the thousand and one annoyances they had to submit to from uncomfortable surroundings and private discords — for no one need think that all the persons and those connected with them who came to Brook Farm were equally inspired and interested — and the risk of personal losses, were part of their pledge and baptism of earnestness.

Mr. Albert Brisbane, of New York, was equally tall with Mr. Channing, but of a type of features that was ordinarily less pleasing; wearing a full beard closely trimmed, intellectual in forehead and face, with a voice one could hardly call musical ; a rapid, earnest talker; the travelled son of a wealthy man, who had spent some years abroad and in France, where he became acquainted personally with Fourier and with his doctrines of association, which had deeply impressed him. On his return to America he advocated them in the New York *Tribune*, and by the publication of two or more volumes, by active interest in a society, and by various writings for papers and magazines.

I do not know whether Mr. Brisbane owned stock in the Brook Farm Association or not. Certainly he never gained any dividend by his labor there, but was an interested observer who boarded at the farm at intervals, sometimes passing a few days only, and finally residing some months, occupied in the study and translation of Fourier's works.

He was an enthusiast, but his over enthusiastic moods influenced the Brook Farmers, it seemed to me, oftentimes unwisely. He saw the full-blown phalanstery coming like a comet and expected every moment. We shortly would be in a blaze of glory ! He loved to talk of the good things to be — of social problems worked out by science and by harmonic modes ; to flatter himself that without great self-sacrifice, devotion and untiring industry, the world was to be regenerated. It seemed to his mind, that it could be done all at once by organization and enthusiasm, and it was only necessary to create enough of them to carry everything before them as in a bayonet charge.

He labored hard with the society to change its name to Phalanx, and to push the movement as far as possible into the formulas and organization described by Fourier, which did not advance it a single step in material or spiritual progress, and acted, as in the case of the constitution, as a dead weight, owing to the burdensomeness of its details, which called for too much labor to keep the accounts of so complex an organization.

Having described a few of the many persons who were members of the Association, I must speak of three noted persons who are very often accredited as belonging to the West Roxbury Community; they are Miss Margaret Fuller (afterwards Countess D'Ossoli), Ralph Waldo Emerson and Theodore Parker. They were all personal friends of Mr. and Mrs. Ripley, and belonged to the Transcendental Club. In the first period of the experiment the two former made lengthy visits at the farm, but during the Industrial Period only one of them, Mr. Parker, that I remember visited the place. I must except a single visit from Miss Fuller, whom I recall as plain-looking, and plainly to old-fashionedly dressed, with a crane-like neck and a long gold chain around it, which reached to her waist. She talked quite easily and freely, and the impression of the blue-stocking was left perhaps unfortunately on my mind.

Rev. Ralph Waldo Emerson — for he had been an ordained minister — wrote for the *Dial*, furnished it with queer poems, wrote articles on the wrongs of labor, and agreed fully with Mr. Ripley on so many points that he has been mistaken many times for a Brook Farmer.

Concord, Massachusetts, Mr. Emerson's home, contained a marked radical centre, and some of the Concord people were affiliated by kinship and by sympathy with the Brook Farm people from first to last during the entire experiment. Mr. Ripley invited Mr. Emerson to join it, but he declined in a letter which may be found in Mr. Frothingham's "Life of George Ripley," Appendix, page 315. I make the following extract: —

"MY DEAR SIR: It is quite time that I made an answer to your proposition that I should venture into your new community. The design appears to me noble and generous, proceeding as I plainly see, from nothing covert or selfish or ambitious, but from a manly heart and mind. So it makes all men its friends and debtors. It becomes a matter to entertain it in a friendly spirit, and examine what it has for us.

"I have decided not to join it, yet very slowly, and I may almost say with penitence. I am greatly relieved by learning that your coadjutors are now so many that you will no longer attach that importance to the defection of individuals which you hinted, in your letter to me, I or others might possess — the painful power, I mean, of preventing the execution of the plan."

Rev. Theodore Parker, the noted liberal Unitarian preacher, of whose close personal relations with Mr. Ripley much might be said, lived two miles away, at West Roxbury, where he preached in the village church, and his afternoon walk every few days was over to the Farm and back for the exercise, and to meet and converse with Mr. Ripley at the Eyry. At the close of their chat you would see them coming down the hill together towards the barn, where Mr. Ripley's duties as milkman took him at that time of day, when they would part — Mr. Parker for his long walk home.

One afternoon they were seen as usual coming down the hill. Theodore Parker had not then become famous, but preached in a little square, wooden church, to his small country congregation, and once on a time, being on a visit to a friend at a distance (we will call the friend's name Smith, for convenience sake), Mr. Smith asked Mr. Parker how Mr. Ripley was getting along with his "Community." "Oh," said the faithless Parker, " Mr. Ripley reminds me, in that connection, of a new and splendid locomotive dragging along a train of mud-cars."

Soon after Mr. Ripley heard what Mr. Parker had said of him, and resolved to pay him in his own coin. So he held him that day in pleasant, lively conversation until he reached the farmyard by the barn at the Hive, and the unsprung joke was running all around the pleasant lines of his face and twinkling in the corners of his brilliant eyes. Towards the close of the conversation, as Mr. Parker was about to leave, Mr. Ripley

casually said that he had met Mr. Smith, and he had spoken of Mr. Parker and his church.

"Indeed," said Mr. Parker, "and what did he say of me?"

"Well, if you must know," Mr. Ripley replied, "he said that you and your little country church over there in West Roxbury, with its few dozen of farmers, reminded him of a new and splendid locomotive dragging along a train of mud-cars."

It would have been worth a month of an ordinary lifetime to be there when Mr. Ripley exploded his joke, to hear his merry peal of laughter, whilst his sides shook again, and his reverend friend stood confounded.

But such little jokes did nothing towards rupturing the sincere confidence and friendship of these two brave men, and soon after this Mr. Parker was writing pleasant notes to the "Archon," as Mr. Ripley was often called. By good fortune, I am the possessor of one of them, and as it shows the playful side of a great man, the side often withheld from the public, I give it here. It is charming. It is without date and reads:—

"ARCHONITE ILLUSTRISSIMO: I have just received a letter from the Secretary of the Navy, who informs me that he has jurisdiction over the *waters* of the U. S. A.. and accordingly over *Brook* Farm. He therefore requests me to investigate your proceedings and report to the department. He thinks of appointing yourself to the command of the fleet destined against Texas, and wishes me to *Sound* you on that point. (How would Little John do for California?)

"I am to come over tomorrow P. M. and make investigations, so have the chips picked up, and the pigs

shut up in the library. Now hold yourself in readiness
to receive *Blanco* White, who thinks you were one of
the greatest men who had appeared since Balaam the
son of Beor. Pray reward him for the honor he has
done you.

"Yours, T."

CHAPTER V.

THE departure from the ordinary mode of living ini-
tated at the farm seemed to stir up every curious, investigating and odd mortal, from one end of the country
to the other, and they all wanted to visit the place.
At first they were made welcome to the table, and to
what there was to spare of the members' time, but when
their name was "legion" the Board of Government
found it necessary to exact a fee for meals. This did
not diminish them; the cry was "Still they come!"
Men, women and children were passing from Hive to
Eyry on every pleasant day from May to November,
and over the farm, back to the Hive, where they took
private carriage or public coach for their departure.
Among these people were some of the oddest of the odd;
those who rode every conceivable hobby; some of all
religions; bond and free; transcendental and occiden-
tal; antislavery and proslavery; come-outers, commun-
ists, fruitists and flutists; dreamers and schemers of all
sorts.

The number of notable persons who visited the farm
at this period was large. I was too young to appreciate
the positions they held, in literature, the church or the
nation, but append a list of names, selected almost at
random, mostly of distinguished persons who were occasional visitors.

Horace Greeley, Parke Godwin, Henry James, Free-
man Hunt, Charles Kraitsir, Henry Giles, S. P. Andrews,
all of New York; Rev. O. A. Brownson, Rev. James
Freeman Clarke, Rev. Henry A. Miles, Rev. Edward E.
Hale, Rev. Samuel Osgood, Rev. Frederick T. Gray,
Rev. A. B. Green, Rev. C. A. Greenleaf, Hon. John C.
Palfrey, Hon. E. Rockwood Hoar, Hon. George H. Cal-
vert, of Newport, R. I.; Hon. Charles Sumner, Judge
Ellis Gray Loring, Judge Wells, Dr. W. F. Channing,
R. H. Dana, A. Bronson Alcott, George B. Emerson,
Samuel G. Ward, — Marcus Spring and Edmund
Tweedy, of New York; James A. Kay, of Phila-
delphia ; — W. W. Story, C. P. Cranch, E. Hicks,
Joseph and Thomas Carew, John Sartain, John A.
Ordway and Benjamin Champney, were among the
many artists who came ; the major portion of all the
above named persons were from New England.

It will not do to forget young and curly-headed John
A. Andrew, who became the war governor of Massachusetts, or Robert Owen, the English communist, well
known for his social experiments at New Harmony, Ind.,
who, at this time, was a ruddy-faced, almost white-haired
person, with a large nose, and carrying well his seventy
years on a vigorous frame.

George R. Russell, Francis G. Shaw and Theodore
Parker, with their wives and members of their families,
were very friendly visitors.

There were numerous ladies, also, who came. I remember Miss A. P. Peabody, Pauline Wright, Mary
Gove and sweet Lydia Maria Child, of New York.

The old record book that lay in the reception room at
the Hive would reveal a list of four thousand names,

registered in one year, to select from, but alas! it is lost forever.

A. Bronson Alcott came one day and brought his friend Lane, who was anxious to visit the "Community," but Lane was opposed to eating anything that was killed or had died, so he ate neither fish nor flesh. Neither would he wear wool, because it was an animal product, for he did not like animal products. Neither would he wear cotton nor use sugar nor rice, because they were the products of slave labor. And finally, he walked from Boston in a linen suit, because he would avoid using a horse, for his argument was that the value of time spent in providing food, lodging and care of animals, was not returned to the owners for the outlay. Lane came from England, and was not a "Yankee crank," as some might possibly think.

Miss Louisa M. Alcott wrote of him in connection with her father and herself, in an article entitled "A Journey to Fruitlands." Judging from my remembrance of all the characters, the picture is faithfully drawn.

Among the odd visitors the climax was reached, when a man came to pass a day and a night, who announced that he had no need of sleep and had not slept for a year. The statement was passed by as a mere whim, we thinking of course that when night came he would not refuse a bed, but he did. After spending the evening at the Eyry, where the visitors were more especially entertained, he was notified that an attendant would show him to his bed, but he politely declined one, and as there seemed to be no other way, he was allowed to remain in an easy chair, with a lamp burning, after the household had retired.

It was late when Irish John Cheevers, *our* odd genius, prowling about the premises on his way to his room at the Cottage, saw the light in the Eyry parlor, and supposing some of the household were awake, went softly up and looked in at the window. There sat the visitor in the chair, *asleep*. He then went in, but his noise aroused the sleeper, and as John couldn't possibly keep his tongue still a minute, he said, " I beg your pardon, sir, I did not intend to disturb your sleep — not in the least, sir," in his palavering way, at which the stranger protested strongly that he hadn't been disturbed, as he had been awake all the time.

In the morning the stranger was there, still sitting in his chair, and declared he had passed the night pleasantly, but had not been asleep. Of course the improbability of the thing made, as the newspapers say, a "sensation." " By gad," said John, " I caught him asleep in the Eyry parlor. I did, upon my word; I did, my very self."

John wasn't inclined to be profane, but when anyone pretended to be what they were not, it aroused his combative spirit, and it was the " blank humbuggery of the thing" that mightily displeased him. But the time came when the laugh was against him. He had been in bed and slept some hours one summer night; it was the time of the full moon, when its transcendent beauty led the young folks to wander over the farm from house to house, to sit a while on the doorsteps or on the knoll at the Hive; to sing " Das Klinket " or such part songs as " Row gently here, my gondolier," or

" The lone starry hours give me Love, when calm is the beautiful night," or anything else to let out the joyousness of their hearts. They were not wild, for they labored enough to take away the wildness that indolence brings, and to sober them down to the cheerful mood; and cheerily would talk to one another of the people around them, and of the hundred little excitements the novel life led them into, that were wanting elsewhere, and often it was an hour or two later than the usual time for rest, before they were in bed.

John had been to his couch, and when he awoke it was broad daylight. He dressed and went down to the Hive, and as some one was going away early to Boston, concluded to get the wagon ready. But first he looked into the kitchen; the door was unlocked, as it always was, day and night; there was no one there, and it was surely time some one should be up. He drew out the light wagon from under the shed, and went for the harness. All the time the universal stillness surprised him. Where could all the people be? He thought he would see how high the sun was, and looking up into the sky, beheld the full face of the most beautiful moon that ever shone on God's fair acres, when a new thought struck him, that he had mistaken moonshine for daylight. He wheeled the wagon into the shed, and then went for another long nap; but some of the young men, who hadn't been in bed a great while, overheard the movements, and had their laugh and fun out of it!

During the first spring and summer of my stay my hours were largely spent in the Farming Series, working in the various groups. I assisted at planting, hoeing and driving or leading the horses at the plough.

I also helped the gardener, who arrived with plants, in the care of them and in the ornamentation of the place.

According to the science of Fourier, everything is naturally arranged in groups and series. A group consists of three or more individuals or things, and a number of similar groups together make a series. To have harmony in society requires the application of this law or arrangement to all the relations of daily life; or in other words, it is natural to be thus arranged in industrial and social life. The Brook Farmers, being ambitious to introduce a resemblance to such an organization — for it could be but very faintly shadowed by their few members — and also desirous to indoctrinate all into the idea of this natural arrangement, organized "groups and series" in the following manner as proposed in the new constitution. "Three or more persons combined for some object or labor" made a group; harmonic numbers for groups — three, five, seven, twelve, etc. A series consisted of three or more groups for a similar object, joined under one head or chief.

To illustrate the system we will suppose it to be the spring of the year. The Farming Series will then consist of the following groups: First, a Cattle Group, which attends to the feeding, grooming and general care of the cattle — horses, cows, oxen, pigs, etc. It may include the milking of the cows, or that may be a group in itself under the name of the Milking Group. Second, a Plowing Group, who attend to the plowing of the fields. Third, a Nursery Group, who have the care of the young trees, grafting, budding, etc. Fourth, a Planting Group, which may later in the season change

into a Hoeing Group, or into a Weeding Group, or into
a Haying Group, or a separate organization for each
may continue till the end of the season.   Each chief of
a group recorded the hours expended in labor in his
group, so that it was possible to tell, at the end of a
season, how many hours had been spent in a given
occupation, as hoeing, weeding, planting, etc. These
groups, each having a chief, formed the aforenamed
series, and the heads, or "chiefs" of all the groups
together elected the head of the series, who kept a
record and had general charge of the work done under
his management.

The Mechanical Series, consisting of shoemaking,
carpentering, sash and blind-makers' groups, were usually the same persons the year around. If, however,
the shoemaker was tired of his group, and could be
spared, he took his hoe and rake, and went into some
group in the Farming Series for a change of occupation;
the hours he spent there were put to his credit on the
book of the group in which he labored in that series.

The Domestic Series had care of the houses and all
domestic work, and was divided into Consistory, Dormitory and Kitchen Groups.   There were also Washing,
Ironing and Mending Groups, and perhaps some others.
The beds, rooms, halls and lamps had to be attended to
every day, water and towels provided, and the "Dormitory" and "Consistory Groups," situated as the
Brook Farmers were, were obliged to go from house to
house to attend to these duties.

There were independent groups on the farm, not
connected with any series, as the Teachers' Group, and
the Miscellaneous Group, who did a variety of mis-

cellaneous work ; and there was a Commercial Agent
who bought and sold goods for the Association. There
was also a group called "The Sacred Legion," who did
exceptionally disagreeable labors, not from the love of
them but from the sacred principle of duty. Only
occasionally some repugnant task had to be undertaken,
and be it to the honor of the leaders, not one of them,
even the most fastidious or cultivated, shirked the
responsibility of it.

The industrial system of Fourier has often been objected to as a mechanical arrangement, by which persons were fixed, automaton-like, and expected to work
where they were placed, and has been opposed with the
criticism that human beings are not automatic — that
they have the restlessness of human nature and will
constantly rebel at such conditions.

Another and a greater criticism has been that the
levelling tendency, as is supposed, of the Fourieristic doctrines, is inimical to every-day experience, and that the
natural differences of characters, ambitions and mental
conditions were not recognized in the system, consequently there would be no place for all these varied
human attributes to work and progress in.

These are very great errors, and are entirely attribu-
table to the superficial knowledge of the man and his
works. If ever there was a man in this universe who
had faith in the Supreme Power, Fourier was that man.
His theology covered the *absolute wisdom* and *absolute
goodness* of God. Starting from these two fixed stand-
points, he believed that the Creator wisely planned the
universe and laid out the destiny of the human race
from its inception, as a wise and beneficent being, fixing

its beginning and its end and all of the intermediate stages between them as parts of the plan. Creating man as a social being, he must, therefore, have created from the first the form of society under which he should, finally, as a race, pass the greatest portion of his sojourn here, and, being an *absolutely good* Creator, he must have created absolutely good social conditions as the destiny towards which all mankind is now tending, and which will finally be reached.

Having also created man with many varied talents, the society or the social order in which he intends him to live, must have room in it for the use and development of the variety he has created: a place for the strong, a place for the weak; a place for the proud, a place for the lowly; a place for the penurious, a place for the lavish; a place for the sober and a place for the gay. Moreover, if the Creator is wise, he has created just the number and variety of mental and physical personages to fill the otherwise empty places, and no others; for, if he has created a surplus of them, he is unwise, and they must be in discord with the rest. If the movements of the heavenly bodies are not left to chance, neither is the destiny nor the place of any human being in creation left to chance, either here or hereafter.

Far from any levelling tendency in Fourier's system, far from any communism, it contains, in itself, room for the completest aristocracy there ever was, the natural and the true aristocracy, ordained by the logical mind of the Creator, implanted in our natures, and which we intuitively admit and admire. But having given man freedom of will, not having made him to associate automatically, as he has, apparently, made the honey-bee, the beaver, the ant, and various social creatures, it is necessary for him to go through a period of ignorance, and, consequently, of some suffering, whilst he is learning by experience to find his powers and his position in creation, even as the little child does, who reaches out its hand for the moon, and stumbles over trifles lying in its way that were easily removed, could it, in its undeveloped condition, have sense enough to do it. But the two conditions are not possible, together. Both ignorance and knowledge of a subject cannot dwell in one person at the same time; therefore it is only slowly and painfully that we find, by degrees, our wonderful powers, the bountiful provision for happiness, and the grand destiny that so peacefully lies in the arms of the future, awaiting our embrace and caress.

Fourier discovered the arrangement in nature of the "Serial Order" or the law of the Groups and Series, which on paper seems formal, but is simply one of the mathematical rules of society, and which, under right conditions, does not intrude itself, any more than the rules of arithmetic do when we are buying a few apples, but are nevertheless ever present. The writer does not wish to impose a dissertation on his readers, but felt impelled to answer, in this place, these objections made by many worthy people.

The workshop, which was being built at the time of my arrival, was two stories in height, sixty by forty feet in size, with a pitched roof; well lighted with windows, and situated some three hundred yards behind the Hive, in a northwesterly direction. At its further end, in the cellar, was placed a horse-mill, afterwards exchanged for a steam-engine, that carried the machinery for all the departments of labor. Our engineer, Jean M. Pallisse, a worthy Swiss, a very intelligent man, had a calm face that fitted well with the quiet wreaths of smoke he sent up on the air, from his almost ever-present cigar. It was our delight to coax him to bring out his violin on dance nights, and give us a charming waltz or two. You would hardly associate his intelligent and pleasant face with the dull work of an engine room, but he was there day by day, faithful and regular as a clock, for he was in earnest. He had the sublime faith in him, and in later years held a responsible position in a wealthy importing house in New York City.

The shop was partitioned off, according to the needs of business, and in the time of our greatest numbers, when crowded with members and visitors, no other place being found to stow people in, beds were placed in its upper story.

The general impression of my first summer at Brook Farm is that it was one of great activity and great hopes. Everywhere the ambition was to enlarge — to increase the number of members, to increase the occupations, to increase the tillage by turning over the grass-grown meadows and "laying down" more land, to increase the nursery for young trees and plants to increase the hay crop by clearing the brushwood and mowing the stubble close. Everywhere were busy people with ploughs and cultivators, hoes and rakes, and I was with them wherever there was work to be done.

The glory of the summer was the hay field. On the fair meadows we turned and gathered the hay. It was a large crop ; although the hay was not all of the best, it was mostly of fair quality. And when the hoeing, weeding and haying were done, the farmers dug meadow-muck for compost.

Ready and willing as I was to try my hand at whatever came along, I went into the meadow and followed the plough with a bogging hoe, and one day tried digging muck but the chief of the group thought the labor was too heavy for me; I would have to wait until I grew stronger.

Coming home one day I was told that one of our number had passed away. She had been sick at the Hive a long while before my arrival. I could scarcely be called acquainted with her, though I had been into her room and called with others. In health she had been a brave worker, and in sickness bore her severe suffering patiently. Messrs. Chiswell and Tirrell of the Carpenters' Group were called on for their help, whilst Mrs. Pratt and others prepared the body for its final sleep. Members of the Direction selected a lovely spot in a little pine grove beyond the Pilgrim House for a grave, and we gathered for a last service.

I expected to hear Mr. Ripley speak, but true to a sensitive instinct of propriety he did not, for though he was at the head of the Association, she had her own faith and creed which he deemed sacred. She was an Episcopalian, and after the service was read by one of our number a solemn procession was formed which followed her body, borne on our light wagon, to the grave, where, singing a hymn, we left her quietly in peace.

Soon after the gardener planted some young evergreens, and placed flowering shrubs and a little fence around the sacred spot.

If one must die, must surrender life, oh, where can it be done better than under such circumstances? From first to last no stranger's hand had aught to do with this sister either in life or in death. No idle or curiously intrusive person came near, and all the surroundings, though simple, were in keeping with the solemnity of the occasion. There was no pomp or rivalry of show, no gaudy deckings, that we in our hearts despise, but which an unhallowed custom forces upon us; but all was done decently, lovingly, peacefully and well. It was a simple name she bore — Mary Ann Williams.

There was an amusement group, the members of which did not receive pecuniary compensation. Its duty was to provide amusement for the people and the scholars, as often as could be afforded, without trespassing on school and daily duties.

Miss Amelia Russell, a little, plump woman, with a pleasant smile, dimpled cheeks, round, laughing eyes, cultivated and easy manners, was chief of this group for a long period. Her title was "the mistress of the revels." Under her direction there were various plays, games, dances and tableaux.

Besides the walks in the fields and woods there was an occasional " children's festival," in the grove of pines, in which a large portion of the elders joined. There were plenty of amusements, for although the amusement group took general charge of them, there was nothing to prevent any person or number of persons from amusing themselves to any extent, and in any way, not interfering with the business of the place.

Being among the minors, the pleasures of dancing and roaming over the diversified country, were most attractive to me; for the young people danced without expense — as we were, anywhere, any time, for five or ten minutes, an hour or an evening, and it never became a dissipation; it was too natural and common to be a dissipation. There were never late hours. There was no dancing for show, or to display handsome clothes, but simply for the love of it, its harmony and love of one another's society and companionship.

When the cares and lessons of the day were laid aside, and the evening meal was over, we sauntered up the hill to the Eyry, and passing near the Cottage, would perhaps find some one at the piano in the music room, and if we numbered four or five, would waltz or dance to one or the other's playing, the players and dancers taking turns until it was time to stop. It might be there was a class in history or in reading at eight, or maybe singing school would soon commence. If so, that terminated the matter. Perhaps there was to be music at the Eyry, — there was no formality, we went without ceremony to hear it.

There were times when there was a regular "dance at the Hive." The mistress of the revels was kind enough to assist young or old, whose "education had been neglected," and who had never been taught their "steps," by forming a dancing class and including all in it; and it would have done your heart good to see the old fogies try for the first time in their lives to put on grace. Grace it was, but often of the oddest kind. Imagine the tall, spare figure of "the General," turned of forty, full six feet in height and stooping in the shoulders, all legs and arms — who could sit in a chair and

wind his legs around each other until the feet changed
places, and sit comfortably so — as pupil of the plump,
little woman, straight as an arrow, and only (at a guess)
four feet six in height, and looking shorter for her
plumpness, taking his "one, two, three," and "forward
and back steps."

Imagine, also, all hands seated at the supper tables,
with the rattle of knives, forks, mugs and plates, and
the full buzz of conversation ; waiters crowding up and
down, supplying the fast vanishing food, and everything
cheerful, when a rapping on one of the tables arrests
the attention of all.   One of the gentlemen, arising, announces, "There will be a dance in this hall this evening, at eight o'clock, to which all are invited." This is
received with applause by the young people.   Perhaps
it is a surprise to them; for some of the pupils who have
a little pocket money, have gained permission of the
authorities, and have sent for the Dedham "feedler," as
our Dane used to call him, to play the violin and call
the dances.

As for music, our orchestra was not very large. I am
almost ashamed to say that one violin, solitary and alone,
or a piano brought down from the Cottage, was often
the only solace and cheer.   But then the room was not
large, and certainly it was not high, so that nothing was
lost in its expanse, and truly the young man played
very well, and I remember there were some brass instru-
ments used on an especial occasion.

You should have been standing outside, looking in at
the window just the time that supper was over.
Wouldn't you have seen some busy young folks, clearing the tables and washing the dining-room ware !   And

you would have seen the clean, white mugs and plates
put up in huge piles in the dining-room closet.
Wouldn't the benches and tables disappear quickly, and
the floor be swept, and the lamps lighted, and everything put in " apple-pie order" ! And then the young
women workers would disappear, and in a few minutes
reappear dressed in their best, like magic pictures of
youth and beauty, adorned in simple garments, with a
rose bud or a wreath of partridge vine (Mitchella) with
its bright red berries, woven into their tresses, or with
some simple adornments ; and then for an hour or two
of enjoyment !

The dance would commence. One by one, after the
young persons were in the midst of the revelry, the
older persons would come in, and the non-dancers
would range around as spectators; and now and then
you would distinguish our leader by the curly locks,
the gleaming eyes and gold-bowed spectacles, his glowing face expressing satisfaction in our enjoyment.

At ten o'clock, the dance ceased; immediately the
tables and dishes would reappear, as if by enchantment,
and in a twinkling the dining room was arranged for
the morning. We had had our pleasure, and were
ready to pay for it by restoring things to immediate
order. Besides, what young man could leave the young
ladies to set the tables alone, after having danced with
them all the evening? After this there were hours
enough left for sound sleep, and there were no headaches
in the morning. The result was, all the young people
grew strong, graceful and healthy.

My peculiar temperament and strong love of nature
made the walks and wanderings in the fields dear to

me. I recall them with the greatest pleasure, and think that some others among the living must do the same. There were no stated, regular hours for walking. The teachers went when their classes for the day were over; the young folks when their tasks were completed, or at twilight, in the long summer days, and often the larger parties were on Sunday afternoons, for then there was greater freedom from care. Some went to West Roxbury to church in the morning, some, maybe, to the Eyry to read Swedenborg or other writers, and unless Mr. Channing or some other minister who desired to preach was present, there were no set services; and even if there were, a walk might be arranged for a later hour in the summer afternoons.

The tall, slim figure of the wife of our president, wearing a Leghorn shade hat, with one or two graceful lady pupils by her side, was often present and leading the procession; then perhaps the manly form of our head farmer, and his stout wife, and his boys and girl; our "poet," always beside some fair maiden, in cheerful conversation; a visitor and the visited; groups of young people together, with muslin dresses, blue tunics and straw hats intermingled; children; and maybe the stately form of William Henry Channing, with his regular profile, and his head carried high, looking upward and off, as into far, pleasant and dreamy distances, walking beside a tall, black haired woman, with a spiritual face of high type, — in all some thirty to forty in number, making a delightfully picturesque group.

Such parties would generally make the large and beautiful pine woods that were near us the *ultimatum* of their walk. Others would take a longer walk, to the thicker woods of " Cow Island " (now covered with houses), or to the Charles River. Leaving the farm they dived into the young oak woods, by a small path in the rear of the Cottage, and entering the magnificent grove of pines after a short walk, found a grassy wood path that led a long distance through them. Soon the party would begin to straggle and divide, some to gather wild flowers and berries, and more to find materials for wreaths, or ferns and mosses for decorations.

The walks ended where walks do that have no definite plan — anywhere in the woods, sitting on the boulders or the pine leaves, or in some shady nook where a topic would be found for discussion, or a pleasant book would be read. When the supper horn sounded, you found the absent ones together again, with bright, rosy faces and good appetites; and only a few of the younger folks would be late, who had strayed farther or walked slower, to enjoy the companionship of those of the same age ; to listen to their sweet voices, and to linger, as only young folks love to linger.

The summer came on with joy and beauty. I recall the long waves of nodding grass, that swayed in the June wind and were chasing each other, fugue-like on the broad meadows. How beautiful it was, tipped with its various hues of green, yellow, red and purple, bending and rising as each breath of wind passed over it ! The crops looked well, and the table was supplied with varieties of garden produce.

If you approached the farm in the middle of the forenoon, you wondered where all the people were, but at the sound of the first horn, half an hour before dinner, " from bush and briar and greensward shade " they would begin to start out like Robin Hood's men, and when the second horn was sounding, the daily, the tri-daily procession was fairly on the move, approaching the Hive from all sides. It was a very pretty and novel sight.

The men had been in the field planting, hoeing or weeding — the farmer's triad of duties in the vegetable field — and as they worked side by side, the questions of the day were discussed with freedom and with partisanship, but with good nature. The one who had a bias for art brought out his art hobby, as did the dress reformer his hobby and the dietetic reformer his notions. Personal questions often came to the front — as how Smith probably voted in the Association meeting in the case of the admission of some mooted person; he was so sly you could not find out! And they quizzed one another, and they laughed and rivalled one another in speed of work, which they did faithfully and interestedly. It was a good school of human nature, and sooner or later each one was sized up with a deal of exactness. With the sounding of the horn the hoes were left in the field or put on the shoulder for the march to the barn, where, in its little room, the toilet for meals was made.

When I think under what disadvantages these toilers worked for five years, I wonder at their patience and firmness. What would our city families say to all going out from their apartments, male and female, young and old, and walking from an eighth to a quarter of a mile — often making their own path through the deep snow of our severe New England winters — three times each day, for the simple meals we had there to eat? What would they say to living in crowded rooms, without private parlors, and the public one at the Hive not much better than an office in a back country hotel, and the other disadvantages heretofore named and many more, simply for the principle of the thing ?

Of course there was enthusiasm, and that sweetens many dull dishes; but for those used to home comforts, to be sandwiched in with comparative strangers—squeezed down, as it were, into a press — oftentimes having the family separated into various and disunited parts of the mansion or into different houses, was decidedly uncomfortable to bear.

These disadvantages could not but make the Association quite early decide that the one thing above all others needed was a new building with suites of rooms, where families could have the comforts and privacy of homes, which with a large kitchen, bakery, dining rooms, parlors, etc., would make a " unitary building " ; approximating to an apartment house of more modern days in many of its details, and improving on it as regards unitary cooking, dining and social conveniences.

The autumn fled rapidly away, and things had to be hurried up and put into shape for the winter. The gardener had no greenhouse, and was growling for fear the early frost might take a fancy to his plants. So the Association built him a temporary one in the " sand bank " by the side of the farm road, and the plan was to bend their energies towards getting the new dwelling started as early as possible in the spring, and to build a permanent greenhouse near it.

I do not know what passed in the General Direction during the winter. They were undoubtedly busy in endeavoring to obtain money for constructing the new building, preparing plans for its interior arrangement, and personally lecturing in various places, to aid in awakening the public to the new ideas, hoping also that some benefit might accrue to their organization, as well as to the cause, from their efforts.

The winter was mild, and it passed rapidly. There were coasting parties of young and old, but it was not often that the snow was favorable. There were literary societies, and we admired "the General" when he recited the part of the lean and hungry Cassius. He didn't stammer then, and he received the additional title of "Shakespeare's hero." These things, with reading, dancing and singing classes, an occasional "social" at the Hive, with private gatherings and chats around the kitchen fire by "Hiveites" (i. e., those living at the Hive), found us with spring at hand before we could realize it.

Among other matters in progress in the spring was the garden. The gardener was urging upon the Association the usefulness and profitableness of the growth and sale of garden and greenhouse plants and flowers; the great benefit they would be in adding attractiveness to the place, and also the importance of starting plants so that they might be growing into sizable shrubs, to return an early profit for their outlay. These facts decided the Association to commence a flower garden, and they located it on a partially level piece of ground behind the Cottage, covering perhaps a half acre, with a chance of future extension by cutting the wood adjoining and cultivating the untilled ground.

There was much labor put on this piece of land, as it

was first reduced to a level by removing the soil and subsoil, and levelling the gravelly bottom; then returning the subsoil and soil to the top. Walks were next laid out with great care, and flower beds made. A border was also dug for the expected new greenhouse, and filled with rich soil and compost, and the end of the summer saw it erected.

But the most important step taken in the spring was the establishment of a journal devoted to the interests of Association and Associative life.

It is easy to see how naturally, independent of the need of an organ for a new movement, the Brook Farmers took to the idea of publishing a journal. In the first place there were at hand men who were abundant in talent; who were used to writing, and well up in literature and fine arts, to whom the idea was grateful as water to young ducks. And, second, there were at least two or three printers and compositors residing on the farm, who were as able in their department as the first named were in theirs. There was in this connection, also, the possibility at some future time of obtaining printing for the Printers' Group, should that branch of labor be well established.

The scheme cannot be better introduced than by giving here the prospectus of the *Harbinger*, the beautiful name of the new weekly paper. You will find in its brave words some of the ideas that the leaders of this movement developed, but more particularly the broad faith they had in human nature and in great principles applied to social life, and the greater trust they had that the Providence under which we live had ordained man for a sublime destiny.

CHAPTER VI.

THE "HARBINGER" AND VARIOUS SUBJECTS.

THE following is the prospectus of

THE "HARBINGER."

Devoted to the Social and Political progress. Published simultaneously at New York and Boston, by the Brook Farm Phalanx. "All things, at the present day, stand provided and prepared, and await the light."

Under this title it is proposed to publish a weekly newspaper, for the examination and discussion of the great questions in social science, politics, literature and the arts, which command the attention of all believers in the progress and elevation of humanity.

In politics, the *Harbinger* will be democratic in its principles and tendencies; cherishing the deepest interest in the advancement and happiness of the masses; warring against all exclusive privilege in legislation, political arrangements and social customs; and striving with the zeal of earnest conviction, to promote the triumph of the high democratic faith, which is the chief mission of the nineteenth century to realize in society.

Our devotion to the democratic principle will lead us to take the ground of fearless and absolute independence in regard to all policical parties, whether professing attachment to that principle or hostility to it. We know that fidelity to an idea can never be reassured by adherence to a name; and hence we shall criticise all parties with equal severity, though we trust that the sternness of truth will always be blended with the temperance of impartial candor. With tolerance for all opinions, we have no patience with hypocrisy and pretense; least of all with that specious fraud which would

101

make a glorious principle the apology for personal ends. It will therefore be a leading object of the *Harbinger* to strip the disguise from the prevailing parties, to show them in their true light, to give them due honor, to tender them our grateful reverence whenever we see them true to a noble principle; but at all times, and on every occasion, to expose false professions, to hold up hollow-heartedness and duplicity to just indignation, to warn the people against the demagogue, who would cajole them by honeyed flatteries, no less than against the devotee of mammon who would make them his slaves.

The *Harbinger* will be devoted to the cause of a radical, organic social reform, as essential to the highest development of man's nature, to the production of those elevated and beautiful forms of character of which he is capable, and to the diffusion of happiness, excellence and universal harmony upon the earth. The principles of universal unity as taught by Charles Fourier, in their application to society, we believe are at the foundation of all genuine social progress, and it will ever be our aim to discuss and defend these principles, without any sectarian bigotry, and in the catholic and comprehensive spirit of their great discoverer. While we bow to no man as an authoritative, infallible master, we revere the genius of Fourier too highly not to accept, with joyful welcome, the light which he has shed on the most intricate problems of human destiny. The social reform of whose advent the signs are everywhere visible, comprehends all others, and in laboring for its speedy accomplishment, we are conscious that we are devoting our best ability to the removal of oppression and injustice among men, to the complete emancipation of the enslaved, to the promotion of genuine temperance, and to the elevation of the toiling and down-trodden masses to the inborn rights of humanity.

In literature the *Harbinger* will exercise a firm and impartial criticism, without respect of persons or parties. It will be made a vehicle for the freest thought, though not of random speculations; and with a generous appreciation of the various forms of truth and beauty, it will not fail to expose such instances of false sentiment, perverted taste and erroneous opinion, as may tend to vitiate the public mind or degrade the individual character. Nor will the literary department of the *Harbinger* be limited to criticism alone. It will receive contributions from various pens, in different spheres of thought, and, free from dogmatic exclusiveness, will accept all that in any way indicates the unity of man with man, with nature, and with God. Consequently all true science, all poetry and arts, all sincere literature, all religion that is from the soul, all wise analyses of mind and character, will come within its province.

We appeal for aid in our enterprise to the earnest and hopeful spirits in all classes of society. We appeal to all who, suffering from a resistless discontent in the present order of things, with faith in man and trust in God are striving for the establishment of universal justice, harmony and love. We appeal to the thoughtful, the aspiring, the generous everywhere, who wish to see the reign of heavenly truth triumphant, by supplanting the infernal discords and falsehoods on which modern society is built — for their sympathy, friendship and practical coöperation in the undertaking which we announce to-day.

The *Harbinger* was launched, and it weathered the storm for four years, until its editors sought other and wider fields for their genius. Besides the motto on the prospectus, they took the following from Rev. William Ellery Channing: "Of modern civilization, the natural fruits are, contempt for others' rights, fraud, oppression, a gambling spirit in trade, reckless adventure and commercial convulsions, all tending to impoverish the laborer and render every condition insecure. Relief is to come, and can only come from the new application of Christian principles, of universal justice and universal love, to social institutions, to commerce, to business, to active life."

It was printed in quarto form, sixteen pages to every number, with clear type and in excellent style. The index of the first volume bears a list of twenty-two names as contributors, and it contains many worthy ones. The New York names were as follows: —

> Albert Brisbane.
> William Henry Channing.
> Christopher P. Cranch.
> George William Curtis.
> George G. Foster.
> Parke Godwin.
> Horace Greeley.
> Osborne MacDaniel.

The New England names were: —

> Otis Clapp, Boston, Mass.
> William W. Story, Boston, Mass.
> T. Wentworth Higginson, Boston, Mass.
> James Russell Lowell, Cambridge, Mass.
> J. A. Saxton, Deerfield, Mass.
> Francis George Shaw, West Roxbury, Mass.
> John G. Whittier, Amesbury, Mass.

Other contributors were: —

> E. P. Grant of Ohio.
> A. J. H. Duganne of Philadelphia.

The Brook Farm writers were: —

> George Ripley.   Charles A. Dana.
> John S. Dwight.   Lewis K. Ryckman.

In the second volume are two more of the Channing family as contributors, Dr. William F. and Walter, and also the name of James Freeman Clarke, of Boston, with an additional writer from Brook Farm — John Orvis.

Mr. Ripley and Mr. Dana wrote most of the editorial Associative articles. Mr. Dana was the principal reviewer, and noticed the new books. Mr. Dwight wrote an occasional article on Association, reviewed, and attended to the musical and poetical department. He also earnestly advocated the doctrines of social and industrial life suggested by Fourier. Translations in prose and poetry were common. Parke Godwin and W. H. Channing assisted in translations or selections from Fourier's writings. George William Curtis wrote the musical correspondence from New York, and among the poetical contributions in the first volume, is one from J. G. Whittier, "To My Friend on the Death of His Sister," and five poems by Cranch, Higginson, Story, Lowell and Duganne; also poetic translations from the German by Dwight and Dana, as well as original poems by them.

The paper was not local. It aimed high as a purely literary and critical as well as progressive journal, and I must ever consider it a fault that it did not chronicle more of Brook Farm life. We look almost in vain through its pages for one word of its situation, finding none except in some allusions to it in the correspondence from abroad. Occasionally the school was advertised in a corner, but for the rest it might as well have been published elsewhere as at Brook Farm. The leaders, feeling that the life there was an experiment, and perhaps a doubtful one, were not disposed to gratify a curiosity which they probably considered morbid, by yielding to it. This was a mistake. It was a mistake, as much as it would be for us to leave out of our letters to our friends the petty incidents of daily life, and describe only grand principles and outside events. It is only to those loved most by us that we recite the trivial things, for we know that those trivialities link us closer than anything else, filling all the chinks in our friendship or love. It was a disappointment to those who desired to know often of the spirit of the workers, and of the little events that happened there, not to find more notices of them.

In many other respects the *Harbinger* was a grand success. In all that pertained to music, criticism, poetry and progress no journal stood higher. I cannot tell of its pecuniary success for I do not find any memorandum of its finances. The first number commenced with a story translated from the French of George Sand (Madame Dudevant) entitled "Consuelo" — in some respects the sweetest story she ever wrote. It was translated by our neighbor, Mr. Francis G. Shaw, who would oftentimes mount his horse, and, with his little boy, a tiny fellow, on a pony by his side, gallop over to see us. How hard it is for me to realize that afterward the same little fellow, as Col. Robert G. Shaw, led his colored regiment through fire and smoke and the whizzing bullets up to the cannon's mouth of bloody Fort Wagner, and there laid down his life for his country.

Francis George Shaw was of a Boston family and a gentleman of means. He took great interest in our experiment and its hoped-for results. I have not words to praise his kindness, and his gentlemanly manner and bearing towards us all. He looked on life from a high standpoint. Wealth did not corrupt him. He was a Christian in large heartedness and philanthropy. He recognized his Maker's image in all men; the garment he saw through; the color he saw through; and he desired above all things the education, progress and culture of all the human family.

Appended is an additional list of all the advertised contributors of the *Harbinger*, during its publication at Brook Farm, not including those already mentioned: —

John Allen, Brook Farm.

Jean M. Pallisse, Brook Farm.

S. P. Andrews, New York, N. Y.

William Ellery Channing, Concord, Mass.

Joseph J. Cooke, Providence, R. I.

Fred. Henry Hedge, Bangor, Me.

Mark E. Lazarus, Wilmington, N. C.

E. W. Parkman, Boston, Mass.

J. H. Pulte, Cincinnati, Ohio.

Samuel D. Robbins, Chelsea, Mass.

Miss E. H. Starr, Deerfield, Mass.

C. Neidhart, Philadelphia, Pa.

The presence of a weekly journal on the farm, with its varieties of current literature, poetry and music, could not but awaken in many of the colaborers most pleasurable emotions. Prose articles and poetry from it were discussed by daylight and by the fireside, by the roadside, in the shops, on the farm — in fact, everywhere. The " Admiral " was wild over Hood's " Bridge of Sighs." It was so quaint; the rhythm was so unique; it was so full of sentiment; it was so tender; it dis-

played so touchingly the sorrows of a young heart, and
was so in harmony with the humanitarian sentiment of
our lives, that he and others could but repeat it over and
over, and the poet's rhymes kept ringing both in our
physical and mental ears.   The lines —

> " One more unfortunate,
> Rashly importunate
> Gone to her death.
>
>   *   *   *
>
> Take her up tenderly,
> Fashioned so slenderly
> Young and so fair."

were repeated times without number. Cranch's, Story's
and Duganne's poems were favorably criticised, the
authors being friendly to the Association, and the verses
of our own members touched tender spots.

When Mr. Emerson's poems were published, there was
quite a desire to know what his sonnet to our friend
William H. Channing was like. The disappointment
was great when, instead of a grand, glowing sonnet to
a great-souled man, it took up only an exceptional point
of feeling in his mind on the Abolition question, on
which they were not quite agreed. Quite a little discussion took place between two young persons as to the
propriety of the lines,

> " What boots thy zeal, O glowing friend,
> That would indignant rend
> The Northland from the South ? "

The one party contended that " boots " was entirely inadmissible in poetic phrase. " What boots? Cow-
hides or patent leathers ? " said he, whilst the other contended that the whole scope of the meaning made the
poetry.   But still the first stuck to his point, that a

grand sentiment needed grand words as well as grand ideas, and "boots" was a homely and inadmissible word with which to express a high sentiment.

Among the many volumes noticed, "Festus," by Philip James Bailey, was a constant source of admiration and criticism in some of our circles, and we had many varied ones. Listen to what Mr. Dwight said of it at the time in the *Harbinger*: "There are more original and magnificent images on a single page of Festus than would endow a dozen of the handsome volumes most in vogue. The conclusion you come to as you read on, is that his wealth of imagination is illimitable, and that you might as well cut a cloud out of the purple sunset atmosphere, as a figure from the boundless atmospheric beauty of this poem."

"Festus" still retains its charm for me.

The *Harbinger*, as may be seen, was to be published by the Brook Farm *Phalanx*, not *Association*. The reason why the name was changed was because "Association" was not a definite one, conveying distinct impressions to the public mind, like "Community"; and the name "Phalanx," although to American ears, new in its connection, was expressive, and was also adopted by a number of social experiments just starting, and it was desirable to have them all associated in name as well as in general doctrine. The name "Community" was rejected because all the societies organized under that name held their property in common, which the "Association" distinctly did not.

There were other changes made at this time, more important in idea than in practice. The name "Areopagus" was applied to an enlarged general council, and our leader got in this connection, without warrant, the name of "the Archon."

"Come!" said jocose Drew to him one day, as he sat on the wagon-seat ready to start for the city, "we are waiting for you!"

"Ah!" was Mr. Ripley's reply, "I see you have the *wag*-on, and are now waiting for the Archon!"

The government was vested in a General Council consisting of four branches: First, a Council of Industry, composed of five members; second, a Council of Finance, of four members; third, a Council of Science, of three members, and fourth a President, who, with the chairmen of the other three councils, constituted a "Central Council." The Council of Industry was appointed by the chiefs of the several series devoted to manual industry; the Council of Finance, by the stockholders; the Council of Science, by chiefs of the series devoted to educational, literary and scientific matters, and the President by the concurrent vote of the three series.

The Areopagus, whose duty was advisory, consisted of the General Council; the chiefs of the several groups and series; stockholders holding stock to the amount of one thousand dollars or more; all members of the Phalanx over the age of forty-five who had resided on the place for two years or longer; and of such other persons as might be elected by this Council on account of their superior wisdom, merit or devotion to the interests of the Association; no person voting who was not a member of the Phalanx.

There was a curious and interesting addition to the constitution in the " Council of Arbiters," which was to

consist of seven persons, "the majority of whom shall
be women." To this council individuals and departments were to bring all complaints, charges and griev-
ances not provided for in other ways. They were to
take cognizance of all matters relating to morals and
manners, and to report to the General Council all cases
wherein their decision was not complied with. The
reader can judge by this that there were men and women
who understood "woman's sphere," and were ready to
assist her to it quietly and naturally, long years ago in
this little band.

A considerable number of arrangements were made
to secure what was considered justice in the relation of
capital to the Phalanx, its members and its stockholders.
The capital stock was divided into three classes, namely:
loan stock, or that which received a fixed percentage for
use; partnership stock, depending on the general product of the Phalanx for its dividend; and labor stock,
that represented the dividend to labor.

The arrangements for the dividends on stock of the
several kinds were quite complicated, and, under the
light of after events, seem farcical; but the constitution makers believed they were arranging matters not
only for the Brook Farm experiment, but for all who
might adopt the social life of the Phalanxes, present and
future. Looking at it in this light, the constitution
might deserve more thought than can be given to it now.

There was a preliminary article, written and signed
by George Ripley, President, from which the following
extracts are made: —

"At the last session of the Legislature of Massachusetts, our Association was incorporated under the name

which it now assumes, with the right to hold real estate to the amount of one hundred thousand dollars.
This confers upon us all the usual powers and privi-
leges of chartered companies.   We have introduced several branches of profitable industry, and established a
market for their products; and finally, in the constitution which follows, we have applied the principles of
social justice to the distribution of profits in such a
manner that the best results are to be expected.

" Nothing is now necessary to the greatest possible
measure of success but capital to furnish sufficient
means to enable us to develop every department to advantage.   This capital we can now apply profitably and
without danger of loss.   We are well aware that there
must be risk in investing money in an infant association as well as in any other untried business, but with the
labors of nearly four years, we have arrived at a point
where this risk hardly exists.   Not that we have surmounted all the difficulties of the enterprise ; these are
still sufficiently abundant.   But we have, by no means
with ease, laid the foundation, and now stand ready to
do our part in rearing a superstructure, which ap-
proaches more nearly to the ideal of human society than
any that has as yet existed —a society which shall establish justice between all interests and all men ; which
shall guarantee education, the right to labor, and the
rights of property to all, and which by actual demonstration of a state of things every way better and more
advantageous, will put an end to the great evils which
at present burden even the most fortunate classes.

" What we have already been able to accomplish
ought to give weight to our words.   We speak not
from abstract conviction, but from experience; not as
mere enthusiasts, but as men of practical common
sense, holding in our hands the means of escape from
the present condition of society, and from that still
more frightful state to which in all civilized countries
it is hurrying.

"Accordingly, we calmly and earnestly invite the aid of those who perceive how little security existing institutions offer against the growth of commercial feudalism on the one hand, and pauperism on the other — of those whose sympathies are with the unfortunate and uneducated masses; of those who long for the establishment of more true and genial conditions of life, as well as of those who are made restless and fiery-souled by the universal necessities of reform.

"But by the increasing number, whose most ardent desire is to see the experiment of Association fairly tried, we are confident that the appeal we now make will not be received without the most generous response in their power. As far as their means and their utmost exertions can go, they will not suffer so favorable an opportunity for the realization of their hopes to pass unimproved."

I cannot say that I think all parties in the Association were pleased with the changes in the constitution. They were not simple enough to be easily applied and quickly comprehended, and were too weighty and cumbersome for the little society.

Early in the second spring (1844) of my sojourn at the farm it was decided to build a large unitary building on the high ground, almost directly in front of the Eyry, though at some distance from it, on the eastern verge of the slope facing the meadow, and nearly in line with the distant town road. It was late when the preparations were concluded and the work was commenced. There was not money enough in the treasury to pay for it, but it was thought that means would come. The result of the season's work was that the foundation walls were laid, the first floor was boarded, and thus it was left for the winter.

It was an oblong, wooden building, with a main entrance on a level with the earth terrace. The lower floor was divided into some five or six apartments, with parlors, a reading room, reception rooms, large dining hall, with an adjoining kitchen and bakery. From the main hall or entry, which was on the left of the centre of the building, arose a flight of stairs which led out on to a corridor or piazza which extended across the whole front of the building. This corridor was duplicated by one above it, and the roof jutted out to a line with the lower story and covered them both. Pillars supported the roof, and were attached to and supported the corridors. On the lower corridor or piazza were the entrances to the suites. There were seven doorways that entered seven houses, as distinct as any other seven houses, except in being connected by the corridors and being under one roof, each house containing two suites. Thus could privacy be maintained and sociability increased.

The building would add wonderfully to the advantages of the Association, and being near the centre of the domain, would diminish the travel which consumed a great deal of time. It would give room for increased numbers; would furnish a suitable assembly room, and more especially would it give to the larger families a chance to place their members together in the natural family order. It would also allow the other buildings to be used exclusively for family purposes, and if success increased the resources of the Association, the main building would be enlarged by adding wings to it.

The proportion of unmarried persons in the Association was large, and young men predominated. They had, in a general sense, a good home in the Association, but there was lacking the family circle to draw around at night, and a good deal of motherly care and sympathy. They were reliable young men, and many of the families would not have objected to having them joined to their evening circles, had they not been crowded themselves; to having a sympathizing care over them, and to looking after many of those trifling things that make the difference between comfort and discomfort.

It was a theory that all should have a home — that the Association, as a general home, should not take the place of the private family; and it was also considered a duty by many to join to their family circles one or more of these single persons. It was proposed in the apportionment of the rooms in the new building, to place a family in each house and proportionately distribute the young men, when desirable to do so, among them. This would give all a more equal chance, and not doom the young and productive members to reside in attics, or in groups in any place convenient for the Association, in its crowded state, to put them.

Extracts from the Financial Report to the Association.

"The Direction of Finance respectfully submit their annual report for the year ending Oct. 31, 1844 : —

The income of the Association during the year from all sources whatever has been	$11,854 41
and its expenditures for all purposes, including interest, losses by bad debts, and damage of buildings, tools and furniture	10,409 14
leaving a balance of	1,445 27
from which deducting the amount of doubtful debts contracted this year	284 43
we have	$1,160 84

which is to be divided according to the Constitution.

" By the last yearly report of this Direction it appears
that the Association has been a loser up to November 1,
1843, to the amount of $2,748.83. In this amount was
included sundry debts against associates amounting to
$924.38 which should not have been included. There
were also some small discrepancies which were afterwards discovered, so that on settling the books, the entire deficit appeared to be $1,837.00.

" To this amount should be added the proportion of the
damage done to the tools, furniture and general fixtures
and depreciation in the live stock, by the use of the
two years which the Association has been in operation
previous to that time. The whole damage of this property by the use of these years has been ascertained by
inventory to be $365.54, according to the estimates and
statements prepared by Messrs. Ryckman and Hastings,
which are herewith submitted.

" Of this sum, $365.54, we have charged one third,
$121.85, to the account of the current year, and two
thirds, $243.69, to the account of the two preceding
years. To the same amount should also be added sundry debts which have since proved to be bad, amounting
in all to $678.08, and also an error in favor of I. Mor-
ton amounting to $17.74, which has since been discov-
ered in his account, so that the total deficit of the preceding years will appear to be as follows : —

Deficit on settling the books	$1,837 00
Damage on furniture and fixtures . . .	243 69
Bad debts, including debts of associates considered doubtful	678 08
I. Morton	17 74
Total	$2,776 51

From this amount is to be deducted the value of the
farm produce consisting of hay, roots, manures, etc., on
hand November 1, 1843, which was not taken into the
amount of last year, but which has been ascertained to
be $762.50, as well as the value, $49.13, of the family

stores which were on hand at the same time, but were also omitted from the amount.

Deducting these two amounts ($762.50+$49.13= $811.63) from the deficit as above stated we have:

Deficit	$2,776 51
Farm produce and family stores	811 63
Real deficit for 1842 and 1843	$1,964 88

"It was the opinion of a majority at least of this Board that this sum must be chargeable upon the future industry of the Association, and that no dividend could be declared until it had been made up. Accordingly the quarterly statement for the quarter ending August 1, 1844, was based upon this opinion, and a deficit of $526.78 declared to exist at that time. It is but justice to say that that statement was made up in the absence of one of the members of the Direction, Mr. Ryckman, who on seeing it objected entirely to the principle which it embodied. Subsequent consideration has convinced the Direction that the statement was in that respect erroneous, and that the transactions of previous years ought not to affect the operations of this, in the way proposed in the statement. It should be borne in mind that the deficit before spoken of is not a debt in itself, but is the difference between the amount of our debts and our joint stock, and the nominal value of our assets. The Association is not bound to pay the sum or to make it good in any way. It pays interest upon it, but can never be called on to pay the principal. The sum total of the actual liabilities of the Association, that is, of debts and obligations which it is bound at some time or other to pay, is much exceeded by the cost value of its property. Its joint stock, which it is not bound to pay, much exceeds the deficit we are speaking of, so that clearly the deficit is not to be paid, but only the interest upon it, that is, five per cent per annum forever. So that it is evident that the principal is by no means chargeable upon the industry of the present or of future years, but only the interest. And even if the said deficit were a debt to be paid it would still, as we conceive, be perfectly just and legitimate to issue stock for its amount to those members by whose labors it was made up. Because in that case we should merely, in consideration of such labor, bind the Association to the yearly payment of the interest aforesaid according to the terms of our joint stock compact.

" This is, as we are persuaded, the only way whereby labor can receive justice. If a hundred dollars in money is invested in our stock, we issue certificates for that amount, and why must we not do the same with an investment of a hundred dollars' worth of labor? The claim in the latter case seems to us even more imperative than in the former. The dividend of each year ought, as we are convinced, to be made with reference solely to the difference between its gains on the one hand, and its expenditures and losses on the other.

" The earlier losses of the establishment must be regarded as the price of much valuable experience, and as inevitable in starting such an institution. Almost every business fails to pay its expenses at the commencement — it always costs something to set the wheels in operation; this is not, however, to be regarded as absolute loss. This is the view which is to be taken of the condition of the Association at the beginning of the present year.

" The true value of any property is precisely the sum on which, in the use for which it was designed or which it may be put to, it pays the requisite interest. The price of railroad stock, for example, is not regulated either by its original cost or by the present intrinsic worth of the property it represents, but by the dividend it pays and by the condition and durability of the railroad. For any other use than as a railroad the property of the road is of course comparatively worthless, but that consideration has no effect upon its value.

The case is entirely the same with the property of this Association. As long as it is able, in the use and under the management of the Association, to pay the stipulated interest—five per cent per annum—upon the stock shares by which it is represented, so long those stock shares will be worth par, whatever may be the nominal cost of the property, or its value for any other purposes than those of the Association.

"In accordance with these views and for other considerations which we shall hereafter allude to, this Direction is altogether of opinion that the results of this year's industry ought to be divided irrespective of the results of former years, and certificates of stock issued to those persons who are entitled to such dividends.

"To some persons it may perhaps seem remarkable that a dividend should be declared when the Association is so much in want of ready money as at present, but a little reflection will show anyone that it is a perfectly legitimate proceeding. A very large part of our industry has been engaged in the production of permanent property such as the shop, the Phalanstery and the improvements upon the farm. These are of even more value to the Association than so much money, and a dividend may as justly be based upon them as upon cash in the treasury.

"As soon as the Phalanstery shall be completed it will become necessary to establish different rates of room rent. It is a matter of doubt whether such an arrangement is not already desirable. In our present crowded condition, indeed, the general inconveniences are distributed with tolerable equality, but still it is impossible to avoid some exceptions, and it might contribute to the harmony of the Association if a just graduation of rates for different apartments should now be established. As far as possible no member should be the recipient of peculiar favors, but when all are charged at an equal rate for unequal accommodations, this is unavoidable. For the same reason a difference should be made between the price of board at the Graham tables, and those which are furnished with a different kind of food. It is only by this means that justice can be done and differences prevented.   " C. A. D."

The first thought that will arrest the attention of some in reading this report is the smallness of the figures. It does not appear to-day that the corporation was much of a financial affair, for there are thousands of persons in our land now who could easily sustain such an institution and pocket its yearly losses; but we must bear in mind that the intervening years have changed the value of money, and its relation to property. A fair price for a mechanic's labor then was a dollar for a day of ten to twelve hours; the same persons would now receive three to four times as much for less hours. We should remember also that the colossal fortunes of to-day were not in existence then. The means at the command of the Association were very small, and the wonder is that with so little money capital the enterprise should have attracted the wide notice it did.

In this report was an allusion to the Graham table. In the dining room there was always, at the time of which I write, one table of vegetarians — those who used no flesh meats, and generally no tea or coffee. They passed under the name of " Grahamities," from the founder of the vegetarian system in America, Dr. Sylvester Graham, whose name is still connected with bread made of unbolted wheat because it was by him considered the very perfection of human food. These persons were of both sexes, different ages and occupations. They worked on the farms, in the schools, the houses and the shops. They had the diet of the place, minus the meat and sometimes the tea and coffee. Little attention was paid at first to this departure from common habits, but by degrees the numbers increased until they began to be a power. Their constancy, their earnest belief, soon swept away all ridicule, and the proof that they could do their share of daily work was not wanting. Among the number were many very devoted and cheerful persons.

Dispensing with meat, with the restricted diet, led some to say : " Our table does not cost as much as the others, for we eat no meat, saving the expense of it to the Association, and we drink no tea or coffee, saving that cost also. Let us have the money we have economized, spent for us in things that we want, in additional fruit and vegetables, or in some articles of diet that we need to replace the food we do not use." The answer to it was that the Association furnished certain things, and if the members did not eat them it was their loss, as it could not be expected that the Association could cater to individual tastes. But after a while the injustice was made apparent, and it led to the notice we have just read in the report.

I have been requested to give my personal testimony as to the effect of a vegetarian diet as seen at Brook Farm. I willingly do so. For two or three years the farmers, mechanics and others worked side by side, and no one could conscientiously say that in ability to work in any field of labor, physical or mental, the vegetarians were out-matched by their companions. Their health was fully maintained and their mental cheerfulness was surpassed by none.

From this report it can easily be learned that no important financial progress had been made at Brook Farm, and that any accumulation of wealth was yet in the future. The Brook Farmers were working in hope. It was still an experiment, and as an experiment it will be necessary for me to point out by-and-by the defects which will answer the often asked question, "Why did Brook Farm fail?" But it is well to bear in mind the starting point. Most men of business go into trade with a capital, some reserved fund, but the Brook Farmers had none, and as they progressed, the want of it was more and more felt. "It is the first step that costs," as the French proverb says, and the Brook Farmers had a great many first steps to take, steps that no others had taken, and inevitable costs and losses must occur. But we pass on into the second spring of my Brook Farm life.

And here another character came into our circle, and joined in work on the farm. He was very enthusiastic. His wife had lately died, and he brought her body to Brook Farm as to Holy Land and buried it in the little grove by the side of our first and only grave, so that there were now two mounds that the gardener ornamented with sods, shrubbery and flowers.

I do not think this new friend had a fine face. His features were not large, and, if we except the full forehead, not very attractive. His mouth was small, and his dark brown hair asserted its rights in spite of brush and comb, and would not lie gracefully down over his brow, and it added to the look of determination there was in the little man's countenance, shown by the lines in his face and the rigid and spare muscles, a "hold on " expression which so well coincided with his character.

New England at this time put its fingers in its ears and stifled the beatings of its heart that kept time with justice, in order that the peace of our country should not be disturbed by men who thought slavery a curse, and proclaimed it so. Rev. John Allen was then in a pulpit, and dared to speak his mind to his people, at which they rebelled and would not hearken. "Speak I must; speak I will," said he, "or we part! Let me but preach a sermon once a quarter on the subject of slavery!" But the church said, "No." "Let me then but preach once in six months," and the church said, "No." Finally he said he would continue with them if they would allow him to preach one sermon a year on the subject — I doubt not that that *one* would have carried flint and steel enough to set fire to all the tinder in the congregation — but the church would not listen, and they parted.

He had one little child, an infant a year or two old, who, deprived of his mother, was brought to the farm and had a great deal of attention and pity bestowed upon it. This little boy brought a misfortune which threatened the lives of the members, the business and life of the Association. He was the pet of his father, who took him to Boston on his lecture tours and brought him back, for Mr. Allen was engaged to lecture for the cause. The child had never been vaccinated, and being ill at the Hive, it was discovered that he had symptoms of small-pox, which disease he had taken somewhere in the city. Imagine the commotion among the persons who had handled and fondled the young

darling, and in the Association in general! But the
bravery of men and women who had dared to leave their
homes and share the fortune and fate of this young Community was everywhere displayed.

The child was isolated and cared for, but in due time
backaches and headaches foretold the coming of the
dreaded disease, and preparations were made for antici-
pated results. The Cottage was vacated, and the sick
were conveyed thither. The disease took a variety of
forms. There were those who had nothing but the
symptoms, or a pustule or two; some had a few dozen
on them, scattered from head to foot; they were almost
absolutely well; they refused to be made invalids of;
they kept at work on the farm or were only disabled for
a day or two when the disease was at its height. The
lighter cases increased in number, and finally the Direction saw it was useless to try to isolate all, and that
the disease must have its run, and they must trust to
fate for final results. The worst cases were in the improvised hospital, under the care of kindly nurses.
"Hired," say you? No; not a bit of it! but dear, kind
women and men volunteered to attend to this sacred
duty, and after weeks of imprisonment, came out with
the glory of having protected every life, and the Associated family lost not a member. There were more
than thirty cases. The simple diet, the pure air and
the healthy mental stimulus of cheerful lives, with the
knowledge that they were something more than in name
a united body, must have had its effect, for the whole
trouble passed away like a summer shower, and left no
permanent impression on the society. There were three
or four extreme cases, but only one or two persons who

bore scars that were defacements, and there was no panic in our midst. The members took the whole matter with wonderful coolness.

Like a shower it wiped out the army of visitors! When any persons came, an attendant warned them of our condition ere they reached the Hive door, and they precipitately retreated. Occasionally only, a carriage or a few persons travelled the accustomed ways. Not until the epidemic had passed did the interminable throng resume its accustomed walk, or strange faces appear at the " visitors' table," and our many constant and cheerful friends greet us again as of yore. The labor of the Association was much disarranged, and there was loss in many ways, but it was truly to be congratulated that it escaped from such an unusual danger as comfortably as it did. From the first days of the Community until its close, there was only one death on the farm, and that of the person described in a former chapter.

CHAPTER VII.

ALL through the spring the talk was of the new building, the " Phalanstery," as we called it. Everybody was thinking what great progress could be made when we should live in it. One day, passing by, I found the carpenters had resumed work, and from thenceforth it progressed until it assumed the resemblance of a mammoth house.

The round of daily life this season was little varied from that of the past, but there was more activity and more crowding. A great many makeshifts were had to enable persons who wished to visit the place to get even lodging for a night, for no one knew who or how many were coming before the evening coach arrived. Oftentimes it came full, when it seemed there was not a sleeping place to be found on the domain. The Association buildings overflowed, and a neighboring house was leased and occupied just across the road, by the Hive. It was sometimes called the " Nest," and had been hired in the first days of the " Community." Even then every corner was filled.

There was some income from this crowd of visitors, and at the same time the work and system of the place were much retarded, for as carriage after carriage and vehicle after vehicle came, each one would require an attendant, who was taken from labor, and when the regular attendants were all occupied the horn would be sounded to see if anyone of the shoemakers or printers or farmers or teachers would leave his work and volunteer for this duty.

Frequently all these visitors would leave as suddenly as they came, and would only give their thanks, not even being of a single cent's immediate value to the place for the outlay of time taken from productive labor. Sometimes a growl would be heard because a trifle was taken for the expense of meals, or about the absence of feathers in the beds, by some visitor who intruded himself uninvited. I pitied the Dormitory Group, running from house to house at edge of evening to find a stray corner to lodge a guest; seeking out the rooms of absent members, and hunting up towels, furnishings and fittings, through all the pleasant summer weather. But this was cheerfully done for "the cause," and much more had to be done.

Our lecturers were wanted — men who were in practical associative life, and they were taken from remunerative work to speak to the public. Thus we entered into the summer, and the beautiful grass waved again on the meadow; the pleasant lights gleamed again from the Eyry windows ; the pure moon looked down on the summer fields; the merry voices of the young and happy folks were heard as the farmers came up from the fields, and the horn sounded its "*toot-toot*" as a signal for all to join at meals.

I was in the gardener's department, assisting him in the care of the greenhouse plants and making flower beds, but our especial work was laying out and planting a large garden which should be a permanent addition to the beauty of the place, and a future source of income. On the farm was a fine imported bull who did not seem to be doing his share of work in our very industrious place, so a ring was put in his nose and he was my especial charge in the way of a team. It appears cruel to one who for the first time sees a bull led by the nose, but there seems to be no reason why a bull should complain, when there are so many humans continually led through life in the same fashion.

In fact the bull throve and had in some ways considerable sense. He was harnessed into a tipcart and we made him work for us. He was a strong, powerful fellow, and has carried his eighty loads of gravel a day, from one part of the garden to the other. At noon I would relieve him of his harness and mount his back for a ride to the barn. I would then be the "observed of all observers." Sometimes, for the frolic, I would load my cart with young misses and dump them at the Hive door, backing up to it in the most approved style of an old "gee-haw" farmer.

"Prince Albert," the bull, was a gem. He worked admirably. He never gave me any trouble, or anyone else human, but when stalled near the oxen he had a peculiar fancy to poke his horns into them. Early one morning, by some mischance, he got loose in the barn, and "going" for one of them frightened him so much that he also broke loose, and in trying to make his escape from the bull, backed into the barn-room. There was a large trap door in it, and the ox ventured on it, breaking it, and fell through. The bull was so close behind that he could not escape, and they dropped together into the little room below, the door of which was open. The ox escaped into the yard, and ran for dear life around the front of the Hive, pursued by the bull. Whether the jar of the fall, his escape, or his quiet disposition sobered him I know not, but he soon fell into a jog-trot pursuit, and was caught and returned by a neighboring farmer.

There was great roaring and noise in the fracas, which was of short duration, but long enough to bring out the men from the Hive to witness the affair. The General, who had been sleeping a little late — probably he had been baking bread the night before — made his appearance from his little room on the ground floor, with boot on one foot and shoe on the other, just as it was all over, with the impatient inquiry, " W-w-what is it all about ? " On an explanation of the affair being made, the next question he asked, in all earnestness, soberness and simplicity, was " W-h-o-i-c-h came out ahead ? " The personal appearance and manner of the General, and the absurd question, uttered in a vehement and stammering way, touched a ludicrous spot in the minds of the spectators so permanently that should you ask one of them to-day, " Which came out ahead ? " he will smile or give you a shout of laughter in return.

It took but little to amuse, sometimes, for on one of the beautiful summer days at nooning time, a group of men were resting in the shade of the arbor that was on an island artificially made in the brook below the terraces in front of the Hive, breathing the pure, balmy air of outdoors instead of the indoor air of the workshop, reclining on the thick greensward, when some two or three essayed the not very difficult feat of jumping the merrily running brook, from embankment to embankment, and dared Tirrell, one of the number, to follow. He was the oldest and a little less supple than the others; and in trying the jump deliberately landed about three inches short of the opposite bank, knee deep in the water. It was, as the young people say, " too funny for anything," but equally funny to the lookers-on to see the amused Chiswell, one of his mates, roll over and over on the greensward in repeated convulsions of side-splitting laughter, whilst the others, standing up, had hard work to keep their perpendicular and writhed in awful shapes as they joined in chorus with him, as Tirrell was slowly wading out of the water up the embankment.

Trouble in financial affairs still existed. Cash in large amount was not received, and it was perilous times with the Direction. When the fall of the year came, it was announced that we must retrench our meagre diet, to enable us to go on until our labor could pay us better — until we could improve our employments and enlarge the institution so that there could be more producers — and it was submitted to without much complaint.

The work on the new building ceased, so that all hope of entering into it before the coming spring was abandoned. There was one motto, " Retrenchment," and it was echoed from all sides with all manner of fun and mock solemnity; but those who were in the inner circle doubtless felt, more than the youngsters did, the seriousness of matters. A more strict account of everything was kept; indeed it seemed that the time spent in keeping all the various items, was out of proportion to the work done. I shall not soon forget, in this connection, the joke of "the Parson," E. Capen, who, holding up a pair of pantaloons that he had just received from the Mending Group, said sharply, "I have just gotten a *reseat in full* for these pantaloons!"

It will not be necessary to go into details of changes made to secure more prosperity. I was undisturbed by them. I could go with crust of good bread all day and be satisfied, growing strong and healthy. I could endure the cold and heat without trouble, and have often braved the winter wind, taking no pains to keep it from being blown on my bare chest, and without discomfort.

The new greenhouse was built in the autumn, just in time to save the plants from frost. It was situated back of the cottage and garden, almost parallel with our boundary wall, and about fifteen feet from it. There was a little sleeping room connected with it, where I lodged summer and winter. Above me in the gable, a variety of beautiful doves, consisting of Pouters, Tumblers, Ruffs, Carriers and Fantails, was installed. They were very tame, and were much admired by our family and visitors. They came at my call, alighted on my hands, head and shoulders, and picked corn from out my hands and from between my lips.

We planted grape vines that bore promises, but were too young for fruit, and we made bouquets and sold them to Boston and West Roxbury parties.

Peter N. Klienstrup, the gardener, was under the spell of the powerful weed, tobacco, and he tried time and again to break from the habit of using it, but as often returned to its enchantment and its witchery.

" Dis is my last piece," I have heard him say many times, showing me the fragment of a " hand," and when that was gone and for some two or three weeks afterwards everything soured him. He was as cross as a bear, but after that time his nerves would gradually become calmer and his complexion clearer.

The gardener would persevere in the disuse of tobacco until the enchanter's spell seemed broken, when some disturbing thing would upset him, and he would turn his pockets inside out, and fumble with his thumb and finger in their extreme corners for the least particle of the " luxury." " John, I *must* have some tobacco," he would say, and in a day or two would be again under the full influence of the weed. I pitied the old man, as I do the thousands of younger men who are to-day under the same enchantment.

Swept into this little nook in the industries of the place, I left the Farming Group forever.

It is often stated that the home circle is the sphere of women, but at times it is a very narrow circle — a very narrowing circle to its occupants. There are thousands who enter it as brilliant young ladies, and come from it at the end of a few years morbid, harassed, depressed; sunk in all the graces and powers that make a woman's life beautiful and distinct from a man's. The circle in many cases is so narrow that there is no room for growth. The humdrum toils, the petty cares and rude contact with hired help, sink many a charming woman into a domestic drudge and scold.

It has been asserted that Associations and Communities may do well for men, but that women can never get along in them. The experience of Brook Farm tes-

tifies against the assertion. If ever there was a clear
record of faithfulness and devotion, of sacrifice, of love
of principle, and earnest, unselfish work for unselfish
ends, the women toilers of Brook Farm can claim it,
and secure it without cavil. Morning and evening, in
season and out of season, in heat and cold, they were
ever at their posts. And the self-imposed toil made
them grow great. It opened their hearts as they daily
saw the devotion of others.

It was for the meanest a life above humdrum, and for
the greatest something far, infinitely far beyond. They
looked into the gates of life and saw beyond charming
visions, and hopes springing up for all. They saw protection for all, even to the meanest of God's creatures;
a life beyond cold charity, up among the attributes of
the Creator's justice; an even garment for all, protecting the weak children of life against the strong, the
strong against the machinations of the weak. How
could they grow otherwise than great?

Wherever woman's hands were wanted to work,
wherever woman's head was wanted to plan, and where-
ever woman's care and sympathy were needed, they
were always forthcoming. Some were witty, too. One
of our ladies, with her hands full of apple blossoms and
her eyes bright as stars, was met by Mr. Ripley, who
said to her, " You have been foraging, I see! " " Oh,
no," she said, with an arch smile, " I do not go *foraging.*"

The pupils of the school took the infection of labor.
At first often haughty and distant, they soon mellowed,
and were ready to assist the young associative friends,
with whom they became acquainted, in various lit-

tle works, and enjoyed the labor. The prevailing tone was health. Sickness was a rarity to either sex. The pupils mingled with the games and sports, walks, rides and parties, and many seemed as devoted as though belonging to the body, and when they returned from vacations, it was with happy greetings to all and from all, and like returning home, rather than to tasks.

Separate and distinct from the school was a room for the young at the Hive, where mothers could leave their children in the care of the Nursery Group whilst they were engaged in industrial work, or as a kindly relief to themselves when fatigued by the care of them; for a primary doctrine was "alternation of employments." It was believed that more and better work could be done by not being confined to one employment all the day of labor; that it was better for the mental as well as the physical system to have a change — in theory as often as once in two hours. In practice, under the conditions which governed our life, an attempt only could be made to alternate labor and to relieve the mothers from the excess of burden that the care of young children often is. Some very sweet and choice ladies attended to this employment, choosing it from their attraction towards it; thus inaugurating the day nursery system, now coming into vogue in our large cities.

In the matter of dress, the women who chose, had made for themselves a short gown with an under garment, bound at the ankles and of the same material. With this dress they could walk well and work well. It was somewhat similar to the dress worn by Mrs. Bloomer and called by her name years after this date.

The question of the " right to vote " for women was

not one that troubled the politicians of Brook Farm.
At all of the meetings for the acceptance or rejection of
applicants and other purposes, women cast their votes
without criticism, for were they not mutually interested?
And now, nearly half a century since, we are asked to
form a party to secure similar rights. Why, men and
women, the party was formed when a majority of persons now living was not born; only it was a very
small party, and, need I add — select!

Only once did we have a wedding ceremony at the
farm, though the friendships commenced outlasted the
Association. The financial conditions for marriage were
not inviting. One pleasant evening, later than this
date as I remember it, we were all invited to the Pilgrim House to a wedding of one of Mr. Dwight's sisters.
Our friend Rev. W. H. Channing officiated.

It was a homelike affair, and after the ceremony " the
Poet " (J. S. Dwight) was invited to speak to us; but
no, he was not in the mood. He was urged — for all
liked to hear his kindly voice, and we thought this a
particularly pleasant subject — so he at last arose from
his seat and commenced with these words: " I like this
making one." It seemed to touch various chords in the
minds of the hearers, for the applause and laughter that
followed silenced the rest of the speech and it was never
finished. Then some one proposed that all should join
hands and make a circle, as the symbol of universal
unity, and a pledge to one another that all were united
in effort to continue and carry on the great work of har-
monizing society on a true and just basis of unity of
interests, attractive industry, mutual guarantees, etc.

> " Come, let us join hands! let our two flames mingle
>   In one more pure;
> Since there is truth in nothing that is single
>   Be love, love's cure,"

sang our Poet after this time in the *Harbinger*, and some
said with double meaning.   I have a list of names of
fourteen married couples whose mutual friendship was
begun or continued through Brook Farm life, and I
have yet to know of an unhappy marriage among them
all.

The question was often debated whether such a life
as was led in Association would have a tendency to
favor early marriages or not, but like a great many other
questions of importance, it was debated without settlement.   One party claimed that from the freedom of
social intercourse and facility of acquaintance, an inti-
macy would spring up that would result in early marriages; and the other party maintained that with the
certainty of true friendship from woman, and pleasant
social relations, marriages would not be hurried, but delayed until the parties' thoughts and temperaments were
well harmonized and all proper and natural arrangements of support and comfort thoroughly secured.

There was with us a variety of female characters.
We had our Marthas who were troubled with much
serving, and our Marys who loved to sit at our leader's
feet and hear the glad tidings and the new doctrines;
and now and then we had an uncomfortable woman,
fully out of place and consequently unhappy.   Such an
one was usually the wife of some man whose whole energies were devoted to his work and who was happy in
himself, on his half shell, and was to be pitied that his

other half lived not in his shadow, but cast a shadow on him.

All Brook Farmers recollect with pleasure, among special cases of devotion, the little, straight, light-haired, smiling woman, who was so long chief of the Dormitory Group, who was at nightfall wandering about with stray towels, sheets and pillows, always making arrangements in the shifting population for every one who came; hunting places for stray visitors, when we were crowded; puzzled and wearied oft — for no one knew at what hour of the day or evening visitors might come and we had oftentimes almost to make a Box and Cox affair of it, for there was no hotel within a long distance. This little woman was at her post again in the morning doing dormitory work, never tired, going from house to house, ever with a smile on her face ; and this position she voluntarily occupied more than two years. Sweet Lizzie Curson !

Then the young folks — the young misses — were full of devotion. Commend me to the young for unselfish work, or was it that the life awoke in them a devoted spirit ? This I know, that the sympathy and friendship which sprung up in those days has lasted all these years, and will remain as long as life. But it was not personal beauty that held me in sway, and still holds me after so many long years — years that have transformed most of those beautiful girls into old matrons and weeping widows, plain and homely — but because it seems to me that there never was a more gentle, kind, amiable, trusting, self-respecting, loving set of young folks anywhere assembled.

And oh, how they learned! How they grew in grace

and in education, both of the practical and the ornamental! How fine in health and figure, from the free life, from the grace learned in dancing, the repose at early hours, the simple diet and the mind filled every day with pleasant thoughts and ideas. I do not know of any one who was not in fine, robust health. They all, without exception, developed into healthy men and women; or, to be a little more exact, as long as they remained on the farm they continued to develop in health, strength, grace and beauty.

CHAPTER VIII.

THE DRAMA, AND IMPORTANT LETTERS.

THE need of especial amusements was not particularly felt at the farm, but sometimes a set, inspired by an active mind, would venture out of the common course and try to do a "big thing," which, like many big things, would prove a failure. There was no hall for performances except the dining hall, and it could not be taken possession of until after supper; consequently, for a dramatic performance where it was important to have the hall prepared before hand, it was useless, and so the Amusement Group secured the lower floor of the shop for a special occasion, and Chiswell, the carpenter, made a portable stage which could be arranged for rehearsals and taken down easily, and all hands went to work, some to learn their parts and others to make dresses, properties and scenery.

The influence of a strong, active mind and persuasive tongue like that of Drew, was felt on this occasion, for he induced the Amusement Group to allow a portion of his favorite poem, Byron's "Corsair," to be acted. With pencil and scissors he went to work, cutting and slashing the "Corsair" with these ungodly weapons until I fear he could not, had he been in the flesh, have fought a brave fight.

I cannot at this late day describe the dresses worn on the occasion; but Glover was the corsair, and burnt cork had to suffer, and I know that there was quite a pretty miss whom he had no especial objection to embracing as Medora. When he said, "My own Medora!" it was quite pathetic — enough to cause a titter among the younger portion of the audience.

Apropos of the audience, it was noised abroad that there was to be a performance at the farm, and there was more than the usual number of outsiders present. Even the Reverend Theodore, who never ventured out in our vicinity in the evening, was tempted to come over for this "great occasion." Some round-faced, pretty daughters of a well-to-do neighboring farmer from "Spring Street" were there also, and with friends and neighbors, the shop was full; for us a large audience.

Well, the "Corsair," clipped as it was, dragged its slow length along to an end. We then ventured to start our great drama, "Pizarro," or the death of Rolla. But here again I am foiled in my remembrance. I know it took the "whole strength of the company" to fill out the many characters needed. Carpenters, shoemakers and farmers were turned into Spanish chieftains and Peruvians; our young maidens were changed into sun-worshippers, and our musical man adapted a portion of one of Mozart's masses, to sing to these words, "The *sun* is in his holy temple," etc., at which some of our people cavilled; but which portion, sung by the maidens, in white, was perhaps the best of all the performance.

I remember, however, that "the Admiral," or some one else, was stationed behind the scenes with a gun to fire at Rolla when he runs away with Alonzo's child;

that one of the great points made was, " By Heaven, it
is Alonzo's child ! " and that rushing over scenic rocks
he should in imagination be shot; but the pesky gun
behind the scenes would not go off until many desperate attempts were made — no report being heard until
the play had further progressed, when all of a sunden
the gun was fired, and frightened individuals had the
temerity to ask " what that gun was for."

I remember this also, that long before the play was
ended, the Reverend Theodore and others of the visitors had departed, thinking their own thoughts, and
that the curative effects of that performance lasted so
long the like was never attempted again ; and although
some were a trifle disheartened by the failure to reach
the summit of their hopes, yet it was a source of merriment to others, and there are those whose eyes may
meet these pages, who will still smile if you quote these
lines to them : " O'er the glad waters of the deep, blue
sea." " List, 'tis the bugle ! " (I can vouch that it
was nothing but the old trumpet we blew for dinner.)
" Ha ! it sure cannot be day ! What star, what sun is
bursting on the bay ? " (It was only the barn lantern
that was raised outside the window, and an awful poor
light at that !).

" Well, how was Drew's play ? " said one wag. " All
blood and thunder, eh ? "

" No ; all thud and blunder," was the rejoinder.

The associative movement had now touched thousands of hearts in this country. The Brook Farm Community, at its formation, was the only community
founded in America on the principle of freedom in religion and social life — all others being founded on

special religious creeds.   The agitation of social questions, the doctrines of Fourier and others, brought
many societies into existence ; but like enthusiasts in
other schemes, the founders of them preached unity, but
did not unite.   The leaders of Brook Farm urged upon
the prominent men in the social belief, to take part with
them in their already established society, with all the
power they could command; but Mr. Greeley and the
New York men joined hands with the North American
Phalanx, an association founded at Red Bank, New
Jersey, and lent their influence and means to its development.   Mr. Greeley thought the land at Brook Farm
was of too poor quality ; that the debts of the organization were heavier than they should be for a beginning,
and that by starting anew, a better chance for thrift
could be had — especially if a location could be selected
with an excellent soil — and he desired it should be
located near the great market of New York.   This departure from a true idea — the idea of concentration —
was certainly a great mistake, and the end proved that
the young societies, with little means, and needing
much, should all have joined together for financial
success.

At a very early date in the movement, there was a
Community formed at Hopedale, Milford, Massachusetts, under the leadership of Rev. Adin Ballou, a
man of considerable ability, whose tenets were those of
peace in absolute distinction to those of war.   The
Community was pledged by its members not to enter
into any hostile act, and to use its influence for universal peace, they being all of a sect called " Non-Resist-
ants."   Our leader, wisely, I think, made overtures to

them to unite with the West Roxbury Community, but the proposition was declined in the following letter : —

"MENDON, MASS., Nov. 3, 1842.

"DEAR BROTHER RIPLEY: Since our last interview I have met our brethren and had a full consultation with them on the points of difficulty on which we are at issue with your friends. We are unanimous in the solemn conviction that we could not enlist for the formation of a community not based on the distinguishing principles of the standard of Practical Christianity so called, especially *non-resistance*, etc. We trust you will do us the justice to think that we are conscientious and not *bigoted*. The temptation is strong to severe, but we dare not hazard the cause we have espoused by yielding our scruples.

"We love you all, and shall be happy to see you go on and prosper, though we fear the final issue. We are few and poor, and therefore you can do without us better than we without you — your means and your learning! But we shall try to do something in our humble way if God favor us. We beseech you and your friends not to think us unkind or unfriendly on account of our stiff notions, as they may seem, and to regard us always as ready to rejoice in your good success. Let me hear from you occasionally, and believe me and those for whom I speak, sincerely your brethren in every good work.

"Affectionately yours,
"ADIN BALLOU."

I remember that the Association, through its leaders, urged upon all the principal men who came within their sphere, with considerable zeal, to unite in their movement. This is a matter of record that should be placed to their credit.

A little later than this I find a letter from Mr. Bris-

bane, who showed his characteristics so well in it, that
I present all its important parts for reading : —

" NEW YORK, the 9th December, 1845.

" MY DEAR RIPLEY : — Yours of the 3d just received, the 5th came to hand yesterday.   I note all its
contents in relation to your views upon the necessity of
developing Brook Farm.   The reason why I have spoken
in some of my last letters of the best means of bringing
Brook Farm to a close, and making preparations for a
trial under more favorable circumstances, is this.   In
the middle of November I received a letter from
Charles in which, in speaking of the varioloid, he stated
the difficulties you have to contend with, and expressed
fears for the future in such a way that I decided you
had made up your minds to bring things to a close.   I
feared that Morton might be foreclosing his mortgage,
which would be a most serious affair.   This is the cause
of my adverting to a possible dissolution and the necessity of looking ahead to meet in the best and most
proper manner such a contingency.

" As to any opinion of what is to be done, it is easily
explained.

" First, we must raise a sufficient amount of capital,
and the amount must not be small.

" Second, when that is secured we must prepare and
work out a plan of scientific organization sufficiently
complete in its details to serve as a guide in organizing
an Association.   For my own part, I feel no capability
whatever of directing an Association by discipline, by
ideas of duty, moral suasion and any other similar
means.   I want organization; I want a mechanism suited
and adapted to human nature, so that human nature
can follow its laws and attractions and go rightly, and
be its own guide.   I might do something in directing
such an organization, but would be useless in any other
way.   As we all like to be active, I would like exceed-

ingly to take part in and help construct a scientific organization.

" How can we raise the capital necessary to do something effectual? I see but two ways. The first is for C. and I — and if he will not do it, then for you and I, if you would possibly engage in it — to lecture patiently and perseveringly in various parts of the country, having the translation of Fourier with us, *and continue at the work* until we have enlisted and interested men enough who will subscribe each a certain sum sufficient to form the fund we deem necessary. Patience and perseverance would do this. One hundred men who would subscribe one thousand dollars cash, would give us a fine capital. Something effectual, I think, might be done with such an amount; less than that would, I fear, be patchwork.

" Second, if C. or you cannot engage in this enterprise, then I shall see what I can do alone. I shall make first the trial of the steel business — that will now soon be determined, probably in a few weeks. There are chances that it may be a great thing; if that turns out nothing, then I shall take Fourier's work and do something of what I propose you or C. and I should do together.

" If the capital can be had, where shall we organize, you will ask? That is a thing to be carefully considered, and which we cannot decide at present.

" Placed under the circumstances you are, all these speculations will appear foreign to the subject that interests you, and useless. You want capital, and immediately, for Brook Farm. Now it seems to me a problem as perplexing to get fifteen thousand dollars for Brook Farm as it does to raise one hundred thousand dollars. Where can it be had? The New Yorkers who have money, G., T., S., etc., are all interested in and pledged to raise ten thousand dollars for the North American Phalanx, to pay off its mortgage. You might as well undertake to raise dead men, as to attain any considerable amount of capital from the people here; I have tried it so often that I know the difficulties.

"The fact is, we have a great work to accomplish, that of organizing an Association, and to do it we must have the means adequate to the task, and to get these means we must make the most persevering and Herculean efforts. We must go at the thing in earnest, and labor until we have secured the means. I really see no other way or avenue to success; if you do, I should be glad to hear your explanation of it. Fifteen thousand dollars might do a great deal at Brook Farm, but would it do the thing effectually — would it make a trial that would impress the public? And for anything short of that, none of us, I suppose, would labor.

"We are surrounded by great difficulties. I see no immediate chance of obtaining a capital sufficient for a good experiment, and until we have the capital to organize upon quite a complete scale, I should say that it would be a very great misfortune to dissolve Brook Farm. No uncertain prospects should exercise any influence; the means must be had in hand before we made any decisive movement towards a removal or organizing in a more favorable location, even if you were perfectly willing to leave New England and the neighborhood of Boston. As I said I spoke of it, and should be urged to make at once the greatest efforts to obtain capital only under the fear that circumstances might force a crisis upon you.

"I have touched merely upon generalities to-day; after further correspondence I will write you more in detail. I will also come on and see you if you deem it advisable. The other experiment keeps me here at present; I think that next week I shall test it. I am greatly rejoiced to hear that you are getting on well with the translation.

"A. BRISBANE."

I present in contrast, the draft of a letter by Mr. Ripley, showing the difference in the ideas of the two men. Among the social organizations at this date, was the Community founded by Mr. John A. Collins, at Skaneateles, New York, to whose friend the letter was addressed. This movement was based on " community of property " which was denounced by the school of Fourier as a fallacy. I commend the letter to careful perusal. It is beautiful in language ; its spirit is transcendent.

" BROOK FARM, MASS.

" MY DEAR SIR : — I thank you for sending me the circular, calling a convention at Skaneateles for the promotion of the community movement.

" I had just enjoyed a short visit from Mr. Collins, who explained to me very fully the purposes of the enterprise, and described the advantages of the situation which had been selected as the scene of the initiatory experiment. I hardly need to say that the movers in this noble effort have my warmest sympathy, and that if circumstances permitted, I could not deprive myself of the privilege of being present at their deliberations. I am, however, just now so involved in cares and labors that I could not be absent for so long a time without neglect of duty.

" Although my present strong convictions are in favor of coöperative Association rather than of communities of property, I look with an indescribable interest on every attempt to redeem society from its corruptions, and establish the intercourse of men on a basis of love instead of competition. The evils arising from trade and money, it appears to me, grow out of the defects of our social organization, not an intrinsic vice in themselves ; and the abolition of private property, I fear, would so far destroy the independence of the individual, as to interfere with the great object of all social reform, namely, the development of humanity, the substitution of a race of free, noble, holy men and women, instead of the dwarfish and mutilated specimens which now cover the earth.

"The great problem is to guarantee individualism against the masses, on the one hand, and the masses against the individual, on the other. In society as now organized, the many are slaves to a few favored individuals in a community. I should dread the bondage of individuals to the power of the mass, while Association, by identifying the interests of the many and the few — the less gifted and the highly gifted — secures the sacred personality of all, gives to each individual the largest liberty of the children of God.

"Such are my present views, subject to any modification which farther light may produce. Still I consider the great question of the means of human regeneration still open, indeed, hardly touched as yet, and Heaven forbid that I should not at least give you my best wishes for the success of your important enterprise.

"In our own little Association we practically adopt many community elements. We are eclectics and learners, but day by day increases our faith and joy in the principle of combined industry and of bearing each other's burdens, instead of seeking every man his own.

"It will give me great pleasure to hear from you whenever you have anything to communicate interesting to the general movement. I feel that all who are seeking the emancipation of man are brothers, though differing in the measures which they may adopt for that purpose; and from our different points of view it is not, perhaps, presumptuous to hope that we may aid each other, by faithfully reporting the aspects of earth and sky as they pass before our field of vision.

"One danger, of which no doubt you are aware, proceeds from the growing interest in the subject, and that is the crowds of converts who desire to help themselves rather than to help the movement. It is as true now as it was of old, that he who follows this new Messiah must deny himself and take up his cross daily, or he cannot enter the promised kingdom. The path of transition is always covered with thorns and marked with the bleeding feet of the faithful. This truth must not be covered up in describing the paradise for which we hope. We must drink the waters of Marah in the desert, that others may feed on the grapes of Eshcol. We must depend on the power of self-sacrifice in man, not on appeals to his selfish nature, for the success of our efforts. We should hardly be willing to accept of men or money for this enterprise, unless called forth by earnest conviction that they are summoned by a divine voice. I wish to hear less said to capitalists about a profitable investment of their funds, as if the holy cause of humanity were to be speeded onward by the same force which conducts railroads and ships of war. Rather preach to the rich, ' Sell all that you have and give to the poor and you shall have treasure in heaven.'

" GEORGE RIPLEY."

Although the working condition of the Association was never better than now; although its organization was complete as it could well be under its disadvantages, it was with sorrow that the Direction heard that one of the earliest members with his family — our head farmer — had decided to leave the Brook Farm life. It was true that he could be spared, that his three children were unproductive and that there was talent enough on the farm to run the Farming Series well ; but it seemed a break in the established order, showing, perhaps, that things were not as successful as they appeared to be, and that maybe the event was a raindrop predicting a storm.

I think no one blamed him, but all were sorry to part

with one whom they loved so well. That his interest in the cause and the Association had not waned is apparent from the following letter, April 3, 1845 : —

"DEAR SIR : — In withdrawing from the Association I cannot believe it necessary for me to say to you that I do not cease to feel an interest, a very deep interest, in the success of the cause in which I have in my humble way labored with you for the last few years. The final success of this attempt to live out the great and holy idea of association for brotherly coöperation, will be to me a greater cause for joy than any merely personal benefit to myself could be.

"I wished, but could not do it, to say to you and others how much I love and esteem you, and how painful it is for me to leave those to whom I am so much indebted for personal kindnesses. You know me well enough to believe that I feel, more deeply than I can express, pained by this separation. God bless you. God bless and prosper the Association individually and collectively.

"Yours truly,

"MINOT PRATT."

It was about this time that a "party" was given by the "Great Apostle," as Mr. Brisbane was called by us. I made a memorandum of it at the time, which aids my memory in presenting it.

The day had been pleasant; it was one of the last in March. The farm work had progressed as usual. Old Kate was at the plough and Cyclops at the wagon. Who was Cyclops? She was a large, raw-boned, gray-white mare, whose feeding did not show well; the more oats and meal and hay she had, the more ribs we counted in her sides — you have seen such an animal! But she was wonderful, because she stepped longer than any other of the horses; worked harder without showing fatigue, and made the nine miles to Boston in a practical if not a graceful way.

She had a fault, and horsemen had to admit it (you know they seldom admit a fault but what is very visible). This was a visible fault, and yet at the same time it was a want of visibility. She had but one eye. And so Glover it was, I am quite sure, named her Cyclops.

By the by, she had one other fault that I had almost forgotten, and that was of elevating her heels against the dashers of wagons, when she had an ugly fit, which took place semi-occasionally, and the peculiarity of it was that she was not particular as to time or place where she made her exhibitions. It might be in Dock Square or State Street, or it might be on the farm, just as all were starting out. It was not over pleasant to be near her when she flung those long hind legs some six feet in air, and the dash-board was flying in pieces.

The "General," with some others, was about to take a ride one day, when she put a hind foot over the dasher, which caused him to dismount precipitately. "For," he said he, when speaking of it, "I thought if she was *g-going* to *g-get* in, it was time for *me* to get out!"

The horn, as usual, rang out its cheerful tones for meals. There were but few notes of preparation shown outside the rooms, for the event of the evening. Up in the greenhouse the gardener and myself were busy picking out choice flowering plants, and clipping off a stray dead leaf or twig, and scouring the pots until they

shone; and as the other teams were busy, I harnessed
my " Prince " to his cart and carried them to the Hive,
where we made the best display of them we could in
the dining room.

We had some mottoes on the walls, as " The Series
distribute the Harmonics of the Universe," " Attractive
Industry," " Universal Unity," etc.

At half past eight o'clock everything was in order.
Side tables were spread with a simple repast, and
around the room were flowering plants, azaleas,
camellias, heaths, geraniums, etc. When the company
had assembled, the choir sang some glees, after which
Mr. Brisbane made a speech, and gave as a sentiment,
" Unity of the Passions." Let me here explain a little
of what is meant by this sentiment.

The twelve passions are what are generally called
" the human feelings or sentiments." They are divided
into the intellectual ones, the social ones and the sensitive ones or those pertaining to the five senses.

There are three intellectual ones, viz., Analysis, Syn-
thesis and the Composite. These exhaust the powers of
the intellect; or, in other words, the mind separates
things, puts things together and compounds things, and
that is all that it can do in its primary intellectual
capacity.

There are four social " passions," viz., Friendship,
Love, Familism (i. e., the family sentiment) and Ambition ; and all our social life is based on one or more of
these four sentiments.

Then there are five sensitive passions, which are aids
and attendants of the body — " sight, smelling, hearing,
touch and taste."

" The five sensitive passions tend to material riches, refinement and harmonies. The four affective passions govern social relations and those of individuals. Friendship tends to social equality and to the levelling of ranks. Love regulates the relations of the sexes, Paternity those of ages and generations; Ambition produces hierarchy of ranks and distinctions among individuals; it establishes in society gradations of all kinds based upon skill, merit, talent, etc.; it is opposite in its effects from friendship." — "Social Destiny of Man," page 453.

The four social passions correspond to the four primary prismatic colors of the Newtonian system, to the common chord in music and to various other natural things. The three intellectual passions correspond to the other three notes of the musical scale and to three other prismatic colors; and the five sensitive passions correspond to the five semi-tones, and also to five intermediate colors of the prism. Now this at first sight looks very much like a scheme or a notion, but the founder of this doctrine lays his claim to a higher judgment. He says practically, " These are facts founded in nature by God himself." Let me give you his own words, often reiterated: " I give no theory of my own, I *deduce*. If I have deduced erroneously let others establish the true deduction." Can words be more simple or more modest?

These " passions," or " faculties," if you like the last word better, as taught in the general schools of theology, are all at war with one another, but as taught by the school of Fourier will all work harmoniously together when right material conditions exist. Or in other words, there is no inherent discord among these twelve sister faculties residing in the nature of man. It is the duty of man on this earth, and his destiny also, to bring them into harmonious relations, first by organizing industry, and bringing man into right relation with nature and his fellows, so that they can commence their natural action : and this is what is meant by the " Unity of the Passions," and is the first step towards universal happiness. Let me give a quotation from the same author:—

" The impulses (passions) have a right and a wrong development. The right development produces harmony, good, justice, unity. The wrong development produces selfishness, injustice, duplicity."

I have no memorandum of what was said by the speaker, but I remember he was enthusiastic beyond bounds, and that he went in fancy from this earth up into the starry vault of spheres that he fancied were peopled by living beings — Jupiter and Saturn being in harmony — and in his enthusiasm cried out, " I *love* those great worlds up there!" looking upwards with outstretched arms and uplifted hands ; and it was telling, for he was eloquent as well as enthusiastic.

After this warm gush of rapture came quiet Dwight in one of those sweet, calm, choice, dignified, exact speeches for which he was noted, and gave as a sentiment, " The marriage of love and wisdom," the idea being that present society, however much it may be filled with love — love for the poor, the needy, the slave and the outcast — can never avail much towards universal happiness until it marries itself to wisdom : wisdom to do justice, to adapt means to ends, to exchange charity, which is a curse to him that gives and him that takes, for even-handed justice, divine law and social order ; so that pauperism and its kindred vices may be done away with forever, and in its place the reign of peace and harmony prevail.

Mr. Dwight was an admirer of Swedenborg's poetic fancies. He thought many of them more than fancies. He believed that he gained through unknown sources some glimpses of a higher life; and some of his doctrines, as that of "correspondences" bore so strong a resemblance to Fourier's "universal analogy" that it was quite striking; but his claims to special theological inspiration, he did not admit. I speak of this because some one might accuse him of plagiarism, the phrase of Mr. Dwight's sentiment being similar to Swedenborg's words. Pardon this digression, and we will return to our party.

Mr. Ripley followed in his free and graceful style, and brought things slowly down to our own door with pleasant word and wit (Ripley was a punster with the rest; one of our wags one day called him a Pumpkin — Pun-King — a paraphrase on New England pronunciation of the word), and in conclusion gave us a sentiment: "The Hive! May it *be* a hive, full of working bees, who make a little noise, a great deal of honey, and sting not at all."

Mr. Dana, the youngest of the four, then followed with a glowing speech, in earnest, clear and chosen words. Not as fluent as either of the other speakers, he yet commanded full attention, and we all knew he meant what he said; there was no doubt about it — the frank manner, the natural gesture, the glowing face, proved it. He gave as a sentiment, "Ambition, the greatest of the four social passions!" He admired it!

It was that which carried life onward and made youth able and strong; the ambition for higher things, for higher life and higher opportunities. It was that which brought this little band together — an ambition to better social life; and it was this passion that would lead them onwards through discords into a higher unity and harmony. But in the present social order a misplaced ambition led men to do a thousand wrongs; it produced war, misery and discord, but when placed on the side of humanity it tended upwards towards God and the heavenly accords. True ambition was the unsatisfied thing that never ends except in something higher, nobler, grander.

Here let me explain again. The four social passions before named correspond to the common chord in music, but ambition corresponds to the seventh note on which no music ever ends. It is always incomplete without the eighth note, the first of the octave above; it runs into it; it is restless, it must never be left alone, but always has an object — the higher unity. Such is true ambition, and such are its results in the natural order.

Applause followed Mr. Dana's speech, and after his remarks the sentiment of the evening turned towards home life. The orators spoke of the earnest endeavors of the men and women by whom they were surrounded; of their constant daily labor to produce harmony and higher social development, and more particularly of their years of personal toil and devotion, and of their own earnest affection for one another, until tears started in some eyes.

Mr. Ripley spoke of the devotion of the persons about

to leave the Association to found "a little colony of their own," for whom he had the highest personal esteem, cemented by years of friendship, counsel and labor together; his sorrow for their departure; his good wishes for them, and his hopes for their present and future welfare, and closed with a sentiment, "The late chief of the Farming Series, Minot Pratt and his family — they can not remain long in *Concord* without returning to *harmony*" (Concord, Massachusetts, was where our farmer was going), for which the modest gentleman returned thanks for himself and wife in a few kind and earnest words.

One after another joined in pleasant remarks, and the simple feast, the music and the conversation were kept up. The ever-present fun and frolic abounded in some corners, but the joke of the evening was perhaps that of the Parson — him of the sharp face and nose, who read so late by the light of the lamp in "Attica" — who commenced his remarks by saying that he desired to offer a sentiment, and must be pardoned if it was of a personal nature. Now the reason why this gentleman got the title of "the Parson" was not from his reading, his gravity or want of gravity, but from the fact of his having been educated for the ministry, which in those days required a great deal more preaching damnation to sinners than now. His unwillingness to do so was the means of his leaving the pulpit, and this gave the pith of the toast or sentiment offered.

Parson Capen's speech was sharp. He did not spill over on every occasion. He had no little spurts of wit like a spatter of water on a hot stove, but when he let out his joke it went off like a percussion cap. The attention of the company being secured, he alluded to his present position as a change, he believed, for the better — from his former relation to society when he was preaching against, to the present time when he was working for, humanity; and gave as a toast, " Ephraim Capen — *thrust into* the pulpit to *damn* mankind, *thrust out* of the pulpit to *bless* mankind."

Laughter followed this sharp witticism, and the hours passed quickly on until it was near midnight, when it was suggested that " Old Hundred " be sung, and all joined in the anthem. As the last note died away, the stroke of the clock announced the hour of twelve, and all departed to their houses to sleep, and dream of the pleasant time they had enjoyed.

CHAPTER IX.

SOCIAL AND PARLOR LIFE.

WE now pass over some months of the life with few words. I have tried to portray it on the farm as it appeared to me, and leave you to think that it continues on and on, ever in the same general current, through the long, clear days and moonlight nights of summer, and the cooler days and misty evenings of the later season, to the time when the warning comes to the farmer to gather in the ripened products of his labor.

I pass over the later autumn — when the fields are cleared of all but the remains of vegetation, and we hear no more the songs of the crickets and the multitudinous insect life that fills the air of the August and September nights, as the full moon looks down on the fields and meadow rich in foliage — to the time when the thought of the farmer is for wood for the winter, for the preservation of the farming implements, for making all things "taut and trig" about the barn and houses to secure their warmth for the coming cold weather and snow; past the day of the New England Thanksgiving, along to Christmas time, saying only in passing that the leaders were much engaged in lecturing, as well as with other duties.

One evening in autumn a party from the farm, myself the youngest of them, started for Boston to hear one of a course of lectures. Mr. Ripley was the chairman, and the ever bounteous joyousness of his nature sparkled out in wit and mirth. These meetings were free, and discussion was invited, but there was present an excitable woman who had a habit of rising at any moment, no matter who was speaking, to make odd remarks and inquiries. She was considered a great nuisance, especially at the meetings of the antislavery societies, where she was often found, and I more than once saw her "suppressed" by police officers. On this occasion, whilst Mr. Brisbane was speaking, she arose to propound questions.

Immediate excitement was visible in the audience, and cries of " Put her out,'" arose. Mr. Ripley was on his feet in an instant. He declared the meeting to be a free one, and that it was ever the faith and duty of those engaged in this liberal movement to give the largest liberty to all inquirers; he appealed to all to be quiet and hear what the lady had to say, for she would, as well as all others, give them credit for having paid respectful attention to whoever wished to make inquiries, and whenever Miss F. had spoken, she could not but acknowledge that they had always and at all times listened to her with the utmost — and he hesitated as if seeking carefully for the exact word, which he uttered slowly and with the utmost gravity — *patience.* At this queer termination the audience laughed loudly, and gave her a hearing, and shortly, pleased at her conquest, she sat down, and disturbed no future meeting of the Associationists.

Again during the discussion Mr. Ripley announced that a contribution would be taken to defray expenses, " but as the speaking was to be continued during the time the box was passing round," the audience was requested to "*put in as many bills as possible so as not to disturb the speaker by the rattling of small change.*"

After the meeting closed, the wagon in which we rode to town was deserted by some half dozen of its male passengers who, with the speed of Indian runners, started for the farm on foot. Being slight of build and not over strong, I would have been left behind, had it not been for the friendship of the Admiral, who awaited my movements, but we still sped on with rapidity, overtaking some, and neared the farm in time to hear the bark of our dog Carlo announce the arrival of the team only a few minutes before us.

The autumn and early winter were very mild. The ground was not frozen on the twenty-fourth day of December, and the gardener had many crocus bulbs unplanted, owing to too much labor in and around the new greenhouse and garden, and being desirous of saving them, commenced to plant them on the Hive terraces in "her majesty's garden." There were hundreds of them. In the morning we prepared our beds and dug our holes for planting. The sky was lowery, and it was afternoon when we commenced to plant.

Shortly the raindrops began to fall, but we continued our work. It rained harder and harder. I had on only ordinary woollen clothing, cotton shirt, no undershirt, and wore over it only an old green baize jacket. Wet to the skin; the rain ran off of me in streams. With my wet hands I assorted and handed the bulbs, four or five at a time, to the gardener, and as they touched the ground or his fingers, the earth stuck to them and mixed mud and plants together. The rain began to grow colder and colder, and our work was not done, but as the shades of night began to fall we finished it. Chilled and cold we wended our way towards the greenhouse, where I changed wet clothes for dry ones. The night came on cold ; the wind howled ; the rain turned into snow and on Christmas morning the ground was covered with a rough, hard conglomerate of snow and ice.

But the next day neither chill nor cold resulted from the long exposure. Was it because our lives were more in harmony with nature than is usual?

At the Eyry all through the winter, in its cosy little parlor, reigned our queens and kings of art and music. I was partial to the room and the company, yet neither felt nor understood the deep music. It is true that I sang songs of my own and made my own harmonies as I wandered over the fields and meadows. The mystic measure of the sunny waltz haunted me happily at times, and my heart kept time to its rhythm even as my feet had kept time in the merry dance; but it seemed to me as though there was a lack of sense in the jingle, and a depth of feeling untouched in me that the music of the parlor had not or could not reach — I did not appreciate it.

It was a pleasure for Mr. Dwight to secure a quartette of singers from the city. I could mention names, but I forbear, yet there are two faces so indelibly linked with those most happy hours, that I must, in order to be true to this sketch of Brook Farm life, twine them into my narrative.

The first face was serene, charming and dignified. Its cheeks were round and gracefully full, and colored with delicious pink, and a dimple rounded in them when the kindly face smiled. Above them reigned a queenly forehead, and over the brown eyes a fine brow. The nose was straight, the upper lip short, and the features were regular. The owner of this face was tall and graceful, and her dark, glossy hair was combed plainly back. She was ever neatly dressed, and her favorite decoration was a wreath of the wild partridge vine, rich with its red berries, which added to her graceful presence. It was her sweet voice, soft and low, that chimed in, in our quartette. She came and went and seemed one of us, as in spirit she was, though in fact only a friendly visitor.

The other face was different and not as pretty, yet it grew upon you more and more.

There was no blue like those eyes of blue, if they were delicately small, and if there was a little drooping expression as though the sun above was a trifle too powerful for them. This was no detriment, however; it lent them a mildness, a soft haze, like that we so much admire in a landscape, and made them more in keeping with the mild, tranquil countenance.

The eyebrows were softly penciled — not bold, not prominent — and were not much arched, and the nose, that was Grecian, was full between the eyes. The lips were of good size as well as the mouth, and the upper lip long enough to indicate strength of character. The chin was finely drawn, and the throat rather large and full. About the mouth, even in repose, seemed to rest the faint semblance of a smile, as though it could not leave its pleasant dwelling place; as though it was akin to the features themselves, as the color of the eyes or hair. The forehead was pure, womanly; intellectual enough, full enough, high enough, but toned down to the sweet, womanly features. It was a fine face; a vigorous, womanly one, unmarked with a single manly symptom, but independent, pure and serene.

And what could set off this face better than that soft, light, blonde hair, that wound into full, large ringlets, looped up in Grecian style? In vain it is for me to describe the tints of it. It seemed as though the Divine Artist had taken the beautiful colors from his palette and mixed them for this especial head. There was a touch of sunshine in it also, and it seems but yesterday that I saw the old gardener take a stray one from the sleeve of his baize jacket, where by chance it had strayed and caught — for the fair owner liked to visit the greenhouse — and hold it admiringly and enthusiastically up in the morning sunlight, and I remember the golden shimmer it had in it, for he called my attention to it. A French writer's words seem to meet its description better than my own: "Non pas rouges — Mais blonde avec des reflets dorés, on delicatement se jouàit la lumière du soleil."

In distinction to the lady named before, the present one was short, of fairly full figure, and not above the average grace. You might even say that the large head was carried a little too far forward for elegance. In distinction also to the calm, quiet manner of the other, she was vivacious, quick and spritely; was fond of conversation, but no matter how trivial the subject of discourse, it grew into earnestness in her mind unless she was wholly playful. But her chief distinction was her love and talent for music, and in the capacity of beautiful singer she was first introduced to us.

I cannot tell how this pure soul first took to the sublime idea of society founded on justice to all, the Christianity of the idea, and the truths of industry, or how the idea came to her that in this one way and only in this one way could the kingdom of God prayed for for eighteen centuries, come to us on earth; but I think it was born in her as jewels are born in the earth, and sparkle when they come to the sun. But this I know, that when they took possession of her she could not withstand their power, more than Saint Paul could the heavenly influences that brought his Jewish heart to love all, and live and die for all the races of God's humanity. Friends, relatives, companions, were opposed to her visits among the Brook Farmers. It was intimated to her that there were suspicious persons residing there. She bravely pinned her informers to facts; she made searching inquiries, and, convincing herself, boldly stood by the idea and the Brook Farmers as living symbols of a better and more Christian life, and triumphed over all in her sublime truthfulness and dignity.

How willing and ready she was to acknowledge her trivial failures! How ready to do for all such kindness as came in her sphere to do, and how quick she was to comprehend great truths. Untied from the dead letter that killeth, she was overflowing with its pure spirit that gave its abundant life, rich, full and charming, to all around her.

One of the young poets of the farm many years ago paid this graceful tribute to her charms: —

OF MARY BULLARD.

Dearly love I to be near her —
Though thought of her is not dearer
    Than friendship may say.
Yet around will I hover;
Bringing joy like a lover,
    To brighten her day.

Ever am I lingering near her —
Her whole soul seems to me clearer
    Than others that are.
And her love-lighted blue eye,
When an aching heart is nigh,
    Beams forth like a star.

It's good for me to be near her —
Should she e'er sorrow, to cheer her
    Out of her sad moods ;
Her dark path to make lighter,
And behold it grow brighter
    Like sunlight through woods.

Still stay I lovingly near her,
Enraptured — sometimes I fear her
    Soul is on its wings —
And ask will it yet return? —
Seems it so pure, so lost and gone,
    Whenever she sings.

Lingering and waiting near her —
The words that she speaks are dearer
    Than birds' songs in May.
With sweet thoughts will I surround her,
As on the day I first found her,
    Forever — for aye.

I have been particular in my description of this lady and friend, because they became the encouragers of the later movement in Boston, where those who remained true to the Brook Farm ideas formed themselves into a society of zealots to propagate the faith, she giving her splendid talents and her warm enthusiasm freely to the movement, and because they were as truly united with us as if enrolled as members on the farm.

It was in the latter part of the month of January that we had the fulfilment of a promise of a long visit from the fair singer. The winter had grown cold and stormy ; the white snow covered the fields, and at times we gleefully slid down the hills over its frozen crust on sleds and improvised vehicles. And there were days of transcendent beauty: I remember especially, a solitary visit to the pine woods after a deep snow storm, and the lifelong impression of it remains.

The evergreens were bowed heavily with the weight of the snow, and across the wood path birches and various trees bent as if in prayer, obstructing the way. The clear air, which was not very cold — for it was one of those subdued days of winter, when the glare of the sun was obstructed by a cloudy mantle — the intense quiet, the strong contrasts of the dark trunks of trees with the heavy evergreens, and the immaculate purity of whiteness laid on by the greatest and sublimest painter were so marked and so lovely that I seemed to be drinking the nectar of the god of beauty, and was soul-subdued.

Up to the Eyry in the evening, I went with others to hear the singing, when Mary, " the nightingale,"— as we sometimes called her — came. I went often and stayed long. Some were at the Hive, reading; some were, perhaps, engaged in Shakespeare; some in their rooms with their families; some at the Cottage practising the piano, and all " following their attractions," to use our common phrase, in their own little sphere — whether it was reading the papers and journals of the day in the improvised reading-room at the Hive, or commenting on the last articles in the *Harbinger*, or doing a little work out of hours for amusement or profit, or attending one of the interminable number of meetings for consultation and arrangement held almost nightly.

There the quartette sang the " Kyrie," and " Gloria in Excelsis " from the masses of Mozart and Haydn. An edition had just been published and forwarded from London, and by degrees they became familiar to us as household words. Did it not seem strange, you may ask, that these radical thinkers and " come-outers " from ordinary forms of society, should turn with pleasure to the emanations of a profoundly conservative church ? I answer that, having freed their minds from sectarian prejudices, they recognized beauty and genius wherever found, and did not care what church or creed they had served, so that they found the gift of beauty from the infinite Father to man in them. With one glorious soprano voice and boundless talent, how much of joy was added to the circle! How we revelled in the choice creations of the masters of harmony, and how, slowly but surely, the missing link that was wanting in my mind to realize that music could cover the void that separated sound from feeling, came to its place — I am tempted to tell.

The sweet songtress was asked to sing. Did she make excuses? Of course she would do so to follow traditional usage. She must have a slight cold, she must think she won't, must be coaxed, and then — why, do it with a grace. But here was a woman so touched with the divine fire of genius and truth, that no excuse came from her lips. She was always ready if you desired it. In her I first learned that music was not a put-on art, an accomplishment, but the outpouring of soul.

One evening when our little party was being filled with music, and the quartette had bravely sung Rossini's "Prayer in Egypt," with the grand vigor and expression that the soprano put into it, she exclaimed with feeling, "How beautiful that is!" From that moment I understood what music meant. She had translated it for me. But instead of inspiring me with joy, it made me sad. It aroused that terrible feeling, "consciousness of self." It waked me to new ideas of duty and destiny, to wondrous thoughts and aspirations; and they would not down at my bidding. Over and over again I tried to banish them, but the inward and spiritual ear was open, and the sad strains of Schubert's

" Elegy of Tears," and " The Wanderer," and the " Ave Maria," seemed my sorrow, my wanderings and my prayers. Sadness was not my nature; I was as cheerful as the bird that sings, save a mighty something which clung to me and overshadowed me like the enormous wings of a terrible genius.

One day it began again to snow; a million feathers from the frost king's fleece were flying in the air. It snowed all day, and in the evening it snowed and whirled and blew around the Eyry, with its little party of choice spirits in its cosy parlor making merry and singing. Perhaps it was the " Wood Robin," or the " Skylark," or one of Colcott's glees, or one of Mendelsshon's two-part songs, or Schubert's " Serenade," or Beethoven's " Adelaide "; or maybe an interlude of piano, one of Mozart's Sonatas, or " Der Freyschutz," and then a Kyrie, Dona Nobis, Gloria, or Agnus Dei, one or all, until it was time to retire. And still it snowed and snowed.

From the Eyry parlor I would go to my quarters in the greenhouse, and there the old man would be anxious for the flowers, that the fire be neither too hot nor too cold, and with a long story to tell me of manners and customs of his youth in Denmark — some of them quaint and strange enough — would slowly finish out the evening, and it was often midnight before we retired.

All the next day it snowed, and piled up its pure whiteness over every projecting thing, whirling and tossing its feathers about, unlike anything else in nature, and at night it snowed still. It snowed steadily for three days and nights, but when the fourth morning broke, it was on one of the clearest and most beautiful days ever known, and to my surprise I awoke full of renewed cheerfulness and physically like my former self. The youthful storm of my life was over.

But the "Ego" had changed. I was living in a poetic atmosphere and imbibing its qualities and its stimulants. Born with artistic tastes, I had imagined an artistic future; but as the procession of realistic lives passed before me, I seemed to see the inward side of the real and the ideal. An artistic life!—a triumph after long years of labor, awarded by the hand-clapping of a few admirers, most of whom had no appreciation of the work, and no sympathy with its higher motives. Would it not be cold? Would it not slowly freeze my heart to the warm love of human beings, with every one of whom I had now something in common? A real life, taking part in active work, in plain, daily toil; touching the great, full, seething heart of humanity on its warm side; working for them; working with them; being one with many — one with her. Which was best? Which was the supremest ideal? I think the latter.

There were other visitors who came, attracted by the little group of singers. There was a young lady, Miss Graubtner from Boston, who touched the piano with the grace of a master. Her German name indicated the stock from whence she sprung, and the training she received from her musical father. There were tenors and basses who were attracted also, but they came and went; the sweetest songstress remained, and the cold days of winter were beginning to give way to the warm March sun when the visit was completed, and we reluctantly gave her back to "civilization."

Among the pleasant occasional visitors was a gentleman who joined in the circle with his flute, who had the reputation, well deserved, of having written some

fine verses — some of them are in the *Harbinger* — and
who was in very friendly sympathy with our music man,
as an old and, I think, college acquaintance. His ac-
complishments were varied. He had graced a pulpit,
and afterwards made his mark with his pen, pallet and
brush: He had a very pleasant gift of imitation, and,
with his modest and, gentlemanly bearing, made quite
an impression on me.

I fancy I see him now, with his tall, graceful, upright
figure, his wealth of dark, curling hair, and his young
manhood, with his sober, dignified face and large forehead, just retiring from our crowded Eyry parlor to the
hall, where under cover, he can more readily introduce
his menagerie — menagerie or barnyard you certainly
would think it was; for from behind the door comes the
imitation of the cow with its young calf; a sow and its
pigs are squealing; the lambs and sheep are bleating;
the rooster begins to crow, and near by the house dog is
heard; soon all is still except his persistent, hoarse bark;
then from a distance we hear the bark of another dog
awakened by the first; soon another, nearer still, wakes
up and tunes his note; presently we hear all the dogs
of the village who are now awake. Then the sound of
the starting up of the locomotive drowns all other
noises, and when it has passed away we hear nothing
but far in the dim distance some one solitary dog still
barking. The frogs begin to peep, and the turtles whis-
tle, and the doves coo, until you are carried away from
the circle, its lights and its pleasant, laughing faces into
the bosom of nature. It is needless to say that all these
sounds came from the throat of Christopher P. Cranch,
the poet-artist, and were clever imitations which were
hugely appreciated by the young folks.

CHAPTER X.

A LADY said to me not long since, knowing it from experience, " There was a great deal of fun at Brook Farm." This was true, and I deem it worthy of particular mention, as I can scarce believe that there ever was in New England a body of men and women who for so long a time, maintained such friendly and intimate relations, and yet kept up such an interminable fire of small fun and joke, puns and *bon-mots*, inoffensively shooting them off right and left at all times and places. Being of an evanescent nature they have mostly vanished from my mind, but the spirit of them remains.

There were " All-Fool's " day tricks played by the young people on such smart, independent geniuses as Irish John; the sending of a letter to him from a supposable lady friend, with a post-mark painted on it by one of the young ladies; putting parsnip ends into his study lamp for wicks, etc. But these are not to be classed with the fun that was present of the genuine sort. There were a few live wits who were Tom Hoods on a small scale, seeing everything with a double meaning, and " double-enders " (*double entendres*) were for breakfast, dinner and supper every day in the week.

Some little children were chasing one another one very warm day. " Why," queried one, " are those children like native Africans?" "Because they belong to the *'hot'* *and* *'tot'* race!"

"Is Mr. —— much of a carpenter?" "Not a *bit* of one, that's *plain*," was the reply.

"What sort of a man is that long-haired fellow opposite?" said one. "He is good in the *main*," replied the other.

"These Grahamites will never make their ends *meet*," said one. "You may *stake* your reputation on that," said the other.

"Mrs. —— is a regular steamboat," said A. "Yes, I know it; she goes by steam — *self* *'steam*," said B. — which was smart, but cutting!

If, for instance, Miss Kettell was to be married, one would ask if she was a "*tin*" kettle, and another would "*go bail*" she was, and the next would say that "the larger the kettle the more tin it would have." "And the more *iron in* (*y*), too!" some one would ejaculate. Then another would say that "after she was married there would be none of the *Kettle* left," and the next wit would say, "And none of the *'tin'* either," and so the badinage would pass about.

It made no difference what the subject was, it was always suggestive. If it was a dog, they would ask. "What kind of a *bark* he had on him?" If it was a pump, "Is it *well* with it?" If it was a shepherd, they would like to inquire "if he was not a *baa*-keeper?" and the first would reply that he would have to "ruminate" on it before he made his answer; and the second would hope his reply would be "*spirited*; if not he had better be *punched* up."

"Have you seen my umbrella?" asked one. "What

sort of an umbrella was it?" was the inquiry. "It had a hooked end," said number one. "I have not seen it," was the reply, "but *I* had a nice one once, and the end was *exactly* like yours; it was *hooked!*"

Passing a rosy-cheeked, unkempt boy, Miss —— remarked to her friend, "Isn't he a little honey?" "Yes," she replied, struck by his traits, "honey without a *comb!*"

"Do you not think Miss B. is beautiful? She bows to perfection." "Yes; but she hasn't bowed to me. Has she to *you?*"

"Who are those girls out in the boat with the old man?" (The name of the boat was "the Dart.") "Why, his *darters*, of course," was the reply.

And how could any one do differently when the great Archon himself was first and foremost in the fray, poking fun at all? "Don't do that," he said one day to me when I put something unusual in the swine's mess, "the hogs will all *die* after it!" with a most serious look on his pleasant face. In my seat at the table, looking down the hall to where the Archon was, I saw him full of frolic, and oftentimes wondered what he could joke so much about.

There was one occasion when he quoted Watts to an offending member in a comical way, which brought him to terms. It was at the Eyry. There was a meeting of the Industrial Council. It was necessary to have a quorum to pass certain important votes, and one of the members, being a trifle weary of business, had stepped out to converse with a friend in the vestibule. After a while, hearing some one coming, he slipped behind the vestibule door. It was the "Archon," who came for

the member to make a quorum. Presently, discovering
his retreat, he hailed him — as he remembered it —
thus : —

> "' And are you there, you sinner d—d,
>   And do you fare so well!
> Were it not for redeeming grace
>   You'd long since been in hell.' "

The unworthy member succumbed and returned to the
meeting, wondering whether the verse was an impromptu
or whether it was part of one of the inspiring Sunday
hymns our grandfathers sang in their cheerless, un-
warmed meeting-houses. In a version of Watts' Hymns
this verse is found : —

> " And are we wretches still alive,
>   And do we yet rebel ?
> 'Tis boundless, 'tis amazing love
>   That bears us up from hell."

It might have been the one Mr. Ripley quoted.

I have heard it said that a prominent literary man
"could not understand the condition of mind it required to make a pun." It would be out of place here
to try to explain that condition to him or to any one
else. It is certainly not an unhappy frame of mind,
and I am not aware that it indicates any depraved condition. I don't know of any very bad men who make
puns, but I have known of many good men who make
bad puns. It is not an avaricious state of the mind, for
who ever heard of "puns for sale or manufactured to
order," or of a man getting rich in the wholesale or
retail pun trade !

In fact, a pun is like an egg — the moment you crack
it the meat is out. Some men carry things to extremes;

I wouldn't myself like to be a punster *in toto*, but only now and then to have a finger in one. But really, the condition of mind seems to be the same as that of some of our criminals who profess they committed the deed because they "couldn't help it," or the boy who was asked angrily "why he whistled?" "He didn't," he replied, "it whistled itself." I imagine our literary friend thinks that a punster draws the steel blade of his intellect, discovers some close-mouthed, hard-fisted sort of a word or sentence doubled up like an oyster and deliberately splits it apart, one shell on one side, one on the other and the soft thing drops out between. I could only despise the sort of brain that would do such a deed.

A pun is a part of the sunshine of words. It gives a sparkle and a glow to language. It is a big pendulum that swings from torrid to frigid zone quicker than a telegram goes. If you hold on to it, you will find yourself in both places in a jiffy, and back again to the spot where you start from without being hurt, and the jog to your intellect, if you happen to have any, is only of an agreeable nature.

But it was not alone in puns and conundrums that the social life of Brook Farm was rich. It was rich in cheerful buzz. The bumble-bees had no more melodious hum than the Brook Farmers. They had thrown aside the forms that bind outside humanity. They were sailing on a voyage of discovery, seeking a modern El Dorado, but they did not carry with them the lust for gold. They were seeking something which, had they found the realization of, would have carried peace to troubled hearts, contentment and joy to all conditions

and classes. They were builders, not destroyers. They
proposed to begin again the social structure with new
foundations. They were at war with none personally;
as high-toned, large-souled men and women they were
ready with their expressions of hatred and contempt for
the unchristian social life of our generation, but they
were never ranters.

In general little was said on the farm of these matters, except in private discussions; all were too busy
with the active work. We felt that we had put our
ears down to the earth and heard nature's whisperings
of harmony; that we had gone back from the uncertain
and flimsy foundations of present society, and placed
our corner stone on the eternal rock of science and justice; that the social laws God ordained from the beginning had been discovered; there could be no possibility of a mistake, and therefore, we felt that our feet
were on eternal foundations, and our souls growing
more and more in harmony with man and God.

Imagine, indifferent reader of my story, the state of
mind you would be in if you could feel that you were
placed in a position of positive harmony with all your
race; that you carried with you a balm that could heal
every earthly wound; an earthly gospel, even as the
church thinks it has a heavenly gospel — a remedy for
poverty, crime, outrage and over-taxed hand, heart and
brain. And every night as you laid your head on your
pillow, you could say: "I have this day wronged no
man. I have this day worked for my race, I have let
all my little plans go and have worked on the grand
plan that the Eternal Father has intended shall sometime be completed. I feel that I am in harmony with

Him.   Now I know He *is* truly our Father.   With an
unending list of crimes and social wrongs staring me in
the face I doubted, and my heart was cast down.   Now
the light is given me by which I see the way through
the labyrinth !   It is our Father's beautiful garden in
which we are.   I have learned that all is intended for
order and beauty, but as children we cannot yet walk
so as not to stumble.   Natural science has explained a
thousand mysteries.   Social science — understand the
word ; not schemes, plans or guessing, but genuine science, as far from guess or scheme as astronomy or chem-
istry is — will reveal to us as many truths and beauties
as ever any other science has done.   I now see clearly!
Blessed be God for the light!"

And after sound sleep, waking in the rosy morning,
with the fresh air from balmy fields blowing into your
window, penetrated still with the afflatus of last night's
thoughts and reveries, wouldn't you be cheerful?
Wouldn't the unity of all things come to you, and
wouldn't you chirrup like a bird, and buzz like a bee,
and turn imaginary somersaults and dance and sing,
and feel like cutting up "didoes," and talk a little high
strung, and be chipper with the lowliest and level with
the highest?   Wouldn't your heart flow over with ever
so much love and gratitude?   Wouldn't it infuse so
much spirit into your poor, weak life that your words
would sparkle with cheeriness, frolic and wit?   I believe so!   I know so!

Such was to me the secret of the fun, wit and frolic
of the Brook Farmers.   The jokes were, it is true,
largely superficial, but they were inseparable from the
position.   The bottom fact was, *the associates there were*

leading a just life, and could go to their labor,
hard beds and simple fare — down to plain bread and
sometimes mythical butter — with cheerfulness just in
proportion as they were penetrated by these great ideas.
They could make merry with their friends over a cup
of coffee, and sought not the stimulants that college
days and college habits might have allowed.

It was with one of our little social groups of friends,
that Mr. Dwight gave the toast, "Here's to the coffee-
pot! If it is not *spiritual*, it's not *material!*"

There was a gentleman who resided with us who had
promised, on a certain day, to assist a department of
our industry with a loan of cash, and had taken the
light wagon to Boston for the purpose of securing the
funds and bringing them home for use. Somewhere
about nine o'clock in the evening the dwellers at the
" Hive " were disturbed by the approach of a team and
the groans of a person. Going out, they discovered
that it was our team, and our member, who had apparently fallen into the back part of the wagon in a help-
less state. They assisted him out and conveyed him to
to his chamber.

He did not seem to be much hurt; but he stated that
in passing through the little patch of woods on the
" back road," some one came out and knocked him off
his seat and then robbed him. He had lain in the
wagon, unable to rise, and the horse had come home of
his own accord. This is the outline of the story. Parties went out on the road with lanterns, but found no
lost pocket-book. The news of the robbery spread. It
was the common talk the next day. There were suspicious circumstances. It might have been a *ruse* to cover

a personal loss of the money, or to deceive us in the pretended loan.   Who could tell?

A few days later a stranger called at the Hive door. He had an announcement to make; he had seen a mystery — doubtless it had something to do with the robbery.   He had been travelling that morning through Muddy Pond woods, in a thick part of which he had seen — what?   Why, a shirt hanging on the bushes to dry; and had heard voices in the woods near.   He had no doubt marauders were encamped there.   We might find there the man who committed the assault and robbery.   His manner was excited, but he seemed to believe his own story.

It was Sunday.   Work would not prevent us.   We would hunt for the robbers.   We would go to Muddy Pond woods and investigate.   We were not over sanguine, but there was mystery in it, and we were bound to solve it.   I don't think anyone of us thought there was any danger in the affair.   A party of volunteers, consisting of some six or eight, was formed, and the valuable Glover placed himself at our head.   " By the by," said he, as we were about to start, " I'll go and borrow Mr. Shaw's pistols."   What insane idea entered his head at that moment who can tell.   Did he have the thousandth part of an idea that he was going to put a bullet into a man's body?   I don't think he had! Returning soon with the pistols, we started on our way.

It would be worth a thousand dollars now if we had a picture of that party on their tramp.   As I remember it, there were some four of us who were of the " young group " and had not quite attained our legal majority.

"The Admiral" and "the Hero," with "Glover," made the older portion of the party, and as we strayed along with our clear, sun-browned, young faces, our classic locks and natural beards — those who had any — with our unique tunics or blouses, with a certain regular quaintness running through them, were picturesque enough. The idea of arming ourselves, suggested by Glover's pistols, soon developed into the improvising of canes and walking sticks from the wayside.

"Glover" paired off with the curly headed Hero, I with the curly headed Admiral, for Glover loved the Hero, and I admired the Admiral's honest, sincere, pleasant ways and heart. The city life we all had tasted, had given new zest to country life. We straggled by the roadside; we sought wild berries; we observed the varieties of foliage and flower, and conversation never flagged. Glover and Hero were ever in earnest talk. There was with them a never-ending story, and I am reminded of the everlasting confidences of school girls when I recall their being together, excepting only that they did not put their arms around each other's waists.

The Admiral's heart was full of music. He could talk of music, poetry and love, and there was a tender spot in him that I did not venture on, although I knew it was there. He was also a deep admirer of nature. Truly we could sing together, "A life in the woods for me!"

It was three miles to the robbers' rendezvous, but what cared we? We dwelt in the bosom of nature, and three miles was but a pastime. We only wanted an excuse of the most feeble kind to start on a tramp, day or night. All along the way we breathed health and vitality; the air was full of singing birds, and our hearts were crying out, "What is so rare as a day in June?" In fact, our June days lasted longer than they did elsewhere — they ran into September, October and November. It is the harmony of our hearts that makes the force of poetry, and not the mere words; and the June feeling may be present in December.

The entrance to Muddy Pond woods was on high ground, and as we approached it we were a little cautious, for near by was the appointed place to find the haunt of the robbers. Filing along singly, we peered into the underbush. Lo, and behold, I see it! It is a white thing hanging on a bush! Yes! And listen, I hear voices! It is the robbers! Why, no, these are only children's voices! They are picking berries, the dear things. Poor children! Don't you know that you may be robbed and murdered by some of these infernal rascals who beat innocent men, take their money and come out here into this wilderness and wash the blood off their garments and hang them on these berry bushes to dry?

Slowly we approached the white garment. Why, this is only an old white rag that has hung here for months, all mildewed and half rotten. Come, boys, we are sold! What an old goose that fellow was to get us out here for such a thing as this! I am going home! I am hungry! Feelings of disgust and mirth took possession of us. Were these the robbers, and was this the bloody raiment? Ha! ha!

There was no use of going further. The exciting problem was solved, and we turned our feet homeward over the hills, across the fields and by stone walls; shying a stone now and then into some gnarled apple tree, just to knock down a wild apple or two, to try if they contained, as Emerson has said of one of them, "a pint of cider and a barrel of wind"; whipping off the heads of the wild daisies with our canes and switches; pulling sprigs of sweet fern and bayberry; mocking the crows and the cat-birds; finding choice flowers, and trying to fill the aching void within us with blackberries and whortleberries, and reaching the farm after the dinner was over.

All but one corner of the dining-room was deserted, and there a solitary waiter was placing plates for the "Waiting Group," who had not been served with dinner. The "Waiting Group" was one of the most cheerful, lively, witty and jolly groups on the place. In fact it contained some of the most eminent persons in our midst, and at dinner the waiters were of the masculine gender solely.

We found there would be room for us to join their table, and that our company was welcome. Alas! alas! How can I describe the dinner? I do not mean the things we had to eat — fine eating was of little consequence if we could satisfy hunger; but the merry cheer was indescribable. It was the Professor (Dana) who sat at the head of the board. It was the brilliant and witty "Timekeeper" (Cabot) who was at one side, and when our party was added to them — "the Hero" (Butterfield), with his full, hearty and musical laugh; Glover (Drew) with his funny and apt quotations, and with the other four to six clear-headed fellows, not a

dull one among them — the gamut of merriment ran to
its highest notes.

Of course the Professor couldn't help making a few
remarks about the " object of our journey " and inquiries about the " success of the enterprise," and of
course our party didn't answer in parliamentary language, but parried wit with wit, fun with fun, joke
with joke. The story had to be told and embellished.
The shirt, it was nothing but a rag, and the children
were probably ragamuffins, and hot muffins at that!
The robber, where could he be! Probably dead, for
there was *berrying* going on, and the children were continually *turning pail*.

But the borrowing of the pistols was the occasion of
the most absurdities. Was Glover *half cocked* when he
borrowed them? Did he *bear-ill* against any man?
Was he going to *brace* up his courage? He wanted a
little more *stock* in hand, eh? It was the only way he
had of getting a little "*pop*"! And if he had "popped"
the robber would there have been any *pop-bier* (beer)
there? "If I had killed him," he said, "there wouldn't
have been any *sham pain*." Pooh, pooh, you could only
have *hocked* him! "I would have made him *whine* any-
how." You might have made him whine but — " *Wine
butt*," did you say?" (Interrupting). "Glover didn't
intend to make any excitement, for where he took the
pistols he left the *wholestir* behind." "But when he
took them," another said, " he thought he was going to
Needham (need 'um). " Ah, no," said another, " when
he took them he felt sure he was going to *Dedham* "
(dead 'um).

You will appreciate the difficulty I have in making any one realize the snap, the vivacity and the quickness of the repartees. Things that seem frivolous when written down — separate from all their connections, with the personality dropped out of them — with the connection unbroken; with youth, friendship and love to join them together, and all the surroundings in keeping, were lively and bright, and added a glow to the toil that made all the difficult surroundings easier to bear. The affair acted over to-day in sober earnest would hardly provoke a smile, but there most trivial incidents were worked up and the result was an increase of happiness for all.

CHAPTER XI.

THE GREAT CATASTROPHE.

Things were looking up in the Phalanx at this time, for from some sources money was coming to finish a portion of the "Phalanstery." Not that it resembled one, but more out of deference to the idea of one did it receive its name. This would admit of additional membership, as well-to-do and able families were to embark in the enterprise, who could not and would not join it in the crowded state of the houses. The feeling among all was particularly hopeful and cheerful at the prospect, as we knew it was the cramped condition of the finances that had prevented the finishing of the building before this time.

Monday, March 2, 1846, was the day of recommencement of labor on it. On the Saturday previous carpenters had put a stove into the building for the purpose of drying it, as it had gathered dampness all through the severe winter. It was now Tuesday, the day after our sweet singer left us, and as we were all cheerful in our new hopes, it was proposed that we should celebrate our good luck with a social dance at the Hive. I shall call on my imagination to people the hall with those who were Brook Farmers, though not all of them were there in person on that occasion, in order to give the effective picture of such an assembly; the realization of it to the mind, rather than the absolute facts.

The first usually to occupy the hall were the young folks living at the Hive, whose labors ended early. The dance commenced without ceremony when one or two sets were ready. The pupils of the school from the Eyry soon arrived, with the young Spanish boys and the well-dressed maidens. Then the "Pilgrims" came, and the few who resided at the Cottage completed the assembly. It was later when the members of the Direction were seen looking in the room. They had been to some of the interminable meetings.

The cotillion was the ruling dance; the plain waltz and hop waltz came in for their share of favor. The polka was new, and hardly yet danced. What fun, what pleasure was there then in that old dining hall among the blue tunics! There the General loomed above the rest, not in tunic, however, but staggering about with his new acquirement, interested and ungraceful; and the old gardener entertained us with a Danish waltz with his fair-haired, plump, round-shouldered daughter. Now they cling together, then swing apart, holding each other by the fingers' ends; now they whirl and twirl in and out, and then come together and waltz around the hall, as all gaze and wonder at the old man's suppleness. Now the spirit of fun takes possession of all as we see Irish John sitting quietly conversing with "Dora," and he must dance a jig! By some chance there may be a girl of his nationality on the place to dance with him; if not, he goes it alone — forward and back, shuffling backward and around; then dancing up as to his partner, and having gone through all the varied motions in grand heel-and-toe style, sits down again or rushes out of the hall door with his giggling laugh, and a loud round of applause for his reward.

I might go on painting various characters and personages, but could not paint the enthusiasm that was catching — how one after another of the older ones put on again the youthful habit long since laid off. There was no selfishness either, in the dancing, because there was plenty of it, and when one of the older persons essayed the graces of youth, instead of its being looked on as an intrusion, it was applauded. I have seen five men whose education was for the ministry enjoying themselves on that small floor at one time.

It was the old courtliness over again. It was the spirit of chivalry revived under a new form, and it was chivalry with interior pride instead of exterior pride — pride of character instead of pride of birth. Did any of these accomplished men and women deem that they lowered themselves by dancing with those who did manual labor? If they had, they would not have been there to do it. And did the "producers of wealth" think that there were those who danced in their company as a favor to them? If they had, it would have been a favor they would not have accepted. The atmosphere was that of mutual respect and mutual good-will.

There was no dancing of clothes-pins from the pockets of the dancers, as Emerson has said, or if it once happened it was probably the intentional freak of a happy schoolboy — a bit of farcical fun, too unworthy even to be mentioned by the "Sage of Concord" in his "Historic Notes." It was poor history and undignified in its connection.

But the reader wishes to know if certain men whose names he has seen and whose reputations he knows took part in these amusements! He may be sure that the " Professor " (Dana) was there, for those charming black eyes and raven hair, and the quick, nervous, volatile, lovely owner of them, with her southern accent, was there to charm him. And he may be sure that the " Poet " (Dwight) was there, for the man of music and song could not despise the poetry of motion, neither could his social soul neglect the opportunity of seeing so much enjoyment, and feasting his eyes on those developing buds of womanhood, those fair-haired, clear-eyed, joyous young girls who were present. And the curly-headed, witty " Time-Keeper " (Cabot) was there because he enjoyed dancing and fun. And the tall, manly, handsome-faced, clear-complexioned " Hero " (Butterfield), whose curls more than rivalled the other, looking for a dark-eyed girl who afterwards became his faithful and loving wife. And the little, thin-faced shoemaker (Colson), with his amiable spouse was there, as also that other one, with head and forehead large enough for Daniel Webster (Hosmer), with his wife.

And that quiet man, whose near-sightedness obliged him to wear glasses, and whose very soul was penetrated with a joke, if you could judge from the internal convulsions and the mounting of the red blood to his face at every good one — " Grandpa " (Treadwell) so different from his light-complexioned wife, who smiled all over her face and indulged in a merry laugh so easily. And John (Orvis) was there — surnamed " the Almighty " — for certain eyes projected their glances on him, which was not unpleasing to his senses. And

Chiswell, the man who desired to be chief of the Amusement Group, was there, of course; and Miss Ripley, " her
perpendicular Majesty," came to look on because she
enjoyed doing so; and the " Mistress of the Revels "
(Miss Russell) was looking after her young nieces.
the Misses Foord, who, with all the other young misses,
were there. And stout " Old Solidarity " (Eaton) was
there, and " Monday (Munday) the tailor's wife ";
Jean (Pallisse) with his " Madame," " Homer the
Sweet " (Doucet), " Chrysalis " (Christopher List),
" Chorles " and Stella (Salisbury), John and Mary
(Sawyer), and all the titled nobility of the place; with
Edgar and Martin, Harry and George, Dan and Wil-
lard, John and Charles — all lads of an age to drink
deep of the fountain of life and pleasure.

But stop! On this occasion the dance was not fairly
under way; it was yet quite early in the evening, and
though in the " full tide of successful experiment," to
quote an old expression, it had not worked itself up to
a high pitch, when an unexpected interruption took
place. Ah, fatal hour! Why was it not delayed?
Why did it ever come? It was this: one of the older
members came in and announced, " The Phalanstery is
on fire!" I remember the loud, derisive laugh that
came from the announcement, and was echoed through
the room. I knew better than all from the sober face
and earnest look of the person who said it — for he
was one of my kin — that the statement must be correct, and I immediately said, "This is no joke, it is true! "

A thing so easily verified needed not argument, and
all rushed for the doors. I hastily changed slippers for
boots and ran out. The barn hid the " Phalanstery "

from sight.   Passing to the other side of it I saw the
flames pouring out of the front, surmounted by a heavy
cloud of black smoke.   Without definiteness of purpose
we all started for the building, and all saw that there
was no chance of saving it.   Ere long the flames were
chasing one another in mad riot over the structure;
running across the long corridors and up and down the
supporting columns of wood, until the huge edifice was
a mass of firework, every part painted in glowing, living
color, yet retaining its distinctive form.

It was a grand and magnificent sight!   The whole
heaven was illuminated with its rosy light, and the
earth was as red as the sky, for the fields, deep covered
with white snow from the long storm, were brilliant
from the reflection of the fire.   Miles and miles away
was the illumination seen.   Men in Boston thought it
was near by, it was so bright, and one man came from
the city across the fields, thinking at every moment he
would reach the object of his search, finding it and himself at last nine miles in the country.

There was a pile of lumber near the building that
we worked hard to save, but the flames were so hot we
had to desist, and some cried out "Save the Eyry!"
Turning on my heel I went to the greenhouse for water
buckets, and entering saw the flowers lighted up with
a heavenly glow of color, and so startlingly beautiful
that in spite of my haste I lingered a moment to look
at them.   Roses and camellias, heaths and azaleas —
whatever flowers there were in bloom looked superbly
glorified in the transcendent light, and I uttered an
exclamation of surprise at the lovely display.

A moment after, armed with buckets, I started for

the Eyry, and at the post of duty worked with a will
to forward water to those above who were wetting the
front of the house and roof to preserve it from the heat.
It was not long before it was seen that danger to that
building was past, and I returned to watch the fire fiend
eat up the remains of our great edifice.

Engines with firemen slowly arrived, but the building was entirely burned, for there was a difficulty in
getting any water, as three feet of snow covered the
ground, and little was done but to extinguish some of
the embers of the burning, blackened main timbers that
had fallen into the cellar.

I pause here to give the account of the fire published
in the *Harbinger* of March 14, 1846. There is little to
add to the clear statement there made: —

"FIRE AT BROOK FARM.

"Our readers have no doubt been informed before
this of the severe calamity with which the Brook Farm
Association has been visited, by the destruction of the
large unitary edifice which it has been for some time
erecting on its domain. Just as our last paper was
going through the press, on Tuesday evening the 3d
inst., the alarm of fire was given at about a quarter
before nine, and it was found to proceed from the
'Phalanstery.' In a few minutes the flames were
bursting through the doors and windows of the second
story; the fire spread with almost incredible rapidity
throughout the building, and in about an hour and a
half the whole edifice was burned to the ground. The
members of the Association were on the spot in a few
moments, and made some attempts to save a quantity
of lumber that was in the basement story; but so rapid
was the progress of the fire, that this was found to be

impossible and they succeeded only in rescuing a couple of tool chests that had been in use by the carpenters.

" The neighboring dwelling house, called the ʻ Eyry,ʼ was in imminent danger while the fire was at its height, and nothing but the stillness of the night and the vigilance and activity of those who were stationed on its roof, preserved it from destruction. The vigorous efforts of our nearest neighbors, Mr. T. J. Orange and Messrs. Thomas and George Palmer, were of great service in protecting this building, as a part of our force were engaged in another direction, watching the workshops, barn and principal dwelling house.

" In a short time our neighbors from the village of West Roxbury, a mile and a half distant, arrived in great numbers with their engine, which together with the engines from Jamaica Plain, Newton and Brookline, rendered valuable assistance in subduing the flaming ruins, although it was impossible to check the progress of the fire until the building was completely destroyed. We are under the deepest obligations to the fire companies which came, some of them five or six miles, through deep snow, on cross roads, and did everything in the power of skill or energy to preserve our other buildings from ruin. Many of the engines from Boston came four or five miles from the city, but finding the fire going down, returned without reaching the spot. The engines from Dedham, we understood, made an unsuccessful attempt to come to our aid, but were obliged to turn back on account of the condition of the roads. No efforts, however, would have probably been successful in arresting the progress of the flames. The building was divided into nearly a hundred rooms in the upper stories, most of which had been lathed for several months without plaster, and being almost as dry as tinder, the fire flashed through them with terrific rapidity.

" There had been no work performed on the building during the winter months, and arrangements had just been made to complete four out of the fourteen distinct suites of apartments into which it was divided, by the first of May. It was hoped that the remainder would be finished during the summer, and that by the first of October the edifice would be prepared for the reception of a hundred and fifty persons, with ample accommodations for families, and spacious and convenient public halls and saloons. A portion of the second story had been set apart for a church or chapel, which was to be finished in a style of simplicity and elegance, by private subscription, and in which it was expected that religious services would be performed by our friend William H. Channing, whose presence with us, until obliged to retire on account of ill health, had been a source of unmingled satisfaction and benefit.

" On the Saturday previous to the fire, a stove was put up in the basement story, for the accommodation of the carpenters, who were to work on the outside ; a fire was kindled in it on Tuesday morning, which burned till four o'clock in the afternoon ; at half past eight in the evening the building was visited by the night watch, who found everything apparently safe, and at about a quarter before nine a faint light was discovered in the second story, which was supposed at first to have proceeded from a lamp, but on entering, to ascertain the fact, the smoke at once showed that the interior was on fire. The alarm was immediately given, but almost before the people had time to assemble, the whole edifice was wrapped in flames. From a defect in the construction of the chimney, a spark from the stove-pipe had probably communicated with the surrounding wood work, and from the combustible nature of the materials, the flames spread with a celerity that made every effort to arrest their violence without effect.

" This edifice was commenced in the summer of 1844, and has been in progress from that time until November last, when the work was suspended for the winter, and resumed, as before stated, on the day in which it was consumed. It was built of wood; one hundred and seventy-five feet long, three stories high, with spacious attics, divided into pleasant and convenient rooms for single persons. The second and third stories were divided into fourteen houses, independent of each other, with a parlor and three sleeping rooms in each, connected by piazzas which ran the whole length of the building on both stories. The basement contained a large and commodious kitchen, a dining hall capable of seating from three to four hundred persons, two public saloons, and a spacious hall and lecture room. Although by no means a model for the Phalanstery, or unitary edifice of a Phalanx, it was well adapted for our purposes at present, situated on a delightful eminence which commanded a most extensive and picturesque view, and affording accommodations and conveniences in the combined order, which in many respects would gratify even a fastidious taste. The actual expenditures upon the building, including the labor performed by the Associates, amounted to about seven thousand dollars, and three thousand dollars more, it was estimated, would be sufficient for its completion. As it was not yet in use by the Association, and, until the day of its destruction, not exposed to fire, no insurance had been effected. It was built by investments in our loan stock, and the loss falls upon the holders of partnership stock and the members of the Association.

"It is some alleviation of the great calamity which we have sustained that it came upon us at this time, rather than at a later period. The house was not endeared to us by any grateful recollections; the tender and hallowed associations of home had not yet begun to cluster around it, and although we looked upon it with joy and hope as destined to occupy an important sphere in the social movement to which it was consecrated, its destruction does not rend asunder those sacred ties which bind us to the dwellings that have thus far been the scene of our toils and of our satisfactions. We could not part with either of the houses in which we have lived at Brook Farm, without a sadness like that which we should feel at the departure of a bosom friend. The destruction of our edifice makes no essential change in our pursuits. It leaves no family destitute of a home; it disturbs no domestic arrangements; it puts us to no immediate inconvenience. The morning after the disaster, if a stranger had not seen the smoking pile of ruins, he would not have suspected that anything extraordinary had taken place. Our schools were attended as usual, our industry in full operation, and not a look or expression of despondency could have been perceived. The calamity is felt to be great; we do not attempt to conceal from ourselves its consequences, but it has been met with a calmness and high trust, which gives us a new proof of the power of associated life to quicken the best elements of character, and to prepare men for every emergency.

" We shall be pardoned for entering into these almost personal details, for we know that the numerous friends of Association, in every part of our land, will feel our misfortune as if it were a private grief of their own. We have received nothing but expressions of the most generous sympathy from every quarter, even from those who might be supposed to take the least interest in our purposes ; and we are sure that our friends in the cause of social unity will share with us the affliction that has visited a branch of their own fraternity.

" We have no wish to keep out of sight the magnitude of our loss. In our present infant state it is a severe trial of our strength. We cannot now calculate its ultimate effect. It may prove more than we are able to bear; or like other previous calamities, it may serve to bind us more closely to each other, and to the holy cause to which we are devoted. We await the result with calm hope, sustained by our faith in the Universal

Providence, whose social laws we have endeavored to ascertain and embody in our daily lives.

"It may not be improper to state, as we are speaking of our own affairs more fully than we have felt at liberty to do before in the columns of our paper, that, whatever be our trials of an external character, we have every reason to rejoice in the internal condition of our Association. For the few last months it has more nearly than ever approached the idea of a true social order. The greatest harmony prevails among us; not a discordant note is heard; a spirit of friendship, of brotherly kindness, of charity, dwells with us and blesses us; our social resources have been greatly multiplied, and our devotion to the cause which has brought us together receives new strength every day. Whatever may be in reserve for us, we have an infinite satisfaction in the true relations which have united us, and the assurance that our enterprise has sprung from a desire to obey the divine law. We feel assured that no outward disappointment or calamity can chill our zeal for the realization of a divine order of society, or abate our efforts in the sphere which may be pointed out by our best judgment as most favorable to the cause which we have at heart."

There was no wind. The building was entirely consumed; and the hungry firemen, on their homeward way, were invited to lunch at the Hive. Peter, the baker, had just turned out from the oven a fine batch of bread. We made coffee for them. The bread was for our morrow's breakfast; they ate it all, and Peter worked all night to supply the deficiency. In the midst of the lunch Mr. Ripley mounted a bench and spoke a few pleasant words of thanks to them, and you would not have guessed that a great misfortune had fallen on our scheme from the serene, cheerful look on his fine face.

He thanked the firemen kindly for coming to our aid.
Their visit, he said, " was *very unexpected* to us," but
he was glad to give them the poor hospitality we had.
" But had we *known*," he said, in that bright, pleasant
way of his, " or even *suspected* you were coming, we
would have been better prepared to receive you, and
given you worthier, if not a *warmer* reception." "Good
enough, good enough!" shouted the firemen.

This calamity did not affect any belief that the Brook
Farmers had in social science, and it did not break up
the Association. Certainly no one departed from the
place at once in fear of disorganization. It called forth
kindly letters from all parts of the country, and our
immediate friends gathered around us as if to shield us
from further harm. The sweet singer returned to pass
a few days with us, and our noble friend Channing
spoke earnest words to all.

It was Sunday; the Direction broke its rule and decided to call the Association together in the evening to
talk over everything connected with its prospects. There
was one reason for doing so, and that was, one of our
prominent members was going next day to New York
to deliver a course of lectures on music, and they desired he should be present at the consultation. I do
not remember that the meeting talked facts and figures,
but that it was a meeting of goodwill and resolution,
where all expressed their sympathies or convictions re-
garding the life then and there led ; their desire for its
continuance, and their hopes and wishes for the future
prosperity of the little band.

I make an extract from an article written by our
president, as showing the state of feeling among the

leaders at this time. After speaking of the various letters received, he says he has selected one for publication
for its practical suggestions, and continues: —

"We do not altogether agree with the writer in the
importance which he attaches to the special movement
at Brook Farm. We have never professed to be able
to represent the idea of Association with the scanty resources at our command; nor would the discontinuance
of our establishment, or of any of the partial attempts
now in progress, in the slightest degree weaken our
faith in the associative system or our conviction that
it will sooner or later be adopted as the only form of
society suited to the nature of man, and in accordance
with the divine will. We have never attempted anything more than to prepare the way for Association
by demonstrating some of the leading ideas on which
the theory is founded. In this we have had the most
gratifying success; but we have regarded ourselves
only as the humble pioneers in a work which would be
carried on by others to its magnificent consummation,
and have been content to wait and toil for the development of the cause and the completion of our hope.

"Still we have established a centre of influence here
for the associative movement which we shall spare no
effort to sustain; we are fully aware of the importance
of this; and nothing but the most inexorable necessity
will withdraw the congenial spirits that are gathered in
social union here, from the work which has always
called forth their most earnest devotedness and enthusiasm. Since our disaster occurred there has not been
an expression or symptom of despondency among our
number. All are resolute and calm; determined to
stand by each other and the cause; ready to encounter
still greater sacrifices than have yet been demanded of
them, and desirous only to adopt the course which may
be presented by the clearest dictates of duty. The loss
we have sustained occasions us no immediate inconven-

ience; does not interfere with any of our present operations, although it is a total destruction of resources on which we had confidently relied, and must inevitably derange our plans for the enlargement of the Association and the extension of our industry. We have a firm and cheerful hope, however, of being able to do much for the illustration of the cause, with the materials that remain. They are far too valuable to be dispersed or applied to any other object, and with favorable circumstances will be able to accomplish much for the realization of social unity.

"We are not so blind as to lose sight of the fact that this enterprise, as well as all others that leave the beaten path of custom and tradition, must experience more or less misrepresentation and consequent hostility. But we rejoice to say that in Boston and its vicinity, where our institution and its members are the best known, we have met with nothing since the occurrence of our disaster but the most cordial and almost enthusiastic sympathy. Our labors for five years have not been in vain in disarming reproach and winning esteem. A universal desire is expressed for the continuance of our establishment, and the success of our experiment; the most friendly hands have been extended to us from all quarters; and if the expression of respect for ourselves and wishes for our prosperity could be of any avail, we might regard our future welfare as certain. If there has been any exception to these remarks it has not come to our knowledge. The truth is, our wisest and best men are deeply sensible, under the pressure of existing evils, of the need of social reform, and they cannot but welcome those whose perseverance and devotion in this work prove them to be in earnest."

These words of our leader expressed clearly the general feeling and hope of the Association, and are worthy of close attention. I will not copy the letter referred to, but put in its place the following shorter one, the writer of whom was an entire stranger to our people: —

"NEW YORK, March 17, 1846.

"GENTLEMEN: — With the greatest sorrow I heard of the destruction of a building of the Brook Farm Association by fire. As an expression of my sympathy please accept the trifle enclosed towards its reconstruction. I am rejoiced at the spirit with which you met this calamity, and think it augurs most favorably for the successful result of your great enterprise.

"The light which some knowledge of the science of Association has poured upon my mind has changed despondency into hope, gloom into cheerfulness. My religious feelings I trust have been purified. I can more intelligently and confidently trust in God, and the reflection that we are all 'members of one another' excites benevolent feelings in my heart. I trust I may live to do something towards spreading the knowledge of this divine science, and that when I die the condition and prospects of the human race may be greatly improved. E."

This great disaster stirred the little commonwealth to its centre. In the hearts of the dwellers were sad spots, were serious thoughts. They felt a deep disappointment, and when the fun and the *bon-mot* were off, that ever sparkled at Brook Farm on the surface of its life of toil and devotion, they met each other in frank, plain talk. I have a great admiration for the simple, straightforward, honest way in which the people, male and female, spoke to each other. There was no beating of the bush; there was no need of it; there was a common interest that united them — a unity, as far as it went — not perfect, it is true, but much higher than I have ever seen it elsewhere.

As we met the morning after the fire at breakfast, which was later than usual, and all through the following days, the talk was about the catastrophe. Each one had his story to tell. Some had been watching the other houses, fearing chance sparks might reach them, but the night was so quiet they did not scatter much. Our Englishman with a spicy name (Peppercorn), cheerful, lively fellow as he was, is said to have observed that "many hanxious heyes were fixed hon that 'ole in the barn when hour 'ouse was hon fire." (It was a square place left open in the gable for ventilation.) Little knots of people gathered together to talk over and over again the same important subject, and foremost among them, tallest among them, was the General, with his disputatious tongue and his occasional unfortunate stammer.

CHAPTER XII.

BROOK FARM was in an exceptionally good position
when the associative movement broke out, like a fever,
all over the country. It was no new organization. It
had started two or three years before the rest. It had
fixed itself in the minds of the thinking part of the
community as a gathering of able, upright, conscientious men and women. There were no slurs on their
moral characters. There were no vices at which to
point the finger of scorn. They were not driven or
urged forward by poverty to take the position they did,
and the "Community" or Association had sprung up so
silently and in such a natural manner, that it seemed a
vital outgrowth from the tree of society. Notices appeared in various prints pleasantly alluding to it.

It was a curious and unique life. It deserved to be
kindly noticed, and not until after the "Fourierite"
doctrines were preached and accepted did there appear
anything in the journals of a defamatory character relating to it. Truth compels me to say that Brook Farm
and its Associates were singularly free from the rude
comments and public assaults that reformers of all kinds
are apt to receive. But while Brook Farm was thus
free, it had to bear its share in the general assaults upon
the doctrines of associative life and "Fourierism" that
were made elsewhere.

Mr. Greeley, in the *Tribune*, had gone into the work manfully, striking heavy blows for the organization of labor; announcing himself as an advocate of the doctrines of Associated Industry, with the freedom of manner and boldness of pen and purpose for which he was noted. The *Tribune* was the leading journal of the country as well as of the Whig party, and the associative idea came into immediate prominence. Mr. Greeley was a man who was not ruled by any party. He had too much of genuine independence to allow himself to follow strict party lines. He was ambitious. He had political enemies ready to strike him in any way that they could to reduce his political power, who did not dare to attack him or his party openly, and they went about seeking flaws in his honest coat of mail, into which they could thrust their lances, caring not how envenomed they were if they could but wound him, thinking by this means to reduce his hold on his party and the public.

I am satisfied that this was the reason of the commencement of the principal attacks on the associative doctrines; but having commenced them, many may finally have believed they were doing justice to society by continuing in their unjust course. The principal ground of attack was that the " Fourierites " were "disorganizers," that they were unsettling the foundations of society and that they wished to make their Associations entering wedges to disrupt the marriage relation and produce promiscuity and general anarchy. Their opponents even went so far as to call the leaders infidels, and made other outrageous and absurd charges against them.

The New York *Express* was early in the field.   The *Courier and Enquirer* and the Buffalo *Advertiser* soon made themselves conspicuous, and finally the New York *Observer*, " a religious newspaper of the Calvinistic school, of large circulation and great influence, actuated in the present case, as must be hoped, by other motives than those that envenomed its associates," says a writer in the *Harbinger*, "added its ability and its power to crush the social reformers."

These attacks, long continued, created great distrust and produced strong suspicions in the public mind derogatory to the morality of the movement.

The Associationists on their part denied that they were Fourierists, or that they had advocated or proposed any change in the marriage relation ; they were united for the organization of industry, and had nothing to do or propose in relation to the marriage system. This denial was not enough for their opponents.   They declared that the doctrines of Association led to certain results, and in proof of it cited Fourier's speculations on the subject, which had about as much to do with the social objects of the Associationists as his cosmogony, his speculations about the Arabian deserts, or his ocean of "lemonade" that had amused so many.   In the study of human nature, Fourier believed he discovered inherently inconstant natures, exceptional men and women, who cannot be constant to one idea, one hope or one love; and believing that this inconstancy was a normal trait of character with some persons, who are the exceptions to the general rule, simply and honestly acknowledged the fact, and speculated on the result and the position such persons would have in the future ideal societies.

Fourier said, "The man has no claim as discoverer. or to the confidence of the world, who advocates such absurdities as community of property, absence of divine worship and rash abolition of marriage."

The Associationists of America made no proposal of any change in the marriage relation. They had no occasion to do so. They considered it one of the best and purest arrangements of present society, and that if there were in that relation oftentimes grave mistakes and errors, there were other greater and more glaring evils and universal wrongs to set right.

"Accordingly our position is that the existing institution is to be maintained in its greatest possible dignity and purity. We believe that with the establishment of *truth* and *justice* in the practical affairs of society; with the guarantee of pecuniary independence to all persons, the most fatal temptations to debase and profane this relation will be removed. . . . But to purer and nobler generations more upright, honorable and generous, we leave all legislation on this subject. It is for us to maintain the institution inviolable."

The above quoted words are taken from a statement made by all the officers of the "American Union of Associationists," for at this time an outside movement of that name had commenced, whose object was to propagate doctrines, and stimulate the various organizations, that were forming, to actualize the new social order in various parts of the country.

At a convention in Boston, held May 27, 1846, where the American Union of Associationists was formed, this resolution was passed : —

" RESOLVED, That we hold it our duty, as seekers of the practical unity of the race, to accept every light afforded by the providential men whom God has raised up, without committing ourselves blindly to the guidance of any *one*, or speaking or acting in the name of any man; that we recognize the invaluable worth of the discoveries of Charles Fourier in the science of society, the harmony of that science with all the vital truths of Christianity, and the promise it holds out of a material condition of life wherein alone the spirit of Christ can dwell in all its fulness; but *Fourierists* we are not and cannot consent to be called, because Fourier is only *one* among the great teachers of mankind; because many of his assertions are concerning spheres of thought which exceed our present ability to test, and of which it would be presumption for us to affirm with confidence; and because we regard this as a holy and providential movement, independent of every merely *individual* influence or guidance, the sure and gradual evolving of man's great unitary destiny in the ages."

After the excitement of the fire and after the enthusiastic meeting for the holy cause, the voice of reason, pure and cold, went forth in whispers over the face of Brook Farm. Inquiries began to be made about prospects. It was considered a great piece of good fortune to have been enabled to commence the first " Phalanstery." Would any one invest in a second one, and was there prospect enough for the success of the industry on the place to secure a livelihood? If not, what must be done? These were important questions. Retrenchment had gone far. The table was too poor to attract visitors; too poor, some thought, for health, but I observed that all kept well.

I am not sure in my details of all the industry on the place just at this time, but I believe that Britannia ware was made by one or two workmen, principally oil hand lamps and teapots; but sales were limited, the market being dull or glutted, and the Brook Farmers had not the capital to manufacture and keep on hand a supply of goods for better times.

Some six to ten were engaged in making shoes and boots. There goods were sold at fair profit, though it was not a particularly remunerative business, and sometimes the group was not full of orders.

There was also the "sash and blind" business, which included the making of doors. I believe that this business could have been made profitable, but here again the inevitable want was capital. In order to make these articles of good quality, it is of the first importance that the stock in them shall be well seasoned, for if it is not, changes of temperature will produce shrinkage and warping. The wood should be either kiln-dried — a novelty then — or dried by long keeping in sheds, and it was important to buy largely when there was a good chance, and store for future use. These things the Brook Farmers could not do, and consequently some of the doors and sashes shrank, much to the disgust of everybody.

The *Harbinger* was the principal work done in the printing line as no outside business, such as job or book work, was secured. I have not found out whether the *Harbinger* paid its expenses or not, but it was considered that it aided Brook Farm by advertising the school in its columns. Certainly there was not much profit in it, for it is well known that the expense of issuing a few copies of a publication is nearly as large as when the number is doubled.

And the farming! Was it paying? A little, of course. Great labor and devotion are needed on a farm at special seasons; I am of the opinion it was a mistaken idea that no day's labor should consist of more than ten hours. Our kind-hearted leader, who had not known the necessity for great personal, physical toil, long-continued, in order to produce special results, frowned on long hours, and did not lend his magnetism to induce persons to toil out of regular time, except possibly in the haying field; and therefore the days were clipped to stated hours, when it would have been better to have extended them occasionally beyond the regular time.

A large crop was hay. Near the main farm was a lot of some fifteen acres of grass land that was a part of the original purchase, but entirely independent of contact, and at some distance towards West Roxbury village. It was called the " Keith Lot " and was the best hay field. All the meadows grew heavy crops of grass; it was not all " herd's grass," but consisted of a variety of species, and went under the name of " meadow hay," which was considered second in quality.

There were the mistakes of beginners made. Some crops were lost that might have been saved and made profitable. Of apples there were not many. The farm could not supply the Association's wants, and we had at times to buy both fruits and vegetables. Besides the cows a few swine were kept. Occasionally a " beef critter " would be killed for home use, either by our stout neighbor with a fruitful name (Orange), or by our little Englishman.

Our practical neighbor's advice and assistance were of use to us. His occupation was especially farming, but he had a "slant" towards killing animals, really liking the business. He could do the butchering of a hog with the best of grace, and had killed, first and last, so many, that I imagine he could tell the number of squeals, or wrigglings of the porcine tail it took to terminate the life of the animal, after he had given it the *coup de grace*. Once, when remonstrated with by a lady for his cruel position towards the race of swine, the "professional" love of his occupation arose above all other considerations.

"Where do you expect to go when you die," said she to him, "if you are so cruel to animals?"

"Well, I don't know," he replied, "but I hope I shall go where there are *plenty of hogs!*"

In the progress of the institution much work was done to increase the amount of grass land and tillage, and where the meadows bordered on the bush and stubble, the bush scythe was freely used. Muck was dug and spread in quantities. Mr. Ripley rather prided himself on the knowledge of the composition and improvement of soils, and when the experiment ceased, the farm had improved in amount of tillable surface and capacity of production. This progress was, much of it, to the Association's cost, and added but little to the immediate income.

I have alluded to the tree-nursery. There were thousands of young trees bought and transplanted for a nursery, and seedlings raised that had to be budded or grafted, and this was faithfully and carefully done by an experienced man, assisted by the Professor and other native talent, and the grounds kept continually in order. There was no immediate return for this outlay, which needed a year or two more of growth and investment, to bring back the first cost and make a profit from the business.

Let me here call attention to the nature of the various occupations started. They contained in general, I am satisfied, as good chances for profitable return as most occupations, and with time, and a market not overstocked, would finally have paid well. Once only were we caught with the *ignis fatuus* of genius, a washing machine — patented, of course — that came to an untimely end with a few gasps.

The greenhouse business was an outgo from first to last. It was a business in prospective. It took two persons from other and more productive labor, and quantities of fuel were consumed through the long winter days and nights with a very meagre return. It had its bright side — it was attractive — and if persevered in would have paid in the end. The garden was still more of an outgo than the greenhouse. The soil was very poor, and the manure for high culture was not forthcoming, for it was all needed on the farm.

The large number of visitors did at times return more than the cash outlay, but in reckoning the incomes of the Association this must be left out, or set down as uncertain. Some boarders were almost always on the place; either interested parties, or members' friends, but this income also was slight, as the table was meagre and the price in proportion. What, then, was there beside these occupations to support and increase the organization? Three things: Income from new members who came with property; income from regular investors, who took stock in the Association, and income from the school.

There was a prospective income from persons who were expected to come and try the new mode of life. There were those who had been promised an opportunity to join us. They were selected from a mass of applicants, and one object in the selection was to secure persons of good standing and means. Such persons represented a desirable class. But now the " Phalanstery " was burned that hope was destroyed, for all the available rooms were occupied with those living on the domain ; and if there was to be no progress in material things, who would wish to invest in stock that had not paid a cent and in which there was but a slight chance of profitable return — nay, more, which stood. ten chances to one of being entirely lost? Of course no one unless he had money to give away. The persuasive eloquence of the gifted leaders could not secure investors for the reasons I have given, and for other reasons of which I shall speak.

The " Associationists " were not united. The centre of the movement was at New York, and from there great stories of the advancement of the North American Phalanx at Red Bank, New Jersey, went forth. It was Greeley's pet. It was the favorite at the centre and mostly with the *doctrinaires*. It was an excellent domain, with water power, splendid fruit-growing land, sufficiently near New York market for an undoubted sale of all its products. Greeley admired the talent and the social life at Brook Farm, but he thought that the leaders engaged at the North American Phalanx had a more practical turn, and their soil was wonderfully better fitted for farming, which always seems to be the hobby of reformers. It was near to him ; he could visit it often, and he invested money in it.

It was intimated that the Brook Farm experiment
had better stop, and that all the material that was
good should be transferred to the North American.
But it is easily seen that this was impossible, and that
the experiment must go on. The leaders and members
had pledged themselves too faithfully to carry out the
Association's ideas, and none among them would be
bold enough to announce such a project. It would
seem like selling out to another organization. Who
would dare to propose to break into the charmed circle
by such discordant words? And so it went on.

Much talent was used in the school. As the Association took to itself a variety of industries; as it added
shoemakers, carpenters and farmers to its original stock
of intellectual workers, a change took place in the selectness of its society. Although the members were
chosen by the organization, yet "practical" farmers,
and "practical" shoemakers, with their wives and
children, are not supposed to have the easy grace of manners, the elegant language and the fluency and charm
of cultivated and scholarly men and women. The little, scarcely organized Community had increased into a
goodly number, so that its dining room was like a small
hotel; and it was no longer held by the "Transcendentalists," but had become a portion of a large and increasing body of men who followed the wild ideas of a
Frenchman named Fourier, and called itself the Brook
Farm Phalanx.

And who was this Fourier? It was just at this time;
it was just as this question was asked by anxious
mothers, that the slanders of the New York Press,
copied into other papers, far and wide, worked mis-

chief to the Brook Farm School. I never knew a pupil who was not pleased and delighted with the school; but the mother who sends a child away from home to an educational institution, especially if the child is a girl, will send it where there are no intimations connected with it of the character of those brought so prominently forward by the New York newspapers. It matters not so much to her that she believes the stories are slanders; her duty seems plain to take no risks.

The "Association" or "Phalanx" now overlapped the school, and it could no longer have the prominence as an industry that it did at first. The school, from being so intimately connected with the Association, began to lose caste. Although conducted with as much talent as ever, and with as much devotion on the part of its teachers, from the fact of the unfortunate odium cast on it, and its peculiar surroundings, was declining, and the high talent, the culture and the knowledge of its teachers, could not retain it in its proud position.

Thus I have gathered together, as in a bouquet, the sources of all the income of the once famous "Brook Farm." How slight they were!

It has often been stated that Brook Farm was a well chosen location for the experiment made there. It was nine miles from Boston. There were no surrounding industries. There was no water power at hand, the little brook being too small for any purpose but ornament. There was no available railroad station — the nearest was four miles away. This necessitated the teaming of lumber, fertilizers, coal, family stores and all stock for manufacturing purposes, from Boston, as it was not practical to send part way by rail and trans-

fer it to teams. A portion of the time we were obliged
to go to the city by the way of West Roxbury Village,
as the nearest way — over the hills — was blocked by
snow during our long New England winters, and this
increased the distance. One or two teams, with men,
were ever on the road. This was expensive and
tedious.

After the manufacturing stock had been teamed thus
far into the country, it was carted back in the shape of
goods over the same road. I must praise the men who
were engaged in this business, for they were not only
teamsters, but errand boys — expressmen we would
call them now — as well as purchasers of provender
and general commercial agents of the Association; and
their combined tasks were hard and difficult. Busy,
driving Glover Drew and Buckley Hastings filled this
office faithfully and long.

For the original purpose of an industrial school the
farm was attractive, but for an experiment such as was
foreshadowed by the name Phalanx, the place was not
at all fitted, and the good sense of Mr. Greeley saw
that the domain of the North American Phalanx was
vastly superior.

In this connection I am reminded that there was but
little machinery invented and employed on farms at
the date of my narrative ; and although our agricultur-
ists, in spite of the stale jokes that have been fathered
on them, were in the advance in this department as in
others, it was only in the third or fourth year of their
occupancy of the farm that they deemed it wise or
prudent to purchase a horse rake, and I recall no other
modern implement used, unless it was a seed drill,

taken on trial. It was the same in the domestic department; there was not even a dish washer or a clothes wringer, and the most extensive and valuable aid in the laundry was a pounding barrel in which the soiled clothes were placed and put under discipline.

There was enough reason and brave common sense among the people to ponder on the condition of things as I have presented them to you. The outlook was not encouraging. I cannot remember the order in which some of the events came to pass which I am to narrate, but the order is unimportant. Certainly there were Association meetings in which prospects were talked over and counsel was demanded and taken from one and another. Unfortunately for this story I was not at them. Doubtless I was in the quiet of the Eyry, dreaming daylight dreams, musing and listening to Fanny Dwight's deft piano playing, while she was filling me with the mysteries of Schubert and Mendelssohn and Beethoven, or else wandering about the farm, with no special aim but to find rest and enjoyment in my leisure hours. These meetings were serious, grave and often protracted. There were some who thought matters could be better managed. This is not strange, for it is always so. There were those who thought that some, particularly among the earlier members, though not absolutely non-producers, should be turned off or made more productive; but this was difficult to do. Expansion was the only true policy, and the fates seemed to be against it. Outside of the meetings and in daily life all seemed to be in harmony.

I had now lived more than two years at the farm. I, the pale city lad, had grown brown under the sun's warm kisses. I fancy I was not rosy, but the bright eyes and the clear complexion, free from speck or blemish, gave the certain indications of health. I had tasted of the actual farm work. I had planted beans, potatoes and melons. I had hoed corn, and on my knees weeded, in the broiling sun, the young onions. I had driven horse to plough, and side by side with others, trying to hoe my row with them, disputed, discussed social questions and ideas, and chaffed one another on our personal gifts and peculiarities while working together in the different groups. I had not hewed wood, but I had chopped brush. I had yoked and driven the oxen, and the first time had a difficulty with them because I tried to yoke the off ox on the nigh side; and when I graduated into the greenhouse group I learned all the mysteries of the care of plants, potting, transplanting, making leaf-mould and doing spade and rake work to perfection; and in the laying out of beds and walks did a full share of shovel-work on the sandy and gravelly soil, and drove the dump-cart.

Oh, the independence of it! To be able to do everything, and with love of it, knowing no high or low of work — all of it honor, and no shame in any of it! It is the surroundings that develop the manhood. Was I working for myself? Was I working for any other man or person? No, it was for all of us that I did it. Did I and we not have the example of great minds and greater hearts? We did. One day whilst the shop was erecting, our mason, who was on the roof building the chimney, was waiting for his helper, who had not returned from his dinner or had been called away; and

as he wanted bricks very much, I carried some hodsful
up the ladder to him in the genuine Emeraldic fashion.
(Arise not from shades profound, to frown on me,
Abraham, thou honest " *Rail Splitter!* " Arise not,
warlike Ulysses, thou " *Tanner.*" Hide thyself away!

Shake not thy cottony locks at me, thou pale-faced
" *Bobbin Boy!* " Be not too jealous of your unique
titles. I shall never aspire to so glorious a one as
" *Hod Carrier.*" I have not earned it. I did it but
once, and shall never do it again! Rest easy!)

And now, at eventide, whilst the Solons of the little
commonwealth were making laws, solving problems and
building defences against the common enemy — the
wolf of penury and hunger — I was sitting on the steps
or on the low window-sills at the Eyry, meditating and
thinking ever of the beautiful things with which I was
surrounded; thinking of the glowworms I found in the
path to Cow Island, their wonderful beauty, and how
like illuminated pearls were their tiny lamps, and when
I touched them how they rolled themselves into a coil
that resembled the pin of pearls my mother wore on her
bosom, only they were more beautiful; thinking that
their lights translated into words were even more beautiful than their phosphorescent hues, for they said,
" Come to me, my love! "

I was thinking of the bobolinks that twittered and
sung, and seemed to tumble upward as well as down-
ward in the air over the waving grass on the meadow!
or I heard behind in the dim oak woods the whip-lash
sound of the notes of the whippoorwill, repeated a hundred times on the air, while the round face of the moon
looked down and made the shadows of the trees and the

forest grow deeper and darker.   Now and then I heard,
when all was still, from his nesting-place, the brave
yet delicate notes of the song sparrow, singing in his
dreams from out a happy, overflowing heart.   Dear little
fluff of feathers!

I was thinking of the brood of young partridges I
scared in the woods, and how like a flash, mysteriously
and totally, they disappeared in the underbrush.   I was
thinking of the tiny newts and wonderful creatures I
found in the shallow water in the meadow ditch.   I was
thinking that if the saracenas were in bloom I would go
to find some of them on the morrow; or if the brilliant
cardinals were, I would hunt for them at the brookside:
or if there were any yellow violets to be had I wanted
to find them, as I had found many varieties.

Then I turned my head and listened more earnestly
to the music or to the conversation in the parlor, of
inspired men and women, talking in low, conversational
tones, with now and then a spice of wit, on art, religion,
science or the lives of great painters, musicians, artists
and reformers.   Or I was looking to see if the " Northern
Cross " had appeared among the constellations above the
horizon.   Or maybe I heard George W. Curtis, who had
come to visit his old teachers, singing the "Erl King "
or "Good-night to Julia " or plaintive " Kathleen
Mavourneen " in his inimitable way.   Perhaps I was
deep in social science or restudying some of Fourier's
pleasant fancies, such as the rivalries of groups of nice
children with his little hordes of brats and " rushers " —
to use a modern word — and how in nature's scheme
their different talents so balanced one another as to
make complete harmony.

I was thinking of the big boulders that join and make
a hole we called "the cave," over which Hawthorne's
fancy made the apostle Eliot preach to the Indians,
giving it the name of "Eliot's Pulpit," and describing
it afterward so prettily in his "Blithedale Romance"; a
book of which Emerson speaks, and truly, as "that disagreeable story," and of some of the sketches in it as
"quite unworthy of his genius." And I was thinking
of the retired little dell in the far "Wisconsin Lot,"
where doubtless he and others have taken their volumes
and note-books, writing and reading to the music of the
hum of the bees, the sighing pines and the redbreasts.

I was thinking of the unfortunate humanity who
lived outside of our charmed circle, and how little they
knew of the magnificent future the infinite Father has
prepared for them and their descendants, and how from
the beginning the plan has been coördinate with man's
help to his brother man and his sister woman ; and my
whole soul was penetrated, even as it is now, with pity
for the blindness, mental and physical, that cannot see
how to use the gifts the Infinite holds out, patiently
waiting for us to take from his indulgent hands. I
was thinking how much, how very much, of all our suffering comes from human ignorance only.

I heard all the songs of nature beside the birds. In
the spring I heard the toads and frogs and turtles making merriment in their little sitting-rooms in the pools
of water in low places. In the summer I heard the
locusts sing and the lazy croak of bullfrog, bearing the
relation of trombone in the orchestra of nature to the
other musicians, whilst the fireflies were dancing in
mid-air all around him — he winking at them with those

wondrous projecting eyes. In the autumn the cricket was my favorite, and he was kind enough at times to come into our musical parlor to rival Mary and Jennie and Helen. But in the winter it was only the kindly birds that came again — sweet chickadee and the talkative crows. None of us injured the birds. I do not remember ever seeing a gun on the place. Thus went the seasons — spring, summer, autumn, winter.

I loved the daily round of life. All were kind to me. I was well mentally and physically. I was in the bud of youth. I was like the pink rhodoras in spring, callow of leaf or fruit but brightly covered with promising blossoms. There remained one thing for me — to know I was happy. Did I know it? Yes, I did. I realized it then as now. I was not a victim of unconscious joy, to awaken to it at some future period. It was not to me a dream. The cup was full! I was truly happy!

CHAPTER XIII.

THE FIRST BREAK.

I DO not know when or where it was first announced, but the announcement came like a clap of thunder from a clear sky. Some one was going to leave us! Who? Was it the " Archon " or the " Professor " ? Certainly this was not expected; but would it be strange if some of the leaders, feeling too much the pressure and the burden of the financial and executive business of the society, should grow weary, depart, and leave their places unfilled forever? Was it any one of the grumblers or the known discontented or disconcerted ones? No, it was no less than Peter, the " General "! Why, if the elm tree in the yard of the Hive had walked off in the night it would not have caused more talk or greater consternation. Could it be possible ?

From that day to this I have wondered how that man could have had such a hold on our hearts. There was not a handsome feature in him. He had a large but uneven forehead. His eyes were small, grayish-blue and deepset. His nose was homely, his teeth were discolored, and he was ungainly and awkward. His best feature was his height, but he stooped in his shoulders, and his dress when about his work was of the plainest description. His baize jacket and slipshod shoes did not become him.

Ever since then I have believed in the effect of virtue and kindness. He was a living sermon — nay, a hundred sermons to me. He was "patient, long-suffering and kind."

A spontaneous regret came from all. Some of the women, who certainly could not be accused of any amatory love for him, shed tears to think that he should go, for he was full of kindness to them. Constantly in contact with their department, he was as gentle as a child, never complaining and yet full of work. Industrious as the day was long, he seemed so like a portion of the very atmosphere of the house, and of the life, that it did not seem that he could be away and the Association be as it was.

The *morale* to the fact of the General's departure also disturbed our people. He was discouraged at the attempt at realization of the new order at Brook Farm. As long as all clung together there seemed to be hope; but the first break was dangerous to our well-being, dangerous to our existence.

Mr. Dwight had gone to New York to deliver lectures on music. When he went away all was enthusiasm, all was harmony. The great loss by fire had shaken no one's faith in the principles or the organization, and as yet the balance of probabilities had not been made or adjusted in men's minds. The word was then to go on at all cost. When he returned he found discussion of means, doubts and fears, uppermost everywhere. As a truth the Association had not prospered financially. Beginning with no real capital, and mortgaged to the debts of the former "Community," it had come to a point where without more means or more money in ready cash it was very difficult to see how it could go on.

The change of social atmosphere in so short a time grated on the sensitive soul of the man of music, and it was my fortune to be present at a general meeting of all the Association where I heard his remarks. He began by stating, as I have done, that when he went away all was harmony and peace. All seemed united by bonds deep and strong; by a common purpose and for a common end. We were all striving for a worthy object, a higher, nobler life than that which surrounded us.

He had been away from this quiet, cheerful, peaceful and just life, among the noise, dust and discord of a great, unwieldy city, and when there he had looked forward to his coming home to this devoted little band with the greatest possible pleasure. He had expected to find them as harmonious and as united as when he left. He trod the precious soil and found all external things glowing in beauty. He mounted the hill, and there came two beautiful white doves flying close to him as he walked on, circling around and around his head and seeming to rejoice in his coming. He regarded it as a symbol of the unity and peace that were with us, as well as a token of welcome.

But when he came to talk with the members, all was doubt, all was distrust. What could it mean? It filled his heart with sad forebodings! Why could we not be as before? Why doubt? why distrust? why not push on? Certainly there would be a way opened for us! It could not be that the years of devotion to one another and to this just cause and just life could end thus! And in pleading tones born out of the depths of his heart, and living sentences to which I can do no manner of justice, he waxed eloquent, and all could not but be touched and moved with his words.

How beautiful it is in looking back to this time, when coming events were casting their sad shadows before them, to think that no one took the opposite side, and that none among all the number argued before us that we had met with a miserable failure; that no one was ready with a rude word to break the bonds of friendship and to use his eloquence to destroy our habit of life, our trust in one another, our faith in God and the eternal justice of His providence, or to hasten in any way the disruption of the institution; and that in those trying hours the strong ties of friendship, love and daily communion were uppermost. All felt that we wished to keep on with our labor, and that Mr. Dwight only spoke the wishes of all hearts. But the inevitable mathematics of finance were against us.

The "Poet," as the young folks called Mr. Dwight, wished that we could manage it somehow, in some manner. He himself would go away. He would go where his services could command higher fees. He would give them to the Association for the privilege only of being sometimes on the domain, and finding there others whom he loved, working still for their sublime purposes.

These well-expressed desires, though availing nothing in the way of adding money to the treasury, stimulated the hearts anew to good fellowship, and helped to keep up the activity of the place to the last. It seems a wonder to me that, in spite of all the changes that took place after this time, as one and another departed, the

industry of the place was still kept in decent working
order.

It was on the third of March that the fire took place,
and the spring and summer were fast passing away; the
beautiful summer — beautiful ever with its fields of
waving grass and its wild flowers, its sunlight and
moonlight glow, its varied charms of growth and ver-
dure; especially beautiful to us, the young, who
watched one another's countenances glowing with
health, innocence and pleasure; who clasped hands
together and danced with nimble feet; and saw the
lithe young forms grow fairer and more womanly and
more manly. With the frank outpourings of friendship
and confidence; with the lavishness of mutual praise in
youth, we enjoyed and joined in merry badinage, in
miffs and flattery. The starry nights echoed our young
voices singing in the clear air. There was a burden of
care taken from us, for was not the Association our
god-father? Had it not also taken from our parents
the dread anxieties that fall to most of common lot?
And while we were there we would be happy, and when
the Association broke up, if it ever did, would we not
unite somewhere again?

Certainly I never heard any one of us doubt, whether
young or old, gray of beard or smooth of face, that
associated life and doctrines would succeed: of this I
am sure. We reasoned that if Brook Farm Association
failed, some other would not. Some new ones would
be formed. The partings were all temporary; and when
we parted, it was with cheerful hearts. It was like
the going forth of a family in the morning to meet again
in the evening; no sad farewells, no heart-breakings.

In a few years all of those engaged in this most interesting experiment will be gathered to their fathers. No one may ever write as consecutive a story of the farm life as I have done; and, with the much that is superficial in my narrative, let me add my convictions of the leading men and women in this movement. They were, in the highest sense, Christians — not technically bound to creeds, but their hearts and intellects were filled to overflowing with the good precepts that are proclaimed as the foundation, aside from technical beliefs, of the Christian doctrine ; to love their neighbors as themselves; to do good to all ; to seek first righteousness in life ; to uphold honesty and honest dealing in *all* earthly relations ; to do unto others as we would they should do unto us; to teach honor to parents ; to make all men love one another ; to inspire a trust in God as a provident Father who stands ready to reconcile all conflicts, with the way open and plain for us, thus doing away with infidelity, unbelief, narrowness of mind and spirit.

The doctrine they taught above all others was the *solidarity of the race*. This was ever repeated. It was their religion that the human race was one creation, bound together by indissoluble ties, links stronger than iron and unbreakable. It was one body. It should be of one heart, one brain, one purpose. Whenever one of its members suffered all suffered. When there was a criminal all had part in his crime ; when there was a debauchee, all partook in his debasement; when there was one diseased all were affected by it ; when one was poor, all bore some of the sting of his poverty. If any one took shelter behind his possessions, wretchedness, poverty and disease found him out.

Ever is Lazarus at the king's gate haunting him, and
he cannot avoid it. At his banquets the ghosts of the
wronged appear to him. Hollow-eyed women and
children point the finger of scorn at him, and phantoms
in his dreams shriek out at him, "Where is thy
brother?" And he has no excuse but the cowardly
question, "Am I my brother's keeper?" His children
inherit the emanations from his cowardly soul and will
not rise up to call him blessed. His mind is not at ease,
because the atmosphere of envy is all around him; he
knows *he* is the cause of evil thoughts, and that he
holds his position by keeping comfort away from many
around him, and his fine surroundings become to him
as tinsel and dross. Dyspepsia, *ennui* and weariness of
spirit claim him. He is a poverty-haunted coward,
ashamed that he is so; and, saddest of all, he is not a
Christian. He does not believe that if he seeks the
kingdom of God, which means only to do aright, all
things of material beauty will be added to him, purify-
ing, comforting, sustaining him, strengthening him,
glorifying him beyond his present power to dream of.

But the Brook Farmers did. They believed that the
Infinite Power ordained social laws so universal and
equitable that the fulfilment of them would make all
unqualifiedly happy, and that it is the mission of this
race of beings to be attached to this earth, to this universe, until their happy human destiny is accomplished,
which destiny must be for *all*, otherwise the Infinite
would be partially and not wholly good and just.

I do not say that all men are conscious of
this as I have pictured it; but the burdens are
lying heavily on their souls and bodies, and they can

be truly happy only when they are taken off from them. Human nature is too buoyant, too elastic, to be conscious of their pressure all of the time ; but often, in every soul, is the keen perception that there *must* be an accounting somewhere, sometime, for all the injustice and wrong done to any one and to every one, and it brings the "dread hereafter" uncomfortably close to their daily lives.

It is too early yet to judge of the result of the work of the Brook Farm socialists. They were progressively ahead of their race. They lived before their time. They existed in the future as well as in the present, and the future will be their judge ; but these are my conclusions justified by actual contact, seeing these men and women under every variety of circumstances of daily life, for the full two and a half years of my actual sojourn at the Farm. The high ideal they carried as their standard lifted them over many of the littlenesses and annoyances of daily life without a disturbing thought.

I find in the *Harbinger* of December 20, 1845, one of the very few special allusions to Brook Farm life, and it is so much to the point that I copy it entire : —

"We speak no less for the whole associative movement in this country than for ourselves when we beseech our friends who are looking upon our operations not to judge of our principles or our purposes by any immediate results which they may have witnessed. The question is often asked of us whether our present mode of life answers our expectations — whether Association is found to be valuable in practice as it seems to be correct in theory, and the like. But all such inquiries betray an ignorance of the actual condition of the enterprise. They suppose the organizations which have gone into

effect in different parts of the country are true specimens of the plans of Association. This is far from
being the case. We do not profess to be able to present
a true picture of associative life. We cannot give
the remotest idea of the advantages which the combined order possesses over the ordinary arrangements
of society.

" The benefits we now actually enjoy are of another
character. The life we now lead, though, to a hasty
and superficial observer surrounded with so great imper-
fections and embarrassments, is far superior to what we
have been able to attain under the most favorable circumstances in civilization. There is a freedom from
the frivolities of fashion, from arbitrary restrictions,
and from the frenzy of competition: we meet our fellow-
men in more hearty, sincere and genial relations; kindred spirits are not separated by artificial conventional
barriers; there is more personal independence and a
wider sphere for its exercise; the soul is warmed in the
sunshine of a true social equality; we are not brought
into the rough and disgusting contact with uncongenial
persons which is such a genuine source of misery in the
common intercourse of society; there is a greater variety
of employment, a more constant demand for the exertion of all the faculties, and a more exquisite pleasure
in effort, from the consciousness that we are not working
for personal ends, but for a holy principle.

"And even the external sacrifices, which the pioneers
in every enterprise are obliged to make, are not without
a sort of romantic charm, which effectually prevents us
from enjoying the luxuries of Egypt, though we should
be blessed with neither the manna nor the quails which
once cheered a table in the desert So that for ourselves we have reason to be content. We are conscious
of a happiness we never knew until we embarked in
this career. A new strength is given to our arms, a new
fire enkindles our souls.

"But great as may be our satisfactions of this nature, they do not proceed from the actual application of associative principles to outward arrangements. The time has not yet come for that. The means have not been brought together to attempt the realization of the associative theory, even on the humblest scale. At present, then, we are only preparing the way for a better order; we are gathering materials that we hope one day we may use with effect; if otherwise, they will not be lost; they will help those who come after us, and accomplish what they were intended for in the designs of Providence. No association as yet has the number of persons, or the amount of capital, to make a fair experiment of the principles of attractive industry. They are all deficient in material resources, in edifices, in machinery, and, above all, in floating capital; and although in their present state they may prove a blessing to the individuals concerned in them, such as the whole earth has not to give, they are not prepared to exhibit that demonstration of the superior benefits of associative life which will at once introduce a new era and install humanity in the position for which it was created.

"But, brothers, patience and hope! We know what we are working for, we know that the truth of God is on our side, that he has no attributes that can favor the existing order of fraud, oppression, carnage and consequent wretchedness. We may be sure of the triumph of our cause. The grass may grow over our graves before it will be accomplished; but as certain as God reigns, will the dominion of justice and truth be established in the order of society. Every plant which the Heavenly Father has not planted will be plucked up, and the earth will yet rejoice in the greenness and beauty of the garden of God."

These are George Ripley's words. Could any one add a word to improve these splendid paragraphs!

CHAPTER XIV.

THE DEPARTURES, AND AFTER LIVES OF MEMBERS.

I AM now to chronicle the last scene in our history, and I know not how to do it, for of all the events of the life it is to me the most dreamy and unreal. The figures of our drama flit before me like shadows. It was like a knotted skein slowly unravelling. It was as the ice becomes water, and runs silently away. It was as the gorgeous, roseate cloud lifts itself up, and then changes in color and hides beyond the horizon. It was as a carriage and traveller fade from sight on the distant road. It was like the coming of sundown and twilight in a clear day. It was like the apple blossoms dropping from the trees. It was as the herds wind out to pasture. It was like a thousand and one changing and fading things in nature.

"It was not discord, it was music stopped."

Who was next to break away from the charm of the life I know not; but when the autumnal season came I was summoned to a family council and advised that I should begin a new occupation where I could at least earn my subsistence. As in duty bound, I acquiesced, and in a few days bade farewell to the Brook Farm life.

I saw no tears shed when I left, but I was sorry to leave my blue tunic behind, it was so comfortable. I left, but it was only my outward self that was gone, not my sympathies or hopes. Behind were family and devoted friends. It was still my home to return to, as it would be for an indefinite period.

For two years and a half I had worn the tunic of the community, and the "swallow tail" and "civilized rig" I put on for my departure transposed my appearance so much that some of the society did not at first know me. With my parents' blessing, I entered on the rudiments of the professional life I have ever since followed, and took the West Roxbury omnibus for Boston, the same I had taken two years and a half before to go to the farm.

The succeeding Saturday night found me at home again. How pleasant the greeting from Willard, Katie and Louise; from Charlie, Abby and Edgar; from Anna and Dolly — from all, old and young! The "Archon" almost screamed when he saw me, I was so "stunning" in his eyes, and poked some of his fun at me. No marked change had taken place. The *Harbinger* was printed as usual, and only one or two persons had gone.

Every Saturday night I returned to the "Phalanx," but soon the shoemakers found occupation elsewhere and their seats were empty. Then the printers went, as the *Harbinger* was transferred to New York. At last the shop was closed, the cattle were sold, and all the industry ceased. I came and went but did not see the actors go, and am glad I did not see the "Archon" take his leave, or the many bright faces I had loved so well.

The Poet lingered near. In Boston he started the *Journal of Music*, and at the Eyry lingered for a while a sweet enchantress, and the spirits of song and music held their revels there. So, also, lingered at "the Hive" some sweet faces and loving hearts besides those of my kin. The greenhouse, where I had spent so much of my time, was closed — the plants all gone. Up the rafter ran the vines I helped to plant, but when the winter came, drear and cold, only a few persons remained on the domain. The dining hall echoed to my voice in its emptiness, and the little reading room at the Hive was where we now assembled at meals.

I wandered around and looked into the empty rooms. I cannot say I felt as sad as I would to-day. Every spot was connected with some little event, but the events were usually of such a cheerful and pleasant nature that I could not be depressed, and a large portion of my intimates were still near me in the city or neighborhood. We could muster a goodly number at call and we tried to keep alive the good work for the "cause" with meetings, social and theoretical. But no longer the stage brought its loads of visitors to the Hive door. Over the hills and the meadows no more resounded the morning horn echoing far and far away, or Miss Ripley's high voice calling "Alfred! Alfred!" who acted as major-domo in the absent General's place.

No more came down from the distant houses school lads and lasses, and the long, tridaily procession of young and old had ceased forever. The din of the kitchen was stopped, and the merry brogue of Irish John was silenced. No more rushed the blue tunics for the mail when the coach came in — alas, it came no more! The fields remained as when last cropped, and if we went to the Cottage no merry sound of music came from the school room. We mounted the stairs without meeting the classic face or the elastic step and figure of the Professor or his fair sister, and in vain did we look for the concourse of books where once he wielded his modest pen and translated his German "*lieder*."

No more mounted in air the beautiful doves that circled and tumbled in their flight — *my* doves, that would come at my call and alight on my hands, head and shoulders, and scramble for the corn I held out to them in my palms. Sunday after Sunday, week after week, I spent in the Hive. I looked out of the window but ventured not to go to the Eyry, for there the music had finally ceased; or if the spirits sang their dirges in those classic walls, my dim ears did not hear them.

Mr. Ripley's books had gone to swell Rev. Theodore Parker's library. Were they surrendered without a pang? I will tell you. " Fanny," said Mr. Ripley, seeing his valued books departing, " I can now understand how a man would feel if he could attend his own funeral." They have been placed in the Boston City Library by the death and last testament of the later proprietor. The flowers I had watered and tended passed into the hands and greenhouse of the translator of "Consuelo." Those who owned any private effects or furniture took them away.

The Pilgrim House, never beautiful, and barren in its immediate surroundings, was entirely deserted. The Hive was my home; and when the warm sun, looking through the barren grape vine into the dining room window, melted the light snow of early spring, and awoke the tender grass into new growth and verdancy, and the remaining poultry warmed themselves by its rays, nestling together by the doorways, as the melting snow dripped drop by drop from the house top — the farm looked beautiful still.

In some of our young hearts, with the coming of early summer, awoke a yearning for one more meeting at the old place; and so we gathered the young people from far and near for one more good time, for one more communion. With what pleasure I recall those few hours. How happy we were! How social and loving and dear we were to one another! In the many years passed since then, there is no red-letter day like that one. We were about twenty in number. There were fourteen of us between the ages of fifteen and twenty-one years. The remainder were older. We filled a table in the reading room. Little we cared if we sat crowded close together, for we chose our mates. Some were pupils of the school, the rest were youths of the Association.

In the afternoon we wandered once more in the beautiful pine woods. We sang once more the "Silver Moon" together as we roved about, or sat on the big boulder on the knoll at the foot of the lightning-struck tree. We recounted old times and seasons; we cracked our merry jokes and ate our simple treat, and then parted. In a few days the wide world was between us, and forever. Some went East, and some West, one to Port-au-Prince, and others to different villages and towns in New England. Of the number, four remained in Boston; I was one of them.

Reader, my reminiscences are told, but not all told! They are like the sultan's story that was to last a thousand years. To all but the one interested there was an unending sameness in it, but to that one, it was his life.

It is natural to wish to know of the writer what became of the persons who formed this little band of devotees. I can but give a meagre sketch in reply, for want of room.

When Mr. Ripley left Brook Farm he was poor. The experiment had cost him money, years of toil and made debts for which he felt responsible. He determined to pay them. As yet the way was not open. The *Harbinger* was changed in form and lived less than two years in its new location, and during a temporary illness of the editor its publication was suspended. Mr. Ripley and wife taught school at Flatbush, L. I.

At the termination of the *Harbinger* he immediately commenced writing for the New York *Tribune*. Its pay roll indicates what he received May 5, 1849; it was $5 for the previous week's work. In July, same year, he was paid $10 per week; April 6, 1850, $15; Sept. 21, 1851, $25 per week. He wrote articles on all the living topics of the day, from the arrival of the last new singer to the death of the last criminal. Things trivial and non-important, grave and gay, of lasting import and the most ephemeral, all came under his pen.

He also wrote, either occasionally or regularly, for a dozen other periodicals. He was an early contributor to *Putnam's* and from its commencement wrote for *Harper's New Monthly*. As editor associated with Mr. C. A. Dana he gave his time and best thought to the New American Cyclopedia, and the first two or three volumes of the series were edited solely by them. In

1871 his salary was raised to $75 per week. When the Cyclopedia was revised he was paid $250 per month for extra work on it. More than a million four hundred and sixty thousand volumes of the two editions have been sold, and a small royalty secured to the editors on each volume.

With prosperity Mr. Ripley never forgot his obligations. The old score of debt was wiped out and paid. He was free, and as a man of letters revelled in that which had been his youthful ideal.

When a student at Harvard College he wrote to his father, " I know that my peculiar habits of mind, imperfect as they are, strongly impel me to the path of intellectual effort; and if I am to be at any time of use to society or a satisfaction to myself or my friends, it will be in the way of some retired literary situation where a fondness for books will be more requisite than the busy, calculating mind of a man in the business part of the community." Thus was one of his youthful dreams fulfilled. His capacity for work seemed unbounded. " He gave all his time and all his energy to literary criticism, and spending on it, too, the full resources of a richly furnished mind and infusing into it the spirit of a broad and noble training."

He passed away July 4, 1880. A great concourse of people attended the obsequies. Distinguished men, divines, critics, scholars, editors, architects, scientists, journalists, publicists, artists and men of affairs were in the assembly. The pall-bearers were the president of Columbia College, the editor of *Harper's Weekly*, an Italian professor, the editor of the *Popular Science Monthly*, the editor of the New York *Observer*, an eminent German lawyer, a distinguished college professor, a popular poet and the editor of the *Tribune*.

His wife Sophia passed from this life nineteen years before him. The story of his romantic after marriage, and many details of his career from birth to death, will be found in Mr. O. B. Frothingham's " Life of George Ripley," told by his kindly biographer.

Deeply interested in his daily toil, thoroughly immersed in it body and brain, yet cheerfully responding to all calls on his unbounded stock of information and good nature, no one knows how often his mind wandered over the intervening distance and saw the old farm with its mingled incidents of pathos, philosophy and heroism, or what regrets were covered up; but the joking allusions he sometimes made to it when speaking of it to those who came to quiz him, were more than repaid to his few intimate friends when he opened his heart to them, and the earnestness of his spirit and the solemnity of his faith in the brotherhood of humanity shone forth. He unveiled to them that he did with undying faith still see in its ideas the elements of the true and heavenly society; that he carried deep down in his bosom intense love for those who were associated with him, and that if it had been founded at this later period, so much has the interest in social problems increased, all the financial support needed would have been freely given.

His friend William Henry Channing urged him to write the story of Brook Farm, saying, " When *will* you tell it?"

His joking reply was, " When I reach my years of

indiscretion!" He knew that the life wrote its own story.

Of the many dear ones I have known whose lives have added to my life faith and trust in the Divine Father and his plans for the good future of the human race; after years of thought and years of life, I give to Mr. Ripley — the leader, the daring man, the brave Christian heart, the torch bearer, himself the harbinger of the bright future of social justice — the first place, the highest seat, the noblest position among them all.

Mr. Ripley paid off the debts of the Community. I do not know all of them. There was an amount due to Hawthorne at one time, probably his original invest-ment, which he growled about, and there was another due to one of the Brothers Morton, who built the Pil-grim House. I am indebted to his daughter, Miss Morton, for the statement that her father received from Mr. Ripley a check in payment of the Community debt to him. Calling her to his side and showing it to her, he said, " There, Hannah, there is an honest man! "

After the institution was incorporated the debts and responsibilities were shared by the incorporators and stock holders.

It has often been stated that it was the influence of Rev. William Ellery Channing that started the West Roxbury Community. His nephew, William Henry Channing, alluding to this in a letter to Rev. J. H. Noyes, author of the "History of American Socialisms," contradicts the statement as follows : —

" Of course my uncle deeply sympathized with his younger friend's heroic effort, and wished all success to the movement, but he did not encourage it, so far as I can understand, for in his judgment he distrusted the prudence of the enterprise," etc. "But it was George Ripley, aided by his noble wife Sophia — it was George Ripley, and Ripley alone, who truly originated Brook Farm; and his should be the honor through all time. And a very high honor it will be sooner or later."

The head farmer, with his wife and family, who were so early in the experiment, spent many years in the quiet town of Concord, Massachusetts. It was he who gave Mr. Ripley courage in his work. He was practical, honest, brave, and had enough of poetry in his composition to take the dry edge off of his daily routine of toil. When ploughing the fields it was with regret he turned under the lovely wild flowers and the wild-rose bushes, and it often struck his fancy to transplant them from the fields to the roadside where they blessed the eyes of the wayfarer. Finally the heavenly voice called him and he went thitherward, deeply loved, honored and respected by all. Minot Pratt's name was a synonym of all that was pure, good and lovely. His wife survived him many years, but in May, 1891, she passed away at an advanced age, the last of the signers to the original agreement.

The ambitious "Professor" lives. The trenchant blade of his intellect is still keen. Sometimes it seems that to overcome obstacles is all with him. His wife was one of the "dear girls" of the Association. Method in business and masterly activity have wrung from fate a fortune, and the editorial and governmental offices he has held have been more than ably filled. Blessed with a charming family, deeply immersed in political as well as other writing, it would almost seem as if the olden days were forgotten by him, were it not that now and then he writes as he did shortly after Mr. Ripley's decease, as follows:—

"It is not too much to say that every person who was at Brook Farm for any length of time has ever since looked back to it with a feeling of satisfaction. The healthy mixture of manual and intellectual labor, the kindly and unaffected social relations, the absence of everything like assumptions or servility, the amusements, the discussions, the friendships, the ideal and poetical atmosphere which gave a charm to life — all these continue to create a picture toward which the mind turns back with pleasure as to something distant and beautiful not elsewhere met with amid·the routine of this world."

Whatever may be said of the tone of the articles that come from his pen, their ability is unquestioned, and it is not a secret that in Mr. Ripley's judgment Charles A. Dana, of the New York *Sun*, was the ablest editor in the world.

The "Poet," as we called him, as editor of Dwight's *Journal of Music*, and also as critic, was deserving of especial credit for his services in musical culture. Earnest, refined, always endeavoring to do right, but strict in his pleasant criticisms, he pointed upward to higher ideals. Living alone in his latter years like a bachelor, he sought solace in his refined tastes with cultivated people. Married to Mary Bullard, the sweet singer of my story, kindred sympathies united them more firmly than marriage vows, but her early death deprived the world of one of the noblest and choicest of womanhood, and his life of its sweetest charm. He went abroad for a short trip, leaving her in full health and beauty; he returned — she had passed from mortal sight.

A number of the members, male and female, joined the Association in New Jersey near Red Bank — the North American Phalanx. There they renewed the social life and experiment, with such result as some other pen can tell.

It was about the time of the closing of the Brook Farm experiment that the "California fever" broke out, or the rush for the gold mines. Some of our theorists argued that the country was too poor for the establishment of the social organizations proposed, and that more wealth was needed. A number of the Brook Farmers went to the new country for gold. The gardener, Peter Klienstrup, was one. I am sorry to say that disappointment awaited him. A foreigner, and sensitive, partly deaf and past middle life, he was not the man for the country or the life. He died there poor. His charming, tuneful daughter, with the beautiful complexion and lovely rounded shoulders, did not long survive him. His wife survived, but one day I stood with only a few who knew her, at the door of an open tomb, and a strange thrill passed over me when one by my side said, as her body was placed within, "This is the last of her race — the family is extinct!"

The good, kind-hearted "General" sleeps within sound of the Pacific waves, for he, too, was one of the early Californians. And the Admiral, the pure-hearted, high-minded and keen-eyed Admiral, has long since laid down his burdens and his aspirations. And so also with many, too many for me here to recount. The two sisters that I have described with flowing hair, grew in loveli-

ness to full womanly beauty and then passed to the
angelic world.

Mr. Ryckman, surnamed the "Omniarch," reigns no
more in this sphere. Peace to his memory.

The downfall of the Association was the wrecking of
Irish John. He seemed homeless and aimless. The
constant smiles on that remarkable face gave way to
soberness profound. Old habits crept back upon him.
He had a friend, one of our number, who took a kindly
interest in him, but could not follow all his wayward-
ness. He departed for New York, ostensibly for business. Not long after this his friend received a note
from there in John's handwriting, saying that if he
would send to a certain number and street he would
find something for him. It was a trunk, and appeared
to contain all of John's effects except the suit of clothes
he had on. What end he made no one knows.

How grand it would be if the social fabric could
keep and guard all its weak ones, surround them by influences that could prevent them from falling into evil
ways, and bear them up until the end comes peacefully
and naturally!

Marianne Ripley, Mr. Ripley's sister, the devoted
soul who reigned over the Kitchen Group and cultivated the flowers on the terraces, spent her later hours
in the West, and passed away at Madison, Wisconsin.
John Allen, the firm preacher, has gone also. His little boy, who conveyed the small-pox to the farm, grew
to manhood, and at an early age fought with Grant at
Vicksburg, where he received the wound that caused
his death.

The dear girl with the loud laugh is still here, but

tears and sorrow have been in her cup. Her kind husband, one of our number, and some children are with the shadows; and the dimpled face of the black-haired girl with the Irish name, whose beauty took my young fancy, long ago joined the larger realm of beauty.

The house dog, Carlo, whom everybody knew, grew rapidly old when the Association broke up. I never saw such a change. It seemed as though regretful remembrances of former times clung to him. There was no more the *music* of "the sounding horn" to awaken him from his drowse, and he passed much of his time under the woodshed. But he was not the sleek and canny dog of yore. He grew thin and weak. Long locks of indifferent colored brown hair grew out of his sides, and hung loosely down. His gait was slow and feeble, and it was not pleasant to look at him. Finally, one cold day, at least a year after the general departure, he was missing, and I could find nothing of him. Inquiries were in vain. It was in the following spring that his bones were found where either he himself had dug a burrow, or the hand of charity had laid him. Good Carlo!

Some very happy marriages sprang from the acquaintance at Brook Farm. There, in a few weeks or months, a better knowledge could be formed, a truer and more absolute and certain estimate of character, than by years of fashionable flirtation. And here let me add, that the women were always well dressed: there were no party dresses, all shine, lace and glitter, and household wrappers all slouched, torn and drabbled. The situation of woman was such as to stimulate her ever to neatness in personal appearance, even if the material

was but a " ninepenny " calico; and the same may be
said to a marked extent of the men.

And many others who stood shoulder to shoulder in
the ranks have shared the common lot. Scattered
through the country, in city, town and hamlet, those
who survive are doing their humble duties, and filling
their stations honorably. There are those among them
who have gained wealth, and none whom I know that
are in poverty. In the circles they occupy, their influence has been felt towards a liberal judgment in all
matters pertaining to government, religion and society.

Our friend Rev. William Henry Channing spent the
major portion of his after life abroad. The war brought
him back to America. He was at one time chaplain of
the House of Representatives of the United States, and
served the country at the front; but he returned to
Liverpool, England, where he preached and educated
his family, passing away beloved by members of all the
prominent churches both conservative and radical.

There were some four and possibly more, who joined
the Catholic Church. This created at the time many
remarks, but it is only an episode for a class of minds
to find themselves at the other end, at the opposite side,
at the bottom instead of the top when they have swung
themselves, pendulum-like, far away from ordinary
moorings. The "Community" people were at the extreme of society, unorganized, without creeds, without
science, and only morality and faith to guide them, and
having given the lie to ordinary social forms; having
lost their faith and trust in society as it was, is it strange
that some should swing to the extreme of conservatism,

that they should try a new departure when met by seeming failure in their radical moves?

But why continue the list? The very boys have become gray-haired men, but proud to say, each one of them, " I was one of the Brook Farmers. "

In closing this picturesque drama, it would not be strange if someone should ask if this is all that is left of the life. Has it been only a failure and a dream that I have chronicled, or has it resulted in something worthy of the aspiration that preceded it? Has it added strength to the lives of individuals, and has it done something for society? As chronicler, I stand in the shade and let my readers judge; but the few words of comment that follow, from well-known individuals, bear strong testimony to an effect that must have been duplicated in a great many other instances: and, indeed, if its influence had gone no farther than to a few persons, that alone would justify the laudable attempt of this "venture in philanthropy." My conviction is that it reached farther than to single individuals, and that it still reaches into and influences more or less all the deep undercurrents of society.

I am confirmed in this opinion by the following statement made by Mr. George P. Bradford in the *Century Magazine* for May, 1892: —

" I cannot but think that the brief and imperfect experiment, with the theory and discussion that grew out of it, had no small influence in teaching more impressively the relation of universal brotherhood and the ties that bind us to all; a deeper feeling of the rights and claims of others, and so in diffusing, enlarging, deepening and giving emphasis to the growing spirit of true democracy."

But if I were to leave my position as narrator, and speak from my individual standpoint, I would say Brook Farm and what it stood for was to world-benighted travellers, seeking for sustenance, like a city set on a hill. It was a small, glimmering light of social truth, shining amid universal darkness. It was a dim foregleam of the great sun of social life and science, that will yet rise and shine gloriously on our earth. It was a spark of that divine justice that, like electricity, has been stored for humanity from the beginning of things — abundant in quantity and power to bless all men — stowed away by the hand of God for us, awaiting only our awakening from the sleep of ignorance and childishness, to use and cherish it. It was an example of trust, a tribute to faith. It was a realization of poetry. It was in touch with the wishes, hopes and prayers of millions of humanity; of untold numbers of saints and martyrs of all nations and climes, and its mission was the highest on earth — universal justice to all mankind.

Albert Brisbane, the *doctrinaire*, has departed also Although allusion has been made to him in the forme pages of this book somewhat in contrast with Mr. Ripley's spiritual gifts, let no person think that I underestimate the mission he undertook or the work he accomplished in his devotion to the master, Fourier. Certainly he deserves very great credit, and there are those who, deep in their hearts, cherish most profound gratitude to him and his memory.

Whatever any one may believe of the feasibility of the carrying out of Fourier's doctrines of united industry or the practicality of any of his theories, they must stand amazed at the bold and often extremely beautiful

conceptions of his brain; such as the actual forecasting
of the development theory before Darwin, Spencer and
Huxley were born — though not exactly in detail with
them; his bolder conception still of the destiny of man,
and his Cosmogony; of the progress of present civilization towards an oligarchy of capital, foretold so exactly,
— as is now seen by thinking minds, three quarters of a
century ago; his profound analysis of the human springs
of action; his discovery of the divine laws applicable to
the future as well as to the present wants of the human
race. For the presentation of all this to the American
people; for all these things and more, we are first indebted to Albert Brisbane, and it is a great debt which
the future will certainly appreciate and pay.

My work would not be finished without alluding
more fully to the wonderful genius whose works and
life made such an impression on the Brook Farmers as
to induce them to brave all the misconception, sarcasm
and obloquy that they must have felt would be heaped
on them when they concluded to follow his formulas,
and bowed their intellects to him in acknowledgment
of his leadership in the field of social science.

The reader will decide, if I have portrayed truly the
men and the principles actuating them, that whoever
they thus acknowledged as worthy of that sublime
place must have been endowed with intellectual, moral
and spiritual capacities, and intuitions of the highest
order. Should it have been the fortune of any one
to come across an occasional allusion to Fourier, it
will be apt to be of such a forbidding nature that there
will be no strong temptation to follow the subject
further; and all through the literature of our country,

in the writings of men whose reading, if not their knowledge, should have taught them better, will be found intimations that "Fourierism" was a system of life based on a plane hardly worthy of being rated higher than mere sensualism.

Against this accusation I place the record of the man whom especially spiritual minded and liberally educated men like George Ripley, John S. Dwight, William Henry Channing and many others delighted to know and to honor.

Charles Fourier was born at Bezancon, France, April 7, 1772. The son of a merchant, he had a collegiate education, and took prizes for French and Latin themes and verses. He was found of geography but more fond of cultivating flowers, and of music. At eighteen years he entered into commercial pursuits. By the siege of Lyons he lost the fortune his father left him, and was forced into the army, where he served two years. This portion of his life was involved in the romance of war and revolution, during which he was doomed to death, but made a fortunate escape from it.

He was always noted for the avidity with which he sought knowledge, and his honesty was outraged at an early age, being punished by his father for telling the truth of goods on sale, thereby losing a purchaser. Again his soul revolted when at Marseilles in 1799, where he was employed, for he was selected to superintend a body of men who secretly cast an immense quantity of rice into the sea, which monopolists had allowed to spoil in a time of famine rather than to sell at a reasonable profit. This last action was to him a crime

of so deep a nature that he entered with more en-
thusiam on his studies for preventing the like.

In capacity of agent he travelled in France, Belgium,
Germany, Holland and Switzerland. He had a prodigious memory, and in his journeys when a building
struck his attention, he took the measurement of it
with his walking stick, which was notched off in feet
and inches; and, one of his biographers says,

"he was profoundly acquainted with every branch of
science, particularly the exact sciences. For forty years
he labored with patience and perseverance at the Herculean task of discovering and developing the theory
and practical details of the system which he has given
to the world."

Says a writer in the London *Phalanx:* —

" The principal features of Fourier's private character
were morality and the love of truth. He had a character both grave and dignified, religious and poetic,
friendly and polite, indulgent and sincere, which never
allowed truth to be profaned by libertine frivolity, nor
faith to be confounded with austere duplicity. He was
a man of dignified simplicity, a child of Heaven, loving God with all his heart, all his soul, and all his mind,
also loving as himself his neighbor — the whole human
family."

Fourier's own words translated says: —

" God sees in the human race only one family, all
the members of which have a right to his favors. He
designs that they shall all be happy together, or else no
one people shall enjoy happiness. . . . The love of God
will become in this new order the most ardent love
among men."

The closing words of an exhaustive review of Fourier's
writings, by Mr. John S. Dwight, in the *Harbinger*, are
these: —

"There is a Titanic strength in all the workings of that wonderful intellect. He walks as one who knows his ground. His step is firm, his eye is clear and unflinching, and he is acknowledged where he passes, for there is no littleness or weakness, no halting or duplicity, in his movement. He is in earnest; he has taken up his cross to fulfil a mighty mission. He doubts not, desponds not; he speaks always with certainty, and though he suffers from impatience of postponement, yet he ceases not to insist upon the truth. He expostulates, perhaps, with deceived and degraded humanity in too much bitterness of sarcasm; but how profound his reverence for Christ and for humanity, how pure his love for man, and how sublime his contemplation of the destiny of man in the scale of higher and higher beings up to God!"

Fourier passed from earth in 1837. His body was buried at Pere la Chaise Cemetery, Paris, France.

The idea of living in combined families is no new thing. From the earliest times to the present, it has cropped out under various circumstances and with various changes. Ever with dawning of new light and the increase of universal education comes the desire — sometimes in great waves — for more united interests, and a truer, more Christian brotherhood; for closer unity in life and for the enlargement of home with all the joy, comfort and peace that word contains.

In this country various outgrowths from the social body have taken positions on this plane. The masses of our people are not now in sympathy with them. They believe that these little social homes or "communities" are dull and monotonous, and are bound so tightly by creeds as to be obnoxious to freedom of life and ideas. My belief is that the creeds adopted and

thrown around them, though often adding to their
financial protection, and possibly often being their only
safeguards from fraud and knavery, have covered from
the public the great dignity, worthiness and beauty of
this mode of life; when, therefore, Mr. Ripley formed
his society free from any pledges or creeds, it touched
a deeper bottom in men's hearts than any like organization had ever sounded.

Whatever of failure there was in their actualization,
Brook Farm ideas remain. They charm philosophers,
poets and statesmen. They work quietly, leavening
the social mass. One must be in sympathy with them
to know how potent is their action and how with a
touch of the old enthusiasm they will be found breaking out again in larger and larger circles of humanity,
for in view of the progress of mechanism, science and
art in the last fifty years, to form the phalanstery in its
material shape would be an easy task.

Rev. William Henry Channing expressed himself in
this wise to his mother, years after the breaking up of
the Association : —

"My dearest mother, I assure you that did I see my
way clear to an honorable independence for my family,
so as to be just, while kind to them, I should joyfully
die in attesting my fixed faith in Association, and I
predict that when, years hence, we meet in the spiritual
world, you will smilingly bless me and say, 'My son,
your personal limitations excepted, you were right.'
You will feel proud of my seeming earthly failures
then; at least I humbly hope so. If this is all romance
it is of that earnest, living strain which I trust ever
more and more to be quickened by."

At a final visit to Brook Farm he said: " Most beautiful was that last day and all its memories; and never did I feel so calmly, humbly, devoutly thankful that it had been my privilege to fail in this grandest, sublimest, surest of all human movements. Were Thermopylæ and Bunker Hill considered successes in their day and generation?"

Lying before me is a letter not intended for publication, showing how one member of the Association affectionately regarded his old home. It is as follows:—

"PROVIDENCE, R. I., 1871.

"MY DEAR FRIEND:— I herewith return the letters you so kindly sent me. I have derived much pleasure in their perusal, and have looked on them with affectionate regard as a mode of greeting from old friends from whom I have been separated for more than a quarter of a century. I do not think any one who was at Brook Farm has that deep and sincere affection for it and its memory that I have. It was my mother by adoption, and what little I have of education, refinement, or culture and taste for matters above things material, I owe to her and the heroic and self-sacrificing men and women who composed its body, social and scholastic. I was but a cipher there, among them by accident, and I was much the gainer even if they were not the losers. What I saw there, and what I learned there, have been of great value to me, and if I have made any progress in material matters or have attained any social position, I am frank enough to confess that I owe it all to dear old Brook Farm. God bless its memory. What I have, and what I am, is the outgrowth of a two years' life at my first real home. . . .

"When I commenced this I intended to write but a half dozen lines, simply making my acknowledgment of your kindness, but my purpose soon changed, and I now find that I have not enough room on this sheet to say one tithe of what comes rushing in my mind 'as a river' about Brook Farm, and I can now only say that I wish you to convey my kindest regards to all of our dear old acquaintances whenever you see them or write to them. All Brook Farmers are to me as brothers and sisters, and I so esteem them.

"WILLIAM H. TEEL."

I am tempted also to add the following extract from a letter written years ago by a friend of the movement in his eightieth year to his son : —

"To many, Brook Farm may have been a dream that ended with the scattering of that little band of workers. That special form of the dream vanished, but the seed was planted, and my confidence in the dream is vivid still. In the past these ideas have been the crude visions of the few, but now they are the absorbing subjects of speculation of the many, and all our best literature is full of them. The highest problems of man and society are the common subjects of discussion. So will it continue to be, by the tiller of the soil, the workman at the bench, as well as the poet and philosopher, until order and harmony are evolved out of this chaos. The good time is surely coming. 'The world,' as Whittier wrote, · is gray with its dawning light.'

"J. A. SAXTON.

"Deerfield, Mass."

Well, the Brook Farm experiment died! There can be only one reason why its friends should rejoice, and it is the same that touched the great mind of Saint Paul, nearly two thousand years ago, when he said, "Thou fool! that which thou sowest is not *quickened* except it *die!*"

FINIS.

APPENDIX

I.

Students' and Inquirers' Letters

II.

Applicants' Letters and Mr. Ripley's Replies

III.

An Outside View of Brook Farm
Associative Articles

APPENDIX. PART I.

Student Life.

BROOK FARM, MASS., Oct. 27, 1842.

MY DEAR FRIEND: — Pardon my delay in writing
you in reply to yours of the 15th ult., but there have
been matters of interest that have occupied my leisure,
and so much so that only now do I find myself free to
exchange good wishes with you and to answer the important questions you put to me as to what I think of,
and how I like, the Brook Farm life.

To reply to these questions I might write a long
dissertation explaining what I like and what I do not
like, or I could answer them by a few brief words; but
my inclination is to do neither, and to give you in
place of both a little sketch of the proceedings here
and make you the judge of what my feelings would
be likely to be under the circumstances that I shall
narrate.

I am still a student, and most of my time has been
spent in studies of various sorts; the languages —
ancient and modern — attracting me a great deal, but
the German and the French the most. I do not " burn
the midnight oil," and yet I think I am progressing
well. Our teachers are all very approachable men and

really seem in dead earnest. You might suppose from rumors that reach you that they would be very notional people, but they are not so, or, to say the least, if they are they keep their notions to themselves. Mr. Dana, Mr. Bradford and Mr. Dwight are particularly kind to me, and all the teachers go out of the way to explain points that come up in the lessons.

After hours, we have had many interesting conversations, class readings, dramatic readings, etc., and visitors come who entertain us in various ways. Miss Frances Ostenelli, for one, who has a wonderful soprano voice, and Miss S. Margaret Fuller from Concord — there is no end to her talk — and also Mr. Emerson from Concord, to whom a good many pay deference.

Whilst he was here there was a masquerading wood party. It was quite a bright idea. Miss Amelia Russell was one of the persons who planned it. Her father has been minister to Sweden and was one of the commissioners who signed the Treaty of Ghent. It was an open-air masquerade in the pine woods, and the affair was worked up splendidly. Masquerades have been, in New England, of a private nature and held indoors. To hold one out " in the garish light of day " was a new sensation, and attracted some of the friends of the Community. The day was lovely and in the woods the privacy was complete. Barring one or two friendly neighbors of farmer stock who looked on, it was truly a select party. One of the ladies personated Diana, and any one entering her wooded precincts was liable to be shot with one of her arrows. Further in the woods a gipsy, personated by Miss 'Ora Gannett, niece to Rev. Ezra Gannett, was ready to tell your fortune. Miss " Georgie " Bruce was an Indian squaw, and " George William " Curtis, a young man, carried off the palm as " Fanny Elssler " the dancer. There was a mixed variety of characters that made up the *tout ensemble* — a Tyrolean songster, sailors, Africans, lackeys, backwoodsmen and the like. The children enjoyed the day much. A large portion of the dresses were home-made. Dances and conversation by the elders filled the day and evening.

Sometimes we have the serious business. Some of the singular persons here affect vagaries and discuss pruderies or church matters, ethics and the like. Or we have some of the Concord people who give us parlor talks. Once in a while they arouse the gifted brothers, and then we have a genuine treat; Mr. Dwight and Mr. Bradford, Mr. Ripley, Mr. Capen, Burton and all hands get dragged in, and in the earnest discussion that follows one cannot but be edified and often very much instructed. Subjects relating to a more rational life and education for the poor and unlearned interest me and arouse my enthusiasm. There are some fine lady as well as gentlemen readers, who show their ability in poetry and prose, and, for the amusement of the young people, some devote their talents on occasions to tableaux, which are delightful and display fine historic scenes and characters.

I rise in the morning at six to half-past; breakfast at seven; chat with the people; get to my studies at eight; work an hour in the garden; recite; dine at noon; take an hour in the afternoon on the farm; drive team; cut hay in the barn; study or recite; walk; dress up for tea at six. In long days the sunsets and twilights are delightful and pass pleasantly with a set of us who chum together. I am so near Boston that I go to concerts and lectures with others, or to the theatres, or to the conventions, the antislavery ones being most exciting. In summer I join the hay-makers. In winter we coast, boys and girls, down the steep though not high hills, in the afternoons, or by moonlight, or by the light of the clear sky and the bright stars; or we drive one of the horses for a ride, or we skate on the frozen meadow or brook to the Charles River where its broad surface gives plenty of room.

One thing I like here — everything but in my lessons I have perfect freedom to come or go and to join in and be one with the good people or not. I am not hampered. I go to church or not, as I desire, and I can do anything that does not violate the rules of good breeding; but I am expected to be in my room at a seasonable hour at night — ten o'clock, sure.

Thus have I given you my programme. Can you think I would do better elsewhere? I might have more style, a better table, and more room to see my friends in, though the parlors here are good enough, but where could I have more genuine comfort? I expect to go home by New Year's, returning, if I can, by March, and am so in love with the life I may try to attach myself to it permanently. In the meantime I will see you, and hope to enjoy with you many hours of conversation after the oldtime way at our house.

As ever,

Your student brother,

CHARLES.

Explanations and Answers to Objections.

BROOK FARM, MASS., Dec. 11, 1845.

FRIEND HARRIS: — As you are a stranger to the associative ideas, and have but little knowledge of our life here, no doubt many questions arise in your mind that you wish answered, and might be answered by me if I knew what they were; but knowing what questions usually appear most prominent to the average mind, I will try my hand at a few of them as they present themselves to me. Number one is, What were my first impressions of the idea of associative life; that is, did the idea strike me pleasantly or not? I frankly reply to this that the idea was decidedly unpleasant. It so connected itself in my mind with some sort of an "institution," as a great hospital or infirmary or "Dotheboys" school, where Smikes or incipient Smikes went daily to a restricted routine, and thrice daily, with the rest of imprisoned souls, to the special amount of grub and rations provided by some personal or impersonal Squeers, that I could not but at once reply to the person speaking of it that I should not like any such institution.

The next question is, How did my mind change on this subject? I answer, by reflection and continued conversation with those who were intimate with the ideas. Mark this: *There is nothing so absurd as the first presentation of great facts to the mind;* the greater the fact, the greater its apparent absurdity, and the greater will be our hate or want of welcome to it if it runs contrary to our preconceived ideas.

Every visible thing is presented to the retina of the eye, the looking-glass of the brain, upside down, and it is by study that begins at birth, and is finished ere remembrance commences, that the child of God and man is able to detect the true relation of material things to himself. We have not yet learned the importance or significance of this arrangement, but why may not we find in future investigations that the mental vision is governed by the same law, and that thoughts strike the brain or mental sensorium in the same inverted way? So universally do law and life differ from their semblances, that it appears to me to be one of our *supreme duties* to learn to *reverse primitive ideas*.

A question also comes to you in this wise: How could one make up his mind to associate with all sorts of people that they might meet in one of these " Communities "? A man in the ordinary chances of life has to meet all sorts of persons, does he not? Ignorant dependents are in your house, sleeping under your roof. Your tradesmen may be rude, unkind and unlettered. Passing from your door you jostle, it may be, the murderer and highwayman on the street; you enter a car, and the driver's breath is perhaps reeking from his last night's debauch; you sit, possibly, between the pickpocket on one side and the patient yet uncured from some epidemic on the other. You pass to your business through a street full of roughs, and in your own store are men wishing you to die that they may take your place, seeking every opportunity to overreach you; and then wonder if I smile when you ask me how *I* could " mix up."

In reply to me, you may say that the relation is

different; that you do not take these persons to your table and associate with them as one is obliged to in one of your "Associations." It is true that you may not sit at meat with these especial persons; but how many live at hotels where the next neighbor at table, to whom, if you are a gentleman, you show politeness, is entirely unknown to you, and may be a swindler, cheat or knave. But you associate with him only as much as it is *necessary* for you to do; and that is just as much as you are obliged to do in an Association, and no more. It does not follow because I sit at meat here at Brook Farm with a hundred, I have intimate social relations with all of them. On the contrary, there are those to whom I seldom speak unless to give them a passing salutation, and some who are civilly disposed, who do no more, or as much, to me.

In a society of which you might be a member, with a full privilege to assist in its organization, you will be better able to choose those of congenial qualities for associates than you ever can in your present position, so that your life, after a while, may be select in its chosen companions, and a great deal more so in its general social features than now.

Since I came here I find my ideas all changed in relation to this subject. Instead of the yoke that I felt would be on me, I find freedom — freedom to speak, to act, and a truly self-imposed government. The yoke I expected to find *is* very easy and the burden is light. I enjoy my life and home. We have not much of worldly goods, but we are united and we look high up — some say to cloud-land; but I assure you that on the average there is nowhere a clearer-headed set of persons on social questions than here, and association is now to me the most beautiful thing on earth. The life and ideas are all one with harmony. Surely is it not better for me to begin life this way than with doubt and distrust of my fellows? Doubt begets doubt; faith begets faith; action begets action. If we can get enough persons to follow us, we can prove whether our ideas are true or not. Surely the dull, monotonous life of "religious communities" like the Moravians, Shakers, Rappites and others find followers; why not this bright, happy, cheering, frank life of ours?

We are expecting a visit from Horace Greeley soon; I have never seen him, but we have heaps of strangers coming every day, some quite distinguished and some plain folks, but the average are wide-awake people.

Truly your friend,

JOHN C. FOSTER.

Letter on Social Equality.

BROOK FARM, MASS., Sept. 9, 1845.

MY DEAR SISTER: Do not think that the great minds here teach *social equality*, as many seem to think they do. To hear outsiders talk one would imagine that the leaders want that all should be of the same pattern; that the tall geniuses should be cut down to an average, and the dwarfs set up on stilts to make them of the same height as the others. How far from it!

Added to this indignity, outsiders appear to think that rations are served as in the army, and that it is an absolute necessity in order to fulfil some absurd law, that every man, woman and child should sit down to-

gether at the same exact time, and eat the aforesaid
rations together; and also, there being some good and
able men here, that they court connection with weak
people of any complexion so as to make a fair average:
and they feel that such conditions, to say the least, are
unnatural; and so would I, if there was truth in the
position, but there is not a particle. It oftentimes seems
to me that people take a sort of pleasure in misrepre-
senting facts, or seem to have a satisfaction in thinking
that they know about as much as the average person,
and that it would be a sin to know a little more. They
are pardoned for their ignorance because nearly, if not
all, the social organizations that have departed from the
common customs of society and have formed "communities" have striven for equality of property rights and
society rights, and often for sameness in dress and religious ceremonies. This is the nut that all persons
who look superficially at us and at the community system, find hard to crack. They feel that if a person has
an ambition to be more than another, to desire more, to
desire to wear a different garment and pray differently
or worship differently, they should have the inherent
right to do so.

And this is the feeling that these common-sense people, these intelligent people of Brook Farm who organized this society, have and believe in, and they have
tried to arrange all their laws and customs to conform
to these evident truths. And also, they never would
have adopted any of the formulas or ideas of Fourier,
had they not believed his Industrial Phalanxes
allowed all the variety of social conditions that make a
true society or social order. No attempts ever under-

taken had the sanction of Fourier, because they had not
the proper number of persons to make a start with.
" By no means," said Fourier, " attempt to organize a
phalanx with less than four hundred persons ; that is
the very least number you can have and have a sufficient
number of characters to produce anything like harmony."
His idea was, that from fifteen to eighteen hundred persons would be the true number.

The Brook Farmers have never preached social
equality, but social *rights*.   Social *equality* is a thing
that comes from individual ability, and is never posi-
tively fixed, but relative, because there are talents superior and inferior mingled in each human being, and the
king may wonder how the cook put the apples in the
dumplings.   With the larger number of individuals
stated, a greater chance is given to find " mates " and
" chums," and the less likelihood there would be in the
imperfectly organized societies of rude contact — for who
could doubt that all such societies, even the very best,
would be imperfect for generations to come ?

I take it that this is the gist of the reason why the
so-called social equality is so repulsive to theorists who
have not comprehended the great difference between
social *equality* and social *rights*.   Once and for all, I do
not believe, we do not believe, in social equality; but
we do believe that societies can be established in such a
manner as to secure in a large degree the rights of all,
and be perfectly practicable, and that in time they will
develop into true harmony.

As ever your sincere

BROTHER CHARLIE.

Religious Views.

BROOK FARM, MASS., June 9, 1845.

MY DEAR FRIEND:— In reply to your question as to what the religious views of the Brook Farmers are, I might, if I wished to be curt, say that they are such as you see by their lives. I am aware, however, that such a reply will not exactly suit you, and that you really mean what are their creeds, as, are they all Baptists, Trinitarians, Unitarians, or what not? And I answer you that I find here those who were brought up in every kind of belief; some who are from the Roman Catholic Church; some from the Jewish; some Trinitarians; some Unitarians; some from the Swedenborgian Church; some who are Liberals; some who are called "Come-Outers," and Mr. P., who professes to be, and is more like an infidel than any other man I ever saw.

They call some of the residents here "Transcendentalists." You may judge from the name that they must be either very good or very bad people, but they represent people of education who are a little "high stilted" in their religious views, and do not take in all the wonderful Mosaic traditions. At least, this is as near as I can explain it to you. It is the fashion to call every one who has any independent notions a Transcendentalist, but I do not know who invented the name or first applied it.

The people here do not dispute on religious creeds; they are too busy. They work together, dine and sup together year in and year out in intimate social relation, and do not either have angry disputes, or quarrels about creeds or anything else. On the contrary, I am much surprised at the earnest inquiry that is often made into the beliefs of others, or rather into the groundwork or foundation from which the churches sprung which have different tenets from their own.

But the majority are Unitarian in their belief. Mr. Ripley, Mr. Dwight, Mr. Dana and Mr. Cabot, with a majority of the ladies, lean that way. Dr. Lazarus and his handsome sister are of or from the Jewish faith, whilst Mr. Hastings leans towards Romanism and Jean Pallisse is Catholic; and by the way, I never until I came here had any sympathy with the symbols of that church, but the intelligent persons by whom I have been surrounded have explained the great beauty of them to me — persons who are not and never can be Romanists any more than myself. Dr. Lazarus has posted me on the Jewish symbols, and Fanny M. and her mother have brought forward the great beauty of the Swedenborgian doctrines.

All Mr. Ripleys's writings on social subjects breathe a religious air. It is true they are not creedal, but his idea is that every act of life should be from a true and earnest spirit, and that this is the substance of all creeds; and strange to say to you, who believe that Associations like ours have a levelling effect, those who have their faiths fixed, say, " I think more of the symbols of my church than ever, since I came here."

" I am a Jew, but a liberal, understanding Jew," says one.

" I am a Catholic, but I am a liberalized Catholic," says another.

" I am a Swedenborgian, but my belief liberates me from the crudities of Swedenborg," say others.

" I look from the centre outward as never before. We all see how the forms of our churches were intended for good, and we all see how many of them have been prostituted. When I go from here I shall respect your forms and ceremonies because you have taught me the meanings of them."

Is this definite enough for a hasty answer? The lesson I have most taken to heart is that by examining with respect the many different faiths, we gain a higher idea of a Being who has an exhaustless variety in his attributes.

As ever yours,

C. J. THOMAS.

APPENDIX. PART II.

APPLICANTS' LETTERS AND MR. RIPLEY'S REPLIES.

[Copies of some of these letters and other documents from the originals were used by permission, in preparing the " Life of George Ripley."]

From a Theological Student.

LONGMEADOW, Feb. 25, 1845.

Rev. George Ripley,

DEAR SIR: Probably you have forgotten the Andover student who spent Thanksgiving with you a year ago, and who made you a short call last September. But he has not forgotten Brook Farm. I write now for the purpose of asking a single question. Are you so full that it will be impossible for you to take one more in the course of a few weeks?

I recollect you asked me last fall if I intended to go to preaching against sin in the church. I agree with you, sir, that there is emphatically sin in the church that ought to be preached against, if anywhere. But the truth is I do not see as much sin either in the church or out of it as my theological teachers have endeavored to persuade me there is. Besides, I think that preaching against it has been proved to be a very ineffectual way of rooting out what sin there is. Indeed, from the very nature of the case, it seems to me that telling men once a week, at arm's length, that they are doing very wrong and will be eternally punished unless they do differently, is not quite what is needed for improving their character and condition. For this reason, and because my faith in other respects also is not sufficiently orthodox, I have braced myself as well as I could against the urgent importunities of my friends, and refused to take a license.

My strongest sympathies are with the cause in which you are laboring, and I am not wholly without hope that I shall yet find something to do in it. I am utterly alone here. I think often of what Carlyle says, "Invisible yet impenetrable walls as of enchantment divided me from all living."

Will you do me the kindness, sir, to answer the inquiry I have made of you as soon as convenient?

Yours most respectfully,

D. B. COLTON.

Letter from a Young Man.

COLCHESTER, CT., Nov. 1, 1843.

Rev. *George Ripley,*

SIR : My ideas of the principles of Industrial Association have been obtained by reading the New York *Tribune.* I am convinced that these principles are the elements out of which may be constructed that true social order which shall develop man's physical well-being, and call forth the mental and moral faculties of the soul.

My intention is to join some association of the kind now forming or already in operation. Your Community has been spoken of as one of the first and best in the country. My object in writing to you is to ascertain the peculiar nature of this organization and management, the terms of membership — the amount of capital required, or whether one without capital would be received — and whether a young man of the following description would find opportunity to *work* and receive a *fair* remuneration for his labor.

What I can *do* you can judge. I am twenty-five years of age, have lived eight years in New York, six years in one of the best wholesale dry goods houses there. Brought up at this place a mechanic and farmer, and am now engaged in wagon making and blacksmithing, for which I don't get a red cent beyond a good living.

The capital that I intended to invest in Association gone to Davy Jones' locker in the wreck of the commercial world.

An answer to these few inquiries would much oblige

Your obedient servant,

HORATIO N. OTIS.

Reply to Preceding Letter.

[The preceding letter has the following draft of a reply to it on a letter sheet in the handwriting of Mr. Ripley.]

MY DEAR SIR : Yours of the 1st inst. is this day received. I dare say that you have received a correct impression of our establishment from the article in the *Tribune*. We are laboring with cheerfulness and hope, in the midst of great obstacles, for the organization of society and the benefit of man. Whoever wishes to join us must be willing to make great sacrifices; to endure severe toil patiently ; to live in comparative poverty; to suffer many deprivations for the sake of realizing justice and charity in the social state.

We are at present on a small scale, but we are making arrangements to enlarge our number and our branches of industry. We should like to establish your branch of business, and could do so to advantage with an efficient and skilful workman and a small increase of capital. An answer to the following questions will decide whether we can have any further negotiations with you:—

1. Are you ready from an interest in the cause of Association to endure the sacrifices which all persons must suffer?

2. Could you by yourself, or your friends, command a few hundred dollars sufficient to start your business?

3. Could you, without help, make and iron off ox carts, horse carts, one horse wagons, etc., in a style that would ensure their sale in the neighborhood of Boston? Can you shoe horses and oxen ?

4. Are you single or married?

5. In fine, have you confidence that by your manual labor in the branches you have mentioned, you could do more than earn your living in Association?

I shall be happy to hear from you as soon as convenient. I am

Yours truly,

GEORGE RIPLEY.

A Model Questioner — a Woman.

UTICA, Jan. 18, 1844.

SIR: I have the happiness of being acquainted with a lady who has some knowledge of you; from whose representations I am encouraged to hope that you will not only excuse the liberty I (being a stranger) thus take in addressing you, but will also kindly answer a number of questions I am desirous of being informed upon relative to the society for social reform to which you belong.

I have a daughter (having five children) who, with her husband, much wishes to join a society of this kind. They have had thoughts of engaging with a society now forming in Rochester, but their friends advise them to go to one that has been some time in operation, because those connected with it will be able to speak with certainty as to whether the working of the system in any way realizes the theory. The first question I would put is, —

1. Have you room in your association to admit the above family?

2. And if so, upon what terms would they be received?

3. Would a piano-forte, which two years ago cost three hundred and fifty dollars, be taken at its present value in payment for shares?

4. Would any household furniture be taken in the same way?

5. Do you carry out Mr. Fourier's idea of diversity of employment?

6. How many members have you at this time?

7. Do the people (generally speaking) appear happy?

8. Does the system work well with the children?

9. Would a young man (mechanic of unexceptionable character) be received having no capital?

10. Have you more than one church, and if so what are its tenets?

11. Have parties opportunities of enjoying any other religion?

12. What number of hours generally employed in labor?

13. What chance for study?

14. Do you meet with society suitable to *your taste?*

Although my questions are so numerous that I fear tiring you, yet I still feel that I may have omitted some inquiry of importance. If so will you do me the favor to *supply the deficiency?*

Please to answer my questions by number, as they are put.

Hoping you will write as soon as possible, and do me the kindness I ask,

I remain,

Yours respectfully,

A. HUDSON.

From a Minister.

NORTH BRAMFORD, CONN., June 1, 1843.

Mr. G. Ripley,

DEAR SIR: — I have an earnest and well matured desire to join your community, with my family, if I can do it under satisfactory circumstances — I mean satisfactory to all parties.

I am pastor of the First Congregational Church in this town. My congregation is quiet, and in many respects very pleasant; but I have felt that my views of late are not sufficiently in accordance with the forms under which I have undertaken to conduct the ministry of Christian truth. This want of accordance increases, and I feel that a crisis is at hand. I must follow the light that guides me, or renounce it to become false and dead. The latter I cannot do.

I have thought of joining your association ever since its commencement. Is it possible for me to do so under satisfactory circumstances? I have deep and, I believe, an intelligent sympathy with your idea. I have a wife and four children — the oldest ten, the youngest seven years old. Our habits of life are very simple, very independent of slavery to the common forms of "gigmanity," and our bodies have not been made to waste and pine by the fashionable follies of this generation. It is our creed that life is greater than all forms, and that the soul's life is diviner than *convenances* of fashion.

As to property, we can bring you little more than ourselves. But we can bring a hearty good-will to work, and in work we have some skill. I have unimpaired health, and an amount of muscular strength beyond what ordinarily falls to the lot of mortals. In the early part of my life I labored on a farm, filling up my leisure time with study, until I entered my present profession. My hands have some skill for many things, and if I join you I wish to live a true life.

My selfish aims are two: first, I wish to be under circumstances where I may live truly; and second, and chiefly, I wish to do the best thing I can for my children.

Be so good as to reply to this at your earliest convenience.

Yours sincerely,

JOHN D. BALDWIN.

From an Ohioan.

CHEVIOT, HAMILTON CO., O., Sept. 23, 1845.

Mr. Ripley,

MY DEAR SIR: — I have been looking somewhat into your plan of Association, and have read carefully Godwin's "Popular View of the Doctrines of Charles Fourier." I see much that I admire and some things that I disapprove in Fourier's views. His views on marriage and his ideas of a future state may do harm to his system of Association: first, in exciting prejudice against it, and so preventing a fair experiment; and secondly, in being adopted by friends of Association in their admiration of their great master.

His views in respect to love are, to my mind, exceedingly exceptionable, and the idea of making provision in

Association for those whose love is inconstant, *appears to me contrary to all sound philosophy.* A vicious constitution ought never to be fostered by indulgence. But I really hope that your Association, which I presume will be the model one for this country, will be careful to reject the exceptionable morality of the French teacher, and while you adopt his practical scheme in its worthy features, will also make it manifest that you esteem Jesus Christ as the true Master.

I may say that the more I compare the principles of Association adopted by you, with the general state of society, the more I admire the former and become dissatisfied with the latter. I feel great anxiety for your success. I feel deeply anxious that the friends of Association should be students of the gospel of Christ, that care might be taken to carry out the glorious doctrines of the Son of God. I do not mean sectarianism. I mean that religion, that pure morality, that spirituality which Jesus Christ exhibited in his own life; not the religion of the *ascetic,* but the social, the benevolent, the philanthropic, the Godward aspirations of the spiritual man.

My wife and myself often converse about the propriety of uniting with you. We become disgusted with the social arrangements with which we are connected. In worldly society we mourn over the outbreaking vices not only of the low, but of those who are highest in rank ; and when we seek satisfaction of mind and heart in the church, lo ! even there selfishness rules supreme, and a profession of religion covers up the meanest propensities of the sanctimonious worshipper. I cry out,

" Help, Lord ! for the godly man ceaseth ; for the faithful fail from among the children of men."

We desire to know through your own candid view of your prospects, as well as present condition, whether we may be justified in so disposing our affairs as to ultimately join your Association. At present I am laboring on my farm, near Cincinnati, having no definite plan of future action.

Please write me definitely upon what terms we may join you, how much I must put into the Association to secure the support of my family and myself — it being understood that we take hold as the rest of you do. Besides my wife I have a son sixteen years of age, another eleven, a third seven and a daughter four. We are all healthy, and I believe are about as well disposed as most families to live by our own personal exertions.

Yours very respectfully,

WILLIAM H. BRISBANE.

Verbatim Letter.

BOSTON MASS. Feb. 23 1844.

Mr. Ripley

DIR SIR I was requsted to pit the following on paper for the consideration of your society. R. H. wife and four children the oldest ten the youngest thre the two eldest boys, the two youngest girles. Furniture wile consist of thre beds and bedding one bedstead one tabel and workstand six or eight chairs crockery ware &c. Tooles and machinery as follows 1 planing machine 1 upright boaring machine 1 circular saw, irons for an upright saw morticing machine 1 turning lathe and belting 1 doz of hand screws 1 copper pot to make varnish in, two dimejons 3–5 gls. each for varnish and oil tooles for cutting bench screws &c likewise 1 cow 3 cosset sheep 1 yew & 2 wethers the cow 11 years old and little lame in one foot otherways a veryry good cow, also a verry light handcart. There are other articles not mentioned perhaps that might be usful to the Association that would be thrown in for the benefit of all.

The Association can consider the above articles and select wat articles would be usful or beneficial and let me know their action thereon at the next meeting of the Association If I should be called to visit my family before the next meeting you will pleas direct a line to me

Yors —

Robert Day.

The Brook Farm wits would say that the writer of the above letter should go to college " for a *spell*."

Seeking Success in Life.

Lockport, Oct. 28, 1842.

Dear Friends, if I may so call you: I read in the New York *Tribune* a piece taken from the *Dial*, headed " The West Roxbury Community." Now what I want to know is, can I and my children be admitted into your society, *and be better off than we are here?* I have enough of the plainest kind to eat and wear. I have no *home* but what we hire from year to year. I have *no property* but movables, and not a cent to spare when the year comes round. I have *three children*, two boys and one girl: the oldest fourteen, the youngest nine. Now I want to educate them. How shall I do it in the country? There is no chance but ordinary schools. To move into the village I could not bring the year round, and the danger they would be exposed to without a father to restrain their wanderings, would be an undertaking more than I dare attempt.

Now if you should presume to let me come, where can I live? Can our industry and economy clothe us for the year? Can I keep a cow? How can I be supplied with fire in that *dear place?* How can I *pay my school bills?* How can I find all the necessary requisites for my children to advance in learning? If I should wish to leave in two or three or five years, could I and mine, if I paid my way whilst there? If you should let me come, and I *think best to go, how shall I get there? What would be my *best and cheapest route?*

How should I proceed with what I have here, sell all off or bring a part? I have three beds and bedding, one cow and ordinary things enough to keep house. My children are all called tolerable scholars. My daughter is the youngest; *the neighbors call her an interesting child.* I have no pretensions to make; my only object is to *enjoy the good of the society* and have my children *educated and accomplished.*

Am I to send my boys off to work alone, or will they have a *kind person* to say, " *Come boys,*" and *relieve me from the heavy task of bringing up my boys* with nothing to *do it with?*

If your religion has a name I should like well enough to know it; if not, and the substance is love to God and good-will to men, my mind is well enough satisfied.

I have reflected on this subject ever since I read the article alluded to, and now I want you to write me *every particular;* then if you and I think best, in the spring I will come to you. We are none of us what may be called weakly. I am forty-six years old; able to do as much every day as to spin what is called a day's work — not that I expect you spin much there, only that is the amount of my strength as it now holds out.

I should wish to seek *intelligence,* as you must know I lack greatly, and I *cannot endure the thought* my children must lack as greatly, whilst multitudes are going so far in advance, no better qualified by nature than they. I want you to *send me quite a number of names of your leading characters.* If it should seem strange to you that I make the demand, I will explain it to you when I get there. I want you to answer *every item* of this letter and as much more as *can have any bearing on my mind,* either way, whether you accept this letter *kindly or not.* I want you to write an answer without delay! Are there meetings for *us to attend?* Do you have singing schools?

I do thus far feel friendly to your society.

Direct your letter to, etc.

M. R. JOHNSON.

A Southern Applicant.

ALEXANDRIA, BENTON CO., ALA., July 13, 1845.
Mr. G. Ripley,

DEAR SIR: Will you step aside for a moment from the many duties, the interesting cares and soul-stirring pleasures of your enviable situation, and read a few lines from a stranger?

They come to you, not from the cold and sterile regions
of the North, nor from the luxuriant yet untamed wilds
of the West, but from the bright and sunny land where
cotton flowers bloom, where nature has placed her sig-
net of beauty and fertility. Yes, sir; the science that
the immortal Fourier brought to light has reached the
far South, and I trust has warmed many hearts, and
interested many minds; but of ours alone will I write.

It is to me the dawn of a brighter day than has ever
yet risen upon the world — a day when man shall be
redeemed from his more than " Egyptian bondage" and
stand erect in moral, intellectual and physical beauty.

I have lived forty years in the world, and divided that
time between the eastern, middle and southern states
— have seen life as exhibited in city and country, have
mingled with the most intelligent and with the unlettered rustic — have marked society in a variety of phases,
and find, amid all, that selfishness has warped the judgment, chilled the affections and blunted all the finer
feelings of the soul. I am weary and worn with the
heartless folly, the wicked vanity and shameless iniquity
which the civilized world everywhere presents. Long
have I sighed for something higher, nobler, holier than
aught found in this world, and have sometimes longed
to lay my body down where the weary rest, that my
spirit might dwell in perfect harmony. But since the
beautiful science of unity has dawned upon my mind,
my heart has loved to cherish the bright anticipations
of hope, and I see in the dim distance the realization of
all my wishes. I see a generation coming on the arena
of action bearing on their brows the impress of their
noble origin, and cultivating in their hearts the pure

and exalted feelings that should ever distinguish those who bear the image of their Maker. Association is destined to do much for poor, suffering humanity — to elevate, refine, redeem the race and restore the purity and love that made the bowers of Eden so surpassingly beautiful. You, sir, and your associates are pioneers in a noble reform. May the blessing of God attend you.

I am anxious to be with you for various reasons. The first is: I have two little daughters whom I wish to bring up amid healthful influences, with healthful and untrammelled bodies, pure minds and all their young affections and sympathies clustering around their hearts. I never wish their minds to be under the influence of the god of this generation — fashion — nor their hearts to become callous to the sufferings of their fellows. I never wish them to regard labor as degrading, nor poverty as a crime. Situated as I am I cannot rear them in health and purity, and, therefore, I am anxious to remove them from the baneful influences that surround them. Again: I look upon labor as a blessing, and feel that every man and woman should spend some portion of each day in healthful employment. It is absolutely necessary to health, and is also a source of enjoyment, even in isolation; how much would that pleasure be increased could I have several kindred spirits around me with whom I could interchange thought, and whose feelings and desires flow in the same channel as my own! O, sir! I must live, labor and *die* in Association.

Again: my heart is pained with the woes of my fellows — with the distressing poverty and excessive labor which are bearing to the grave a portion of the human family. Gladly would I bear my part in raising them to a higher and happier condition; and how can I better do this than by uniting myself with the noble reformers of Brook Farm, where caste is thrown aside, and rich and poor constitute one family. I have not a large fortune, but sufficient to live comfortable anywhere. A large part of it is now invested in houses and lands in Georgia. Such is the low price of cotton that real estate cannot be sold at this time without a serious sacrifice. Most of my Georgia property rents for more than the interest of its cost at 8 per cent. I have also houses and land in this state, but cannot for the above named reason find a purchaser. Therefore, if I go into Association I shall be obliged to leave some of my possessions unsold, and be content to receive the rent until I can effect a sale.

I have no negroes — thank God. Now if you are not full at Brook Farm, and do not object to myself, wife and two daughters, one four years and the other six months old, presenting ourselves as candidates for admission, and $2500 or $3000 will be sufficient for an initiation fee, I shall, as soon as I can arrange my affairs, be with you.

I will thank you to write to me, informing me with how much ready cash, with an income of $500 or $600 per year, I can be received. Mrs. Clarke and myself will wish to engage daily in labor. We both labored in our youth — we wish to resume it again.

Very respectfully,

JOHN CLARKE.

The following letter is in manuscript without date and is

One of Mr. Ripley's Replies.

DEAR SIR: — It gives me the most sincere pleasure to reply to the inquiries proposed in your favor of the 3d inst. I welcome the extended and increasing interest which is manifested in our apparently humble enterprise, as a proof that it is founded in nature and truth, and as a cheering omen of its ultimate success. Like yourself, we are seekers of universal truth. We worship only reality. We are striving to establish a mode of life which shall combine the enchantments of poetry with the facts of daily experience. This we believe can be done by a rigid adherence to justice, by fidelity to human rights, by loving and honoring man as man, and rejecting all arbitrary, factitious distinctions.

We are not in the interest of any sect, party or coterie; we have faith in the soul of man, in the universal soul of things, and trusting to the might of a benignant Providence which is over all, we are here sowing in weakness a seed which will be raised in power. But I need not dwell on these general considerations with which you are doubtless familiar.

In regard to the connection of a family with us, our arrangements are liberal and comprehensive. We are not bound by fixed rules which apply to all cases. The general principle we are obliged to adhere to rigidly is not to receive any persons who would increase the expenses more than the revenue of the establishment. Within the limits of this principle we can make any arrangement which shall suit particular cases.

A family with resources sufficient for self-support, independent of the exertion of its members, would find a favorable situation with us for the education of its children, and for social enjoyment. An annual payment of $1000 would probably cover the expenses of board and instruction, supposing that no services were rendered to diminish the expense. An investment of $5000 would more than meet the original outlay required for a family of eight persons; but in that case an additional appropriation would be needed, either of productive labor or cash, to meet the current expenditures. I forward you herewith a copy of our Prospectus, from which you will perceive that the whole expense of a pupil, without including board in vacations, is $250 per annum; but in case of one or more pupils remaining with us for a term of years, and assisting in the labor of the establishment, a deduction of $1 or $2 per week would be made, according to the services rendered, until such time as their education being so far completed, they might defray all their expenses by their labor.

In the case of your son fifteen years of age, it would be necessary for him to reside with us for three months at least, and if at the end of that time his services should be found useful, he might continue by paying $150 or $200 per annum, according to the value of his labor, and if he should prove to have a gift for active industry, in process of time, he might defray his whole expenses, complete his education and be fitted for practical life.

With the intelligent zeal which you manifest in our enterprise, I need not say that we highly value your sympathy. I should rejoice in any arrangement which might bring us into closer relations. It is only from the faith and love of those whose hearts are filled with the hopes of a better future for humanity, that we look for the building up of our "City of God." So far we have been prospered in our highest expectations. We are more and more convinced of the beauty and justice of our mode of life. We love to breathe this pure, healthy atmosphere; we feel that we are living in the bosom of nature, and all things seem to expand under the freedom and truth which we worship in our hearts.

I should regret to think that this was to be our last communication with each other. May I not hope to hear from you again — and with the sincere wish that your views of the philosophy of life may bring you still nearer to us, I am, with great respect,

Sincerely your friend,
GEO. RIPLEY.

From a Lady Teacher.

NEW YORK, March 18, 1843.

DEAR SIR: For the last ten years I have been employed as a teacher in a boarding school in this city. A year ago the lady with whom I was associated died, and though I do not love business as such, there were many and weighty reasons why it seemed right for me to commence a school of my own. I have had during the winter past a school of twenty-three pupils consisting of children and youth. My success hitherto in teaching, in my own judgment, has been dependent on an earnestness of manner, a sincere love of knowledge and a deep interest in the welfare of the young. I know how to work and would not fear to undertake any kind of household occupation which devolves upon woman.

Early in life I embraced a religious faith, and, seeking to obey God according to my light, connected myself with a church. Years have passed away; experience, reflection and light from other minds have produced a radical change in my views. I stand in the eye of the world as one of a sect, but my spirit does not recognize the union. I am, from my position, subject to painful restraints. I cannot be just to the truth which is in me. The alternative, I need not say, with me is to hold fast to the popular faith or give up my bread.

I am much interested in those ideas which your Association is attempting to find a realization of. The state of things resulting from a full expansion of the principles upon which your society is based would seem to meet many spiritual wants. I can understand that so high an aim can be reached only through lowliness of life. The prospect of becoming one day a co-worker in your cause is very agreeable to me. I should like to know that I may be permitted to cherish the idea.

With much respect,

R. PRENTISS.

Application for an Unfortunate.

[The person who indited the following was a friend of the organization, and probably saw as well as anyone the absurdity of making a reformatory institution of the great experiment, but from kindly and personal considerations put the question and the best face on the matter that he could.]

New York, Sept. 14, 1845.

My Dear Friend : I have been applied to by a very respectable widow lady of this city, at the instance of Dr. —— (who it seems is fast getting over his want of sympathy for Fourier and his disciples), to see whether you will not convert Brook Farm into a sort of hospital for the cure of young men who won't mind their mothers. But, as the case is a serious one, I must treat it seriously as it deserves.

The lady is a Mrs. ——, who is connected with one or two of our wealthiest families, and who has a son about twenty-five years of age whom she desires to get a place with you.

He is said to be a person of the most kind and amiable disposition, and willing to do the hardest kind of work, but unfortunately he is surrounded by evil companions in this city, who draw him into bad habits. His mother is exceedingly distressed by his weakness, and has been counselled to send him to sea, but Dr. —— has advised her to come to me and ask whether he could not be taken on trial at Brook Farm, in order to ascertain what might be the effect of good influences. The young man is well educated, a good accountant, has worked considerably on a farm, and is exceedingly anxious to escape from his present position, where his *infirmity of will* betrays him under temptation. His general disposition and deportment are excellent, and under proper circumstances would make an estimable member of society.

If you have room for him, and are willing to undertake his case, his mother can contribute a few dollars a week toward paying his board, until it shall have been determined whether his longer stay would be mutually satisfactory. Should he be able to stay, no doubt his friends here would raise an amount of capital for him which might be an object worth considering.

Very sincerely yours,

P. GODWIN.

Wanted to Speak against Slavery.

COLLINSVILLE, CT., March 22, 1844.

FRIENDS: I call all people friends who have for their object the elevation of the human race and are opposed to all oppression in any form, who do not wish to build up one class at the expense of the other.

I have been reading on the subject of Association for the last six months all the publications I could find, which has pleased me much. I think it is just such a system that is wanted. Massachusetts being my native state, and also being acquainted with the vicinity of Roxbury, which I think is a delightful place, especially in the summer, I thought that I would write you to inquire if you have an opening for any more this spring providing I can bring recommendations to your satisfaction.

I was brought up a farmer; the last twelve years I have been to work in a scythe shop. I have a wife — no children. My wife is a tailoress, makes all kinds of men's clothing and is acquainted with all kinds of housework. We are both forty-two years of age. I shall want to buy four hundred dollars' worth of stock and pay for it when I join. If I am rightly informed of your system, it does not interfere with anyone's religion or his politics. Being an abolitionist, I shall want the privilege of voting and speaking against slavery in every respect.

Please write me as soon as you receive this and inform me what recommendations will be required and all other particulars.

Respectfully yours,
JAMES C. SMITH.

From a Wesleyan.

TRINITY, NEWFOUNDLAND, June 30, 1845.

SIR: Having been informed by Mr. Brisbane that an establishment on the united interest principle has been commenced near Boston, I hasten to address you to inform you that for some years I have felt impressed with its superiority to the individual system; and have been, and still am, anxious to engage heart and soul in so good a cause. I have been in this country between four and five years, and have a comfortable situation; but feeling confident of the ultimate advantage of an Association, and feeling assured that I could render myself valuable in such an establishment, I prefer casting my lot with those who feel desirous of acting for the restoration of man.

I have to inform you that from my youth I have chiefly engaged in the dry goods business, ironmongery, grocery, etc., and have a general knowledge of trade. I am of industrious habits and with an active turn of mind, and together with my wife, I may justly say, few will be found more useful and desirous of acting for the general good. I am about forty-two years of age, and my wife is a little older; my son is fourteen, and we are fully prepared for active life. I have no knowledge of any mechanical trade, but am fond of it as well as agriculture and gardening; I possess a fair share of health; am fond of writing and bookkeeping; only occasionally disposed to gaiety, but rather for scientific relaxation; not fanatical in religion, but a regarder of the great commandments and charitable for the feelings and the convictions of others.

I have, sir, given you an unvarnished statement with regard to myself, and I should feel obliged by your informing me at your earliest convenience if myself, wife and son can be admitted by my investing two hundred dollars for the furnishing of the apartment assigned to us. Are there any Wesleyans with you, and what is the distance to the Wesleyan chapel?—as my wife is a member of that body. From what I have learned from Mr. Brisbane's letter and newspaper he was kind enough to send me, I should judge your establishment to be such as we could safely and comfortably join, and I trust you will give me in your answer additional reason to think so.

I remain, sir,

Your obedient servant,

H. GAWLER.

From a Printer.

BANGOR, ME., Jan. 1, 1845.

Mr. George Ripley,

DEAR SIR: While on a visit to Brook Farm Association last August, it was intimated to me that it was probable, on the completion of the arrangements then in progress for the accommodation of an additional number of members, that a printing press might be introduced, a weekly paper published and something done at the printing business generally; further, that though there were two or three practical printers in the Association, yet others in all likelihood would also be required; in which case, a selection from the number of candidates would be made. Should it be the intention to adopt the plan, which was then in doubt, I beg most respectfully to present myself as a candidate for the acceptance of the Association.

I am at present situated as foreman of a daily paper in Bangor, and previous to this time, have had a somewhat varied experience in other branches of the business. Though now rather favorably located, in the ordinary acceptation of the term, yet I would prefer a thousand times mingling even in the struggles of an infant Association, founded upon what I deem to be substantial principles, than the most desirable possession in an overgrown and distorted civilization.

Touching the requisite of character, I believe I can make out a case in my favor; but with respect to capital — when I say I am a *printer*, I say also that I am in the predicament of the most of my profession, with nothing to recommend us but a willing heart and a ready hand; albeit, if the taking of one share of a hundred dollars will entitle me to membership, the amount may be forthcoming.

With sentiment of great respect,

I have the honor to be, sir,

Yours most obediently, etc.,

GEORGE BAYNE, Jr.

A Wife's Eloquent Appeal.

KINGSTON, Sept. 5, 1845.

Mr. George Ripley,

SIR: After taking the *Phalanx* and the *Harbinger* and visiting Brook Farm, our attachment and love for associated life has become so strong, and the idea of our present life so cold and to a benevolent mind so difficult, that I very much doubt of remaining any longer happy in our present state. For these reasons I write to inform you that we wish to make an application to be received as members of — so it looks to us — your happy Association; and, "delays being dangerous," we would ask an answer soon to it, as, living on a farm, it is necessary to know whether we shall dispose of our crops, cattle, etc., in the market, or store them in barn and cellar for another *lonely* winter — so my husband expresses it; though I assure you it is not lonely for lack of numbers, but he is doubtless expressing the feeling many of us have experienced of solitude in the midst of a crowd of uncongenial spirits.

As it is a busy time — we have to work from 5 A. M. until late at night, with scarce a moment to rest our weary limbs — it is not convenient to visit you personally; we wish you to return us a written letter stating whether we can have any encouragement and what are the requirements. Being strangers to you we would probably need recommendation.

Thus far I have acted as amanuensis for my husband. Hoping that it may not offend, I now address you of and from myself.   ELIZABETH BREWSTER,

for Elisha Brewster.

Mr. Ripley,

DEAR SIR: In the cause my husband urges I would plead. Had I skill I would do so with all the eloquence ascribed to woman's tongue; nay, more, had I an angel's tongue tipped with burning eloquence, I would exert its utmost efforts to urge my husband's suit. I feel deeply that his present and future earthly happiness depends on what answer may be received from you. That is saying much, but I believe it is strictly true. And if his happiness depends on it, surely that of the rest must, for what happiness does a woman desire but that of those connected with her? Husband has been for three years a devoted associationist; his whole heart and mind have been with them and he has ardently desired the associative life.

Not so myself. I was willing, it is true, to go anywhere he desired and would be happy where he was happy, but I dreaded to leave such a beautiful home, for the place we would leave is no ordinary one. The prospect from it is considered as almost without a parallel. We have plenty of fruit, flowers, fine grove and shade trees, in fact everything to make rural life agreeable and we know how to appreciate a beautiful location and prospect. Then I have had a fear of being a pioneer, lest there should be too heavy work or duties imposed or required of me. Such ideas combined, prevented me from seeing unitary life as one ought who knows that it is in the form of a heavenly society, and that as we desire perfection here on earth we must imitate the heavenly model.

Since visiting you my fears have given place to an

ardent desire to become one of your Community, not to
come as an alien and a stranger but as a sister in full
communion, with a heart full of love and affection and
with a strong desire to act my part fully and to do all
required of me.

You will find I have great skill and ingenuity in
work, understanding almost all kinds, and have, I am
told, a good faculty to plan and perform it, so I hope
that I shall be of real use to you. You will not think
I am trying to flatter you or myself. Husband's idea
is this: he says when people trade they place their com-
modities in the best light and speak of their desirable
qualities, and this is so much like trading ourselves off
that we have a right to give some idea of ourselves as
an offset for what we expect to receive.

Mr. Brewster has sound, unbroken health, untiring
strength and great skill and ability to work. He often
says he would not go where he could not work — but he
would like more time to read than he gets here. He
has great power and skill in doing heavy work and great
patience and industry in doing small and light work;
talents not often combined in one individual. He is
just as handy and skilful in planting and weeding and
planning a flower garden, or in potting plants and tending them, as in doing the heaviest work. He loves birds
and flowers, but *bees* are his *hobby*; he loves them as a
mother loves her children. If he comes among you, you
must let him have a hive of bees or I fear he would tire
of Association. Ah! a new thought just strikes me.
Bees are *associationists* and that accounts for his great
love of them.

I cannot believe that you will ever regret the possession of such a working man. Furthermore, you will rarely find two united with more willing hearts and hands and more cheerful tempers. We have never been, so far, either of us unhappy in any situation. Our family is not large; it consists of three daughters, one of eleven, one eight and the last three years of age, twenty-fifth of May last — they all have one birthday. We shall probably bring with us, if you make no objection, a girl who is bound to us, and there remains three years of unexpired service — a very stout, strong girl, who loves coarse work and who is Mr. Brewster's mesmeric subject.

Mr. Brewster is a lineal descendant of old Elder Brewster, of the fifth generation on the paternal side and a lateral descendant on the maternal side. He thinks that accounts for his being so ardent an associationist, as Elder Brewster started his colony on that plan and failed — and perhaps this E. Brewster will do the same thing. But seriously, because the first failed it is no reason that the second should, for the world was not as well prepared for unitary life then as now. Mr. Brewster thinks he would rather help you provide for winter than to be doing the same here.

May the blessing of Heaven attend you all at Brook Farm.

E. B. B. BREWSTER.

APPENDIX. PART III.

AN OUTSIDE VIEW OF BROOK FARM.

From the Dial of January, 1844.

Wherever we recognize the principle of progress our sympathies and affections are engaged. However small may be the innovation, however limited the effort towards the attainment of pure good, that effort is worthy of our best encouragement and succor. The institution at Brook Farm, West Roxbury, though sufficiently extensive in respect to number of persons, perhaps is not to be considered an experiment of large intent. Its aims are moderate ; too humble, indeed, to satisfy the extreme demands of the age ; yet for that reason, probably, the effort is more valuable, as likely to exhibit a larger share of actual success.

Though familiarly designated a " Community," it is only so in the process of eating in commons; a practice at least as antiquated as the collegiate halls of old England, where it still continues without producing, as far as we can learn, any of the Spartan virtues. A residence at Brook Farm does not involve either a community of money, of opinions or of sympathy. The motives which bring individuals there, may be as various as their numbers. In fact, the present residents are divisible into three distinct classes; and if the majority in numbers were considered, it is possible that a vote in favor of self-sacrifice for the common good would not be very strongly carried.

The leading portion of the adult inmates, they whose

presence imparts the greatest peculiarity and the fra-
ternal tone to the household, believe that an improved
state of existence would be developed in Association,
and are therefore anxious to promote it. Another class
consists of those who join with the view of bettering
their condition, by being exempt from some portion of
worldly strife. The third portion comprises those who
have their own development or education for their principal object.

Practically, too, the institution manifests a threefold
improvement over the world at large, corresponding to
these three motives. In consequence of the first, the
companionship, the personal intercourse, the social bearing, are of a marked and very superior character. There
may possibly to some minds, long accustomed to other
modes, appear a want of homeness and of the private
fireside; but all observers must acknowledge a brotherly
and softening condition, highly conducive to the permanent and pleasant growth of all the better human
qualities. If the life is not of a deeply religious cast,
it is at least not inferior to that which is exemplified
elsewhere, and there is the advantage of an entire absence of assumption and pretence. The moral atmosphere, so far, is pure; and there is found a strong desire to walk ever on the mountain tops of life; though
taste, rather than piety, is the aspect presented to the
eye.

In the second class of motives we have enumerated
there is a strong tendency to an important improvement
in meeting the terrestrial necessities of humanity. The
banishment of servitude, the renouncement of hireling
labor and the elevation of all unavoidable work to its

true station, are problems whose solution seems to be charged upon Association ; for the dissociate systems have in vain sought remedies for this unfavorable portion of human condition. It is impossible to introduce into separate families even one half of the economies which the present state of science furnishes to man. In that particular, it is probable that even the feudal system is superior to the civic ; for its combinations permit many domestic arrangements of an economic character, which are impracticable in small households. In order to economize labor, and dignify the laborer, it is absolutely necessary that men should cease to work in the present isolated, competitive mode, and adopt that of coöperative union or Association. It is as false and as ruinous to call any man " master," in secular business, as it is in theological opinion. Those persons, therefore, who congregate for the purpose, as it is called, of bettering their outward relations, on principles so high and universal as we have endeavored to describe, are not engaged in a petty design, bounded by their own selfish or temporary improvement. Everyone who is here found giving up the usual chances of individual aggrandizement, may not be thus influenced; but whether it be so or not, the outward demonstration will probably be equally certain.

In education Brook Farm appears to present greater mental freedom than most other institutions. The tuition being more heart-rendered, is in its effects more heart-stirring. The younger pupils, as well as the more advanced students, are held mostly, if not wholly, by the power of love. In this particular, Brook Farm is a much improved model for the oft-praised schools of New

England. It is time that the imitative and book-learned systems of the latter should be superseded or liberalized, by some plan better calculated to excite originality of thought and the native energies of the mind. The deeper, kindly sympathies of the heart, too, should not be forgotten; but the germination of these must be despaired of under a rigid hireling system. Hence Brook Farm, with its spontaneous teachers, presents the unusual and cheering condition of a really " free school."

By watchful and diligent economy, there can be no doubt that a community would attain greater pecuniary success than is within the hope of honest individuals working separately. But Brook Farm is not a community, and in the variety of motives with which persons associate there, a double diligence and a watchfulness perhaps, too costly will be needful to preserve financial prosperity. While, however, this security is an essential element in success, riches would, on the other hand, be as fatal as poverty, to the true progress of such an institution. Even in the case of those foundations which have assumed a religious character, all history proves the fatality of wealth. The just and happy mean between riches and poverty is, indeed, more likely to be attained when, as in this instance, all thought of acquiring great wealth in a brief time is necessarily abandoned, as a condition of membership. On the other hand, the presence of many persons, who congregate merely for the attainment of some individual end, must weigh heavily and unfairly upon those whose hearts are really expanded to universal results.

As a whole, even the initiative powers of Brook

Farm have, as is found almost everywhere, the design of a life much too objective, too much derived from objects in the exterior world. The subjective life, that in which the soul finds the living source and the true communion within itself, is not sufficiently prevalent to impart to the establishment the permanent and sedate character it should enjoy. Undeniably, many devoted individuals are there; several who have, as generously as wisely, relinquished what are considered great social and pecuniary advantages, and, by throwing their skill and energies into a course of the most ordinary labors, at once prove their disinterestedness, and lay the foundation for industrial nobility.

An assemblage of persons, not brought together by the principles of community, will necessarily be subject to many of the inconveniences of ordinary life, as well as to burdens peculiar to such a condition. Now Brook Farm is at present such an institution. It is not a community; it is not truly an association; it is merely an aggregation of persons, and lacks that oneness of spirit, which is probably needful to make it of deep and lasting value to mankind. It seems, after three years' continuance, uncertain whether it is to be resolved more into an educational or an industrial institution, or into one combined of both.

Placed so near a large city, and in a populous neighborhood, the original liability for land, etc., was so large as still to leave a considerable burden of debt. This state of things seems fairly to entitle the establishment to re-draw from the old world in fees for education, or in the sale of produce, sufficient to pay the annual interest of such liabilities. Hence the necessity for a

more intimate intercourse with the trading world, and
a deeper involvement in money affairs than would have
attended a more retired effort of the like kind. To
enter into the corrupting modes of the world, with the
view of diminishing or destroying them, is a delusive
hope. It will, notwithstanding, be a labor of no little
worth, to induce improvements in the two grand departments of industry and education. We say *improvement*
as distinct from *progress ;* for with any association short
of community, we do not see how it is possible for an
institution to stand so high above the present world as
to conduct its affairs on principles entirely different
from those which now influence men in general.

There are other considerations also suggested by a
glance at Brook Farm, which are worthy the attention
of the many minds now attracted by the deeply interesting subject of human association. We are gratified by
observing several external improvements during the
past year; such as a larger and more convenient dining
room, a labor saving cooking apparatus, a purer diet, a
more orderly and quiet attendance at the refections,
superior arrangements for industry, and generally an increased seriousness in respect to the value of the example which those who are there assembled may constitute
to their fellow beings.

Of about seventy persons now assembled there, about
thirty are children, sent thither for education; some
adult persons also place themselves there chiefly for
mental assistance; and in the society there are only four
married couples. With such materials it is almost certain that the sensitive and vital points of communication cannot well be tested. A joint-stock company,

working with some of its own members and with others as agents, cannot bring to issue the great question whether the existence of the individual family is compatible with the universal family, which the term "Community" signifies. This is now the grand problem. By mothers it has ever been felt to be so. The maternal instinct, as hitherto educated, has declared itself so strongly in favor of the separate fireside, that the association, which appears so beautiful to the young and unattached soul, has yet accomplished little progress in the affections of that important section of the human race — the mothers. With fathers, the feeling in favor of the separate family is certainly less strong; but there is an undefinable tie, a sort of magnetic *rapport*, an invisible, inseverable umbilical cord between the mother and child, which in most cases circumscribes her desires and ambition to her own immediate family.

All the accepted adages and wise saws of society, all the precepts of morality, all the sanctions of theology, have for ages been employed to confirm this feeling. This is the chief corner stone of present society; and to this maternal instinct have, till very lately, our most heartfelt appeals been made for the progress of the human race, by means of a deeper and more vital education. Pestalozzi and his most enlightened disciples are distinguished by this sentiment. And are we all at once to abandon, to deny, to destroy this supposed stronghold of virtue? Is it questioned whether the family arrangement of mankind is to be preserved? Is it discovered that the sanctuary, till now deemed the holiest on earth, is to be invaded by intermeddling scepticism, and its altars sacrilegiously destroyed by the rude hands of innovating progress ?

Here "social science" must be brought to issue. The question of Association and marriage are one. If, as we have been popularly led to believe, the individual or separate family is the true order of Providence, then the associate life is a false effort. If the associate life is true, then is the separate family a false arrangement. By the maternal feeling it appears to be decided that the coëxistence of both is incompatible — is impossible. So also say some religious sects. Social science ventures to assert their harmony. This is the grand problem now remaining to be solved, for at least the enlightening, if not for the vital elevation, of humanity. That the affections can be divided, or bent with equal ardor on two objects so opposed as universal and individual love, may at least be rationally doubted. History has not yet exhibited such phenomena in an associate body, and scarcely, perhaps, in any individual.

The monasteries and convents, which have existed in all ages, have been maintained solely by the annihilation of that peculiar affection on which the separate family is based. The Shaker families, in which the two sexes are not entirely dissociated, can yet only maintain their union by forbidding and preventing the growth of personal affection other than that of a spiritual character. And this, in fact, is not personal in the sense of individual, but ever a manifestation of universal affection. Spite of the speculations of hopeful bachelors and æsthetic spinsters, there is somewhat in the marriage bond which is found to counteract the universal nature of the affections to a degree tending at least to make

considerable pause, before they can be blended into one
harmony.

The general condition of married persons at this time
is some evidence of the existence of such doubt in their
minds.   Were they as convinced as the unmarried of
the beauty and truth of associate life, the demonstration
would be now presented.   But might it not be enforced
that the two family ideas really neutralize one another?
It is not quite certain that the human heart cannot be
set in two places; that man cannot worship at two
altars?   It is only the determination to do what parents
consider the best for themselves and their families,
which renders the o'er populous world such a wilderness of selfhood as it is.   Destroy this feeling, they say,
and you prohibit every motive for exertion.   Much
truth is there in this affirmation.   For to them no other
motive remains, nor indeed to any one else, save that of
the universal good, which does not permit the building
up of supposed self-good, and, therefore, forecloses all
possibility of an individual family.

These observations, of course, equally apply to all the
associative attempts, now attracting so much public
attention; and perhaps most especially to such as have
more of Fourier's designs than are observable at Brook
Farm.   The slight allusion in all the writers of the
" Phalansterian " class, to the subject of marriage, is
rather remarkable.   They are acute and eloquent in
deploring woman's oppressed and degraded position in
past and present times, but are almost silent as to the
future.   In the meanwhile, it is gratifying to observe
the success which in some departments attend every
effort, and that Brook Farm is likely to become com-

paratively eminent in the highly important and praise-
worthy attempts to render labor of the hands more
dignified and noble, and mental education more free
and loveful. C. L.

ASSOCIATIVE ARTICLES.

"*Association the Body of Christianity*," *by John S.*
Dwight.

THE world has been divided between infidels and
bigots. In Association there will be neither, for it will
remove their causes. The framework of society is false
which drives to such extremities. For most assuredly
these opposites proceeded from one common centre, and
will most gladly gravitate back again to that, so soon as
the general order becomes just and genial to the real
character and purpose of each individual soul.

Unbelief is torment, as much as any obstinate refus-
ing of food, and no one courts it because he will, but
only accepts it because he must. On the other hand,
exclusive religionism has too much consciousness of
secret sympathy with its avowed antipodes, to enjoy
itself much better. They are only opposite forms of
the same denial; opposite feelings from the same great
central wrong. They seem to hate each other; it is
only because they are not permitted to embrace: let
them transfer their hate to that which separates them.
And what is that?

It is the want of unity and of all recognition of unity
in the material interests of men. If the material interest of each harmonized with the material interest of all,

as fully as their spiritual interests do, the immediate result would be that the material and spiritual would harmonize with one another. Then religion would not have to renounce the world to save its very life ; nor would the believer in natural reason and the lover of justice cry, " Away with all religion, since it leaves the world so bad! "

There are certain instincts and convictions in every human soul which call for love and truth and justice. There is a revelation from God which confirms them all. One noble life was all made up of these high qualities, a present incarnation of these seemingly almost unattainable ideals, and freely gave itself for man. Some say it was very God ; all acknowledge that such virtue is the divinest thing known, that such love stands for the Most High, and that to reverence and obey it, is to obey the very saving principle of human nature ; that such obedience, in fact, is perfect freedom. So that, leaving intellectual dogmas and theories out of the question, the essence of what is called Christianity is the natural faith of the human heart, and all men do in their heart of hearts long to have a Christian spirit and to have that prevail throughout the world.

But while the spirit of Christ is unity, the material interests of men are without unity. In the whole body politic of life, the unity of the human race is not at all implied. On the contrary, everything contradicts the idea. Every man in seeking his material interests becomes the rival and antagonist of every other man. To gain his bread he must sacrifice friendship, generosity and even honor. He must keep his convictions of nobleness and justice for a beautiful and holiday idea;

he must consign them to the keeping of religion; and she, like the gentle wife at home, has careful instructions not to show her beautiful face in the market place. It is hard; since in the market place mankind are doomed to spend the most part of their life; and very many men and women and children *all* their life, except what nature claims for sleep.

If there be no way, then, of realizing the unity of man with man, of growing into the beauty of Christian love and fellowship, by the very act which earns us bread; if there be no reconciling of religion with this worldliness; if there be no possibility of raising in the very market place the song, " The Lord is in his temple " ; if religion calls us one way and necessity another; if business is to be based on principles which render ineffectual every prayer for the spirit of love and charity; if work is the dissevering of all the bonds which thought and speech and sentiment and blessed dreams and holy influences, with all the help, too, of God's Holy Spirit, strive to weave; — then is Christianity impotent, a heavenly voice that mocks mankind.

But no! As surely as Christ taught the love of God and of the neighbor, so surely did his prediction imply a change in the material organization of society which should fit it to be the container of this heavenly spirit. Did he think to "put new wine into old bottles"? Must not the spirit of Christianity create unto itself a *body?* It is a fruitless abstraction until it does. And this, if we read the signs aright, is the demand of this age. This is the tendency of all social movements. The material basis of our life, our social and industrial system, is entirely incompatible with the moral convic-

tion and duties of this age. Our social economy all
represents and preaches selfishness; but the idea of
Christian love, the vision of unity and brotherhood, is
born in the mind, and makes terrible and unendurable
contrast with this state of things. The world is nearly
ripe for the kingdom of heaven — the organization of
society precludes it.

ASSOCIATION is the word that solves the problem.
The earnest and believing hearts of this day everywhere
have certain hopeful lookings towards that; and at this
providential moment science comes and offers us the
key which shall unlock the whole sphere of material
interests to its true lord, the spirit of religious love and
unity. The organization of attractive industry will be
the reconciliation of spirit and matter, of religion and
the world; it will be the admission of Christ into all
our spheres; it will make all nature holy, and clothe
religion in the garb of nature.

*Extract from a lecture on Association in its Connection
with Religion, by Charles A. Dana.*

IT is now more than eighteen hundred years since
that annunciation of the coming of peace on earth and
good-will to men, at which the world might well have
trembled with a new and mighty hope. The Divine
Infant, whose birth the celestial choirs thus celebrated,
grew up to man's estate, still bearing within him that
blessed promise ; he went about on earth, imparting
new life to the broken-hearted and forlorn, and uttering
words of such heavenly significance, that to this day
there is nothing that thrills the hearts of men with so

true a power. At last he gave his life a testimony to
those eternal truths, and died in great bodily agony,
still publishing the prophecy that welcomed his birth,
still announcing the kingdom of peace and love, the
kingdom of God on earth.

His followers have since grown to cover great continents; whole nations acknowledge those few words of
his as their most sacred possession; great temples are
built in which his life and death are solemnly com-
memorated, and men gladly yield their hard-won treasure to carry his history to distant regions that his name
has never reached. And yet, my friends, where is that
kingdom of peace and love; where, where in the whole
wide world is the will of God done as it is in heaven?
Is it even thought of as anything but a dream, an im-
possibility? Does not a sceptical smile steal over the
faces of men, when an earnest and enthusiastic person
speaks of it as a thing yet actually to be?

And yet it is only what Christ taught us to hope for
and pray for. We are not deceived; no one of us is
mistaken in the vision that in innocent and blessed
moments visits us all. No man who utters that sacred
petition prays in vain. For the kingdom of God, the
reign of peace and good-will among men, shall surely
come. Not in mystical raptures, not in feverish trances,
not in imagination, but in reality — in actual outward
peace and beauty, and in the abiding spirit of love, filling humanity and sanctifying the earth to be the worthy
temple of so divine a presence.

And yet, who that beholds only the present condition
of the Christian church, to which these sacred ideas
have been especially entrusted; who that sees the body

of Christ thus torn and discordant, would imagine that
a consummation of this imperishable hope was any
longer possible? Might we not despair, seeing these
centuries of terror, of revolution, of injustice and of
perpetual hatred, and seeing that the very disciples of
the spirit of love have lost the memory of their Master
— might we not despair, and cry out with them, that
the earth was given over to evil, and that the kingdom
of God would never come?

No, my friends, we may not so despair, we cannot if
we would. That old prophecy, however long delayed,
still finds an involuntary echo in our souls. And now,
in this hope of a true and brotherly society, its fulfilment seems at hand. Say it is enthusiasm, say it is a
mistake, say it is irreligion, if you will, and still I reply
that the time is not distant. It is in the combined
order, where men are held together by inward laws
only, and not by outward constraint and outward necessities, that the kingdom of God is to come down and
possess the earth.

It is in Association, then, that the promise of Christianity is to be fulfilled — fulfilled by making the
incarnation of the great law of love an actual and
universal fact. Hitherto Christianity has been in the
world a spirit pining and dying for want of a body.
She has wandered up and down on the earth, possessing
here and there an individual, but never obtaining her
birthright, which is the whole of humanity, never able
to exercise her prerogative, which is to bathe the earth
in the aroma of harmony and peace. The forms of
selfish and egoistical society, the forms of society here
in Boston, and throughout the civilized world, are not

of Christianity, but of the primeval curse, which they perpetuate. Into them Christianity cannot fully enter, any more than light can dwell in the midst of darkness.

The relations which Christianity seeks to establish between man and man, are indicated in these words, "Love one another." But how is this possible in a competitive society, where the interests of all are hostile? How can vital and true love operate between me and my neighbor, when his misfortune is my advantage, and my loss is his gain? What does it avail that on Sundays the better spirit is feebly awakened; what does it avail that then I aspire and long to love all men, if on the other six days in the week my hand is of necessity set against them all?

Do you tell me that if my love is deep and pure enough, it will modify my whole life, and of itself, without hindrance from circumstances, appear perfectly in all my actions and relations? This is the old heresy, this is the error of the individualism and egoism which has hindered us so long. Let us meet it fully and fairly.

In all results there are two elements, namely, that which acts and that which is acted upon. The character of the individual never does and never can form his circumstances, but can only modify them. No man is an artist or a poet by virtue of inward genius alone. No matter how great his gifts, unless he find a congenial atmosphere and favorable conditions, his high office is not fulfilled. Precisely so is it with that sacred energy which we call love. It can act entirely and sincerely only in circumstances that harmonize and correspond with itself. In order to carry Christianity into

my daily life, the forms of my daily life, all my relations
to others, my household and my business, must be in
harmony with it.

If these forms are contrary to Christianity, the first
thing for me, as a Christian, to do, is to change them,
to put them off, to be free from them at whatever cost.
If I am indeed filled and impelled by that divine in-
junction, "Love one another," I cannot rest, I shall
give myself no peace, until it be possible for me to do
so, not in my inward spirit only, but in all my outward
actions also. But how is this to be done? How are
the ultimate forms of my life to be brought into correspondence with its central impulse? Plainly not by
any spontaneous and unconscious power, but by intellectual inquiry and voluntary action. *Inspiration can
discharge its whole mission only by the aid of science.*

Besides, the end of Christianity is not the salvation
of individuals, but the transfiguration of humanity; it
cannot be accomplished in you and me, but only in the
whole race. It promises the kingdom of peace and
love, not to a few solitary souls, but to man. He is
indeed a servant of Christianity, who has learned its
universal purpose and labors therefor; who does not so
much seek to be saved himself, as to bring salvation
to all the world, who sees that his own private life
and development are forever involved in the universal
progress. He is ignorant of the true idea of Christianity, who has not understood that it demands not so
much that one should be careful about his own spiritual
perfection, that he should watch himself, and by private
remorse and tears seek a far-off heaven, as by a generous
self-forgetfulness and self-devotion, seek to build up

the kingdom of peace and love among men, and make heaven a reality here, and not the hope only of a distant future and a different sphere of existence.

It is time, my friends, that this long divorce between the natural and spiritual worlds should be broken off, and that we should know that even now we may breathe the celestial ether, and have our common life transformed and illumined by infinite spiritual glories.

We have said that the end of Christianity is not the salvation of individuals; but do not let it be thought that we overlook the worth of individual character. For heroism and holiness we have an unspeakable reverence. The saints and poets and sages of all time are the choicest gifts of God. The virtue, the beauty and the devotion that now shine in the lives of private men and women, still assure us that all is not and cannot be a failure. The ultimate result of the life of humanity will doubtless be found in symmetrical and harmonious individuals; and in a perfect Christianity we shall look to see an angelic love radiant from every face. But while there is disease and imperfection in any part of the human body, there cannot be perfect health in any other part; just so while there is disease and imperfection in humanity, of which the human body is an image, there cannot be perfect health in any individual. Perfect men and women are possible only in a perfect society.

Finally, the sum of our remarks on the relation of Association to Christianity, is briefly this: Association fulfils the promise of Christianity; it shows the means whereby peace on earth and goodwill among men are to be realized. It harmonizes the forms and relations of

society with the spirit of Christianity; in a word, it
makes them forms and relations of brotherly love, and
not of selfishness and discord, and thereby renders
possible the accomplishment of the final aim of Christianity, which is the salvation and spiritual life of
universal humanity.

The Temptation in the Wilderness, from the Harbinger, by William Henry Channing.

A prophecy in the spirit of this age announces that a
new era in humanity is opening, and sounds forth more
fully than ever before the venerable yet new gospel,
that the kingdom of heaven is at hand.

Doubtless, in all generations, the seers and the seekers
— who are usually one and the same — have felt that
their times were the culminating points of history, the
mountain of vision, the border overlooking the promised
land.   Doubtless, the great of all nations and ages have
felt that they were a peculiar people, called to a peculiar
work, inspired and led by divine guidance to sublime
ends.   No age, no people, have wholly wanted such
signs of providential commission.

And doubtless, too, the works, bravely attempted
from such high promptings, have always in actual results seemed fruitless.   Yes! compared with his vision,
the gains of the martyr's labors seem tantalizing — a
dropping shower upon the droughty earth.   Always the
ideal entering the soul of man, like a god descending
to the embrace of a mortal, seems to engender a son but
half divine.   Yet this disappointment is a delusion of
the moment.

Quite opposite are the facts. No man yet upon earth ever boldly aspired, and faithfully obeyed his clear convictions of good without transmitting through his race an all but omnipotent energy. Winds waft, streams scatter, birds of the air carry in their beaks, each seed that drops in ripeness from the tree of life. The failures of man have been from infidelity to his faith. Infinitely grander consequences than the doer could estimate, have followed every executed purpose of heroism and humanity and holy hope. Each age has been right in feeling that its mission was all-important. Each prophet has chanted, as if for very life, his warning and cheering, for God spoke through him in the language of his land and era.

The Infinite Being, who through generation upon generation, progressively incarnates himself in the human race, and so manifests his glory upon earth, calls this age to its heavenly mission, and speaks through it with an eloquent longing, that cannot be uttered, his welcome and promise. The word whispers through the nations: " Man made One; a World at Peace; Humanity, the Earth round." At the nativity of this great hope, of this present Immanuel, the angels of our highest aspirations bend from their cloudy thrones, —

> " Harping in loud and solemn choir,
> With unexpressive notes, to Heaven's newborn heir."

And the burden of the song that interprets their symphony is this: —

> " Justice and Truth again
> Shall down return to men.

Orb'd in a rainbow; and, like glories wearing,
Mercy will sit between,
Throned in celestial sheen,
With radiant feet the tissued clouds down steering,
And Heaven, as at some festival,
Will open wide the gates of her high palace hall."

The hope of universal unity has been born, cradled in the rude manger of labor; nurtured by charity, ever virgin; worshipped by shepherds, guarding humble, humane thoughts, like flocks in the fold of their hearts; it has sat with the doctors in the temple, unsullied by timidity and prudence, and has astonished them at its profound doctrine of unbounded love; it has grown in favor with God and man, and answered to its half doubting, half hoping parents of the church and state, " Wist ye not that I must be about my Father's business?" and now is it driven away into the wilderness of poverty and hard toil, of loneliness and mortification, to be tempted of the devil.

Let us first consider awhile these temptations; then review the forty days' meditation upon the divine mission of this principle of perfect love; and so be ready to preach, " Repent, for the kingdom of heaven is at hand."

To the scattered band who, few and weak, are here and there withdrawn from the thoroughfares of life, to commune together and to coöperate in the grand movement of the age, the world comes in with scarce dissembled sneer, and ironically says, " *If* Association is really this Messiah to the ages, this pledge of universal prosperity, of overflowing wealth, then let it make these barren fields into gardens, these thick growing woods into palaces, these stones into bread."

And all the while the shrewd, the rosy, sleek and full-fed world, with title deeds in pocket and scrip and stock in hand, thinks of its factories on rapid streams; its warehouses of three thousand dollars' rent; its dividends at seven per cent half yearly; its iron-limbed and tireless steeds, hurrying with the spoils of myriads of acres; its carpeted, curtained, glowing, shining, pictured, sculptured, perfumed homes. The victorious world, so confident and easy and jocular, so beautiful in its own right, so wrapped about in kingly purple — how strangely is it metamorphosed to the eyes of the child of God! Its factories change into brothels; its rents to distress warrants; its railroads to mighty fetters, binding industry in an inextricable net of feudalism; from under the showy robes of its success, flutter the unseemly rags of an ever-growing beggary; from garret and cellar of its luxurious habitations, stare out the gaunt forms of haggard want; the lash of the jailer, the gleam of swords, the glitter of bayonets, are its garters and stars of nobility.

If Association has been elated by the thought of its miraculous power, or meditated to use it for selfish ends, it deserves the taunt of the yet more selfish world. And it is reason for great rejoicing, that the difficulties of transition from the isolated to the harmonic mode of life are so great. God thus *sifts* his people. None are worthy to enter upon this work who are not *dusted*. We need to hunger. We need to feel dependence, in order that we may judge competition in contrast. We need to know actually how pinching is necessity; how deep it ploughs its furrows into brow and brain ; how tight it knots up the muscles and cramps back and limbs, by exhausting toil.

Association must be in its very essence disinterested ; holding power as something given from above, to be used not for self alone, or chiefly, but for universal good ; consecrating itself as a servant. And its answer to the boasting world is, "Man liveth not by bread alone, but by every word that proceedeth out of the mouth of God." We are learning, in these trial times, the beauty of reciprocation, the wealth of sharing all ; we are study-ing experimentally the law of coöperation ; we are esti-mating the value of justice by its practical application ; above all, are we opening our hearts to the glad convic-tion that it is possible, ay, easy, for men to grow more kindly by adversity, and to love each other better for each other's wants.

The word which is proceeding out of the mouth of God to Associationists now, to all the true-hearted and brave and devoted and hopeful of them is, "Union with fellow beings by usefulness is the very life of life." Let patience have its perfect work. Let no man be so mean as to emphasize the "If thou be," etc. Let no doubt enter from present humiliation. Association is the divine form of humanity. So ends in piety the first temptation.

Then the Satan of selfishness takes counsel of his cunning, and subtly states a new suggestion. "If As-sociation is this glorious truth to renovate the nations, then glorious should be its announcement ; loud, wide, startling, should be its call ; sudden, as from the skies, its appearing. Here on the pinnacle of the temple of peace(or of Salem), shalt thou stand, and cast thyself

down among the multitudes like an angel. Some
splendid boldness should introduce thy reign. Take
no heed of care and caution ; count not the cost; risk
all in a providential career. Surely thou shalt be
guided safe. God's angels will bear thee up, that thou
dash not thy foot against a stone.

O bragging, advertising, placarding, circular-scatter-
ing, auctioneering, humbuging world ! And you would
thus prove Association to be also a windbag and a lie !
Just in so far as Association has been rash and precipi-
tate, and swollen with promises and dizzy in its tower-
ing pretensions, it has been truly carried to the pinnacle.

The child of God waits for opportunities. There will
be occasions soon enough for manifestation. According
to the hour is the duty ; and the duty now is performance. Calm, wise, large and balanced plans, discrimi-
nate selection of persons, discreet preparations of industry, a sober estimate of the greatness of the undertaking,
and a summoning of all energies to its fulfilment, is the
vocation just now of Association. Enough for the day
it is, honestly, honorably, humanely, to lay the foundation in the earth unseen for the glorious fabric which
the future shall rear in light.

In so far as the inculcation of principles, the instruc-
tion of the national mind, the calling out of enthusiasm
and courage, of hope and heroism, demand publicity, of
course Association must not be backward. It must no
more be behind than before the time. But the special
call to-day is, in practical endeavor to prepare the way
for a future gospel preaching. We need complete
science, clear understanding, solid judgment. We
need to solve innumerable problems, to comprehend

principles exactly by their detailed development in practice. We need inward concentration, to gain singleness and unity of purpose.

"Thou shalt not tempt the Lord thy God," either by anticipation or by tardiness. If Association is the salvation of mankind, there will be time enough to let mankind know it. Meanwhile, let us give ourselves wholly up to God, to be filled with his love, inspired with his wisdom, strengthened with his might, and so made ready for the sublime work of manifesting man made one in a perfect society. We will humbly wait the opening of opportunities by Providence. And so ends the second temptation in patience.

Thus baffled twice, the Prince of this world gathers up his routed forces for the final charge : —

"Surely the power of united effort is irresistible. What has it not already accomplished? — tunnelling mountains, bridging oceans with boats, wringing from the gnomes of the mines their wealth long buried in sparry palaces of salt and diamond, of gold and silver, — preparing to sever the bond that unites twin continents, summoning storms and staying them, making the desert yield an hundred fold, using the lightning for post boy, giving iron weavers coal for bread and fire for drink, that they may spin garments for the nations, — prodigious power of combined effort, what may it not do!

"We will appeal to the rich and mighty. We will show them how they can multiply their means seventy times seven. We will unite the race in one grand effort of prolific production and unlimited voluptuousness. We will be kings upon earth. All these things that

thou seest from this high mountain of exceeding enterprise, all these kingdoms and their glory shall be thine,
if thou wilt but give thyself up, O Association! body,
soul, spirit, to the worship of worldly power and splendor and enjoyment."

Ah, Satan! that was thy wiliest web. What! no
poor, all nobles, all fat, all glittering in court raiment,
all surfeited with sweets, all bathing in Johannisberg
and champagne, all tended by houries, all pillowed on
orange-scented beds, and covered with gauze or eider
down, according to the season? Charming Satan!
Selfishness made universal will be selfishness no more.
Thou art an angel of light!

Just in so far as Association, using the tact of worldly
training, has in its plannings and pleadings, lowered itself to exaltation of the outward, by merging the inward,
it has permitted the magic of sin to dazzle its vision.

It is indeed a splendid prospect, this of a world re-
claimed, of overflowing plenty. And it shall be realized.
Perfect beauty shall one day enwreath this earth with
its clustering vines. The long folded petals of this little
planet flower on the tree of the sun, shall open and dis-
til sweetness; its gorgeous fruit of consummate joy shall
swell and ripen. Far more than all the voluptuaries
of all ages have dreamed of shall exist, heightened by a
purity they could not conceive of.

Yes! O devil, the kingdoms and the glory of them
are there before us. But know this — they do not belong unto thee to give. Thou poor devil, always
mocked and always mocking. Have not six thousand
years taught thee yet, that self-love is always a suicide?
Thou wilt give the kingdoms of the world as thou al-

ways hast, first by stealing them for thy slaves, and then stealing them from thy slaves? No! thou forlorn devil, thy rule is ended, thy sceptre snapped into shivers; henceforth thou art so wholly accursed, that God and man will heartily forgive thee, whenever thou canst forgive thyself.

"Duty of Associationists to the Cause," by Horace Greeley.
From the Harbinger of Oct. 25, 1845.

Through the last four or five years, the doctrine of Association has been widely disseminated through the country. The labors of its ardent advocates, few but faithful, have been ably seconded by some portion of the press, and both have been immensely aided by the course of events. The great themes of political discussion in our day — the tariff and the currency — lead directly to a consideration of the conditions of labor, of the relations between producers and products, of mutual rights and respective interests of employers and employed. The existence of extreme destitution and consequent misery in the midst of general prosperity and plenty, of willing hands vainly seeking employment amid unsurpassed industrial activity and thrift, cannot have escaped attention. The disasters resulting from industrial anarchy, from "strikes" of operatives for higher wages or fewer hours of labor, the stoppage of work by combinations if not by outright violence, arrest general attention.

Truly the remedy for these errors and evils has yet been perceived and embraced by comparatively few, but the conviction that the present organization of industry cannot be advantageously maintained, and some radical change is at hand, must have already forced itself upon very many intelligent and candid minds. The readjustment of the relations of capital and labor on a basis of harmony and mutual advantage, is manifestly the great problem of the age. But that a change is at hand is evident: the practical question regards not its probability or certainty, but its character.

The more intelligent and wealthy class have it in their power so to mould this change as to render it peaceful, gradual and universally beneficent ; or they can turn a deaf ear to the calls of humanity, and let the demagogue, the envious, the selfishly discontented, pervert it into an engine of convulsion, destruction and desolation. As in the days of King John, the barons laid the foundations of English political liberty, so in our day the intellectual and philanthropic may guide the car of progress, and in establishing industrial harmony may secure to all but the stubbornly vicious or incurably afflicted, true independence and ample means of subsistence and development ; or they can indolently leave all to the benighted and malignant, and see reproduced a war of classes, different indeed in its weapons and its physical aspects, but not different in its essential character from the ravages of France by the *Jacquerie* or the butcheries of the reign of terror.

In this crisis of events, with an industrial war plainly threatened and partially commenced, the doctrine of Association appears as a mediator and reconciler. Its bow of promise shines broadly in the lurid sky ; it irradiates the murky visage of the gathering, muttering tem-

pest. It awakens a hope, and the only well grounded
hope, of averting the miseries of an insane struggle between those who ought to be the closest allies, to see
which can the more injure the other. Need I urge
that in this crisis the friends of Association ought to be
most earnest and untiring in the promulgation and ad-
vocacy of their faith; that they ought to improve the
opportunities which are daily presented of commending
the truth to others whose minds are but newly prepared
to receive it? What Associationist so dull that he cannot improve every "strike," every collision respecting
the hours or the wages of labor, to the advancement of
the good cause?

To do this with effect, we must be, in the true sense
of an abused term, catholic. We must not suffer Association to be merged in mere partisanship for any class
or calling, or blind hostility to any abuse or oppression.
We are not the champions of the slave or the hired servant, the factory girl or the housemaid, the seamstress
or the washerwoman. We are not the advocates
merely of labor against capital, of the employers as
opposed to the employed. Ours is the cause of all
classes and vocations, and our success is the triumph of
all. We are in danger of becoming partial and one-
sided ; let us take special care to overcome it.

But it is not enough that we give our testimony in
behalf of this benign truth; it behooves us to be doers
of the work as well as hearers and commenders.
Friends of Association! scattered over the face of our
wide country! do you realize this? Do you feel that
your works ought to justify and fortify your words?
We are surrounded by a world full of want, vice and

misery, which Association realized would greatly modify
and ultimately cure. But those who know nothing of
this truth will never cause it to be realized; it would
be absurd to expect anything of the kind. The work
must be accomplished by us, and by those whom our
acts rather than words shall win over to a knowledge
of the truth. Is not the work of sufficient importance
to incite you to embark heartily in its furtherance?

But, says one, how can I engage practically in realizing Association? My family and friends are vehe-
mently adverse to it; I am engrossed by responsibilities
and duties of various kinds which I cannot uprightly
escape, and which confine me where I am. I am not
yet prepared, if I ever should be, to embark in Association.

Very well, you are not required to embark in it in
the way your objection contemplates. You are urged
only to contribute to the great work according to your
ability and in a mode not inconsistent with the proper
discharge of all your duties. But many who cannot
personally enlist in the pioneer groups who for the next
ten years will be engaged in preparing the ground on
which Associations are ultimately to arise, are yet able
to contribute something of their time and means to the
cause of humanity's emancipation from brutal drudgery.

And this something is eminently needed by that
cause. The great work of disseminating and defend-
ing the principles of social science needs pecuniary aid;
who will offer it? The secondary work of founding
and sustaining pioneer Associations also languishes for
want of means. Ought it to do so? I say founding,
not that I would encourage the commencement of any

new undertaking, but because I consider no Association founded as yet. We have a few beginning to clear the ground for the work, and that is all.

But in this work noble men and women are engaged; to it they have consecrated their energies; for it they suffer hardship and privations, and are willing to suffer. But they cannot make their labor truly effective without a large increase of capital, in every instance within my knowledge. They commenced with little means, in no case sufficient to pay for their land and buildings, and generally not half enough. They were in need of everything, even of experience and skill to render their labor effective, and for a long time two out of every three blows they strike are ill-directed or render no immediate return. Thus they toil on, needing machinery, power, buildings, everything, to give them a chance for rapid progress; and even Associationists stand ready to wonder at their snail-paced advance, or reproach their occasional failures !

As one Associationist who has given his efforts and means freely to the cause, I feel that I have a right to speak frankly. I know that the great number of our believers are far from wealthy; yet I know that there is wealth enough in our ranks, if it were but devoted to it, to give an instant and resistless influence to the cause. A few thousand dollars subscribed to the stock of each existing Association would in most cases extinguish the mortgages on its property, provide it with machinery and materials, and render its industry immediately productive and profitable. Then manufacturing invention and skill would fearlessly take up their abode with our infant colonies; labor and thrift would flow thither, and a new and brighter era would dawn upon them.

Fellow Associationists! I shall do whatever I can for the promotion of our common cause; to it whatever I have or may hereafter acquire of pecuniary ability is devoted; may I not hope for a like devotion from you?

A Prophecy. From the Introduction to Fourier's "Theory of Social Organization," translated by Albert Brisbane.

" Among the influences tending to restrict man's industrial rights, I will mention the formation of privileged corporations which, monopolizing a given branch of industry, arbitrarily close the doors of labor against whomsoever they please. These corporations will become dangerous, and lead to new convulsions on being extended to the whole industrial and commercial system. This event is not far distant and it will be brought about all the more easily as it is not apprehended. The greatest evils have often sprung from imperceptible germs, as for instance, Jacobism, and if our civilization has engendered this and so many other calamities, may it not engender others which we do not now foresee? The most imminent of these is the birth of a commercial feudalism or the monopoly of commerce and industry by joint-stock companies, leagued together for the purpose of usurping and controlling all branches of industrial organizations. Extremes meet, and the greater the extent to which anarchical competition is carried, the nearer is the approach to *universal monopoly*, which is the opposite excess. Circumstances are tending towards the organization of the commercial and industrial classes into federal companies or affiliated monopolies, which, operating in conjunction with the great landed interest, will reduce the middle and laboring classes to a state of commercial vassalage, and by the influence of combined action become the masters of the productive industry of entire nations. The small operators will be reduced to the position of mere agents working for the mercantile coalition. We shall then see the reappearance of feudalism in an inverse order, founded on mercantile leagues and answering to the baronial leagues of the middle ages.

"Everything is concurring to produce this result. The spirit of commercial speculation and financial monopoly has extended to all classes. Public opinion prostrates itself before the bankers and financiers who share authority with the governments and devise every day new means for the monopoly and control of industry.

"We are marching with rapid strides towards a commercial feudalism and to the fourth phase of our civilization. The economists accustomed to reverence everything which comes in the name and under the sanction of commerce, will see this new order spring up without alarm, and will consecrate their servile pens to the celebration of its praises. Its *debut* will be one of brilliant promise, but the result will be an industrial inquisition, subordinating the whole people to the interests of the affiliated monopolists."

Albert Brisbane prefaces this wonderful prophecy by these remarks: "In 1805 or 6, amid the preoccupation

of war and military politics, he [Fourier] foresaw and
described with accuracy the future formation of vast
joint-stock companies destined to monopolize and control all branches of industry, commerce and finance, and
establish what he called ‘An industrial or commercial
feudalism ’ — a feudalism that would control society by
the power of capital, as did the old baronial or military
feudalism by the power of the sword, and as despotically.
Under the dominion of the great barons who leagued
together to control the social world there was a monopoly of the then existing wealth, namely, the land and
the laboring classes. Now, society having passed out of
the military *regime*, and entered the industrial and commercial, it is threatened with another vast system of
monopoly.”

He concludes as follows: “ This was written seventy
years ago [it is now almost ninety years] when public
attention was absorbed in military conquests and glory.
To-day advanced thinkers on social questions are beginning to see the conquest of the industrial and commercial worlds by the power of associated capital. To-day
the new feudalism has more than half entangled society
in its meshes, and its complete establishment stares us
in the face. What perspicuity to have foreseen so
clearly what is now being realized ! If prescience is a
test of science — if the foretelling of future events is a
test of the laws that govern them and from which they
are deducible, then Fourier must have discovered at
least some of the laws which govern social evolution.

“A vague opinion prevails among men that society
is moving onward to its appointed state by what is vari-

ously termed the 'force of circumstances,' 'the instinct
of the race,' 'the general law of progress,' 'Divine
guidance.' These loose opinions are speculative fancies
adopted in the absence of real knowledge; whereas the
fact is, that society can only reach its true state by the
conscious and calculated efforts of human reason under
the direction of an exact social science. Men act on
this principle when they try to organize any part of the
social system. When, from necessity, they are forced to
frame political institutions and organize governments,
as they often are after revolutions, they do so by conscious calculation and reasoning. True, being without
a scientific guide, their institutions are imperfect and
arbitrary; yet these efforts show that man recognizes
the necessity of calculation and thought in one branch,
at least, of the social organism. He knows that to have
a government, he must think, plan and devise; but he
does not know that the other branches of the social organism are subject to the same conditions, and can only be
normally constituted by the exercise of conscious reason
guided by scientific principles. Construction and organization — the same in principle in all departments of
creation — can only be the work of mind, conscious of
its operations, planning with forethought; analyzing,
comparing and combining; adapting means to ends and
calculating the relations of cause and effect. Instinct
cannot organize; Divine Providence does not interfere
to do the work of reason; no science is revealed to man;
no constructions or other means are furnished him by
nature.

"When the human mind shall rise to the conception

of the possibility of a scientific organization of society, it will at once undertake, as the work of paramount importance, the elaboration of a system of exact social science. First, however, the laws on which the science is to be based must be discovered and combined into a system that will enable the mind clearly to comprehend and apply them."

www.ingramcontent.com/pod-product-compliance
Lightning Source LLC
Chambersburg PA
CBHW021114270326
41929CB00009B/880